Healthy Heart
One-Dish Meals

Oxmoor
House®

Healthy Heart One-Dish Meals from the Today's Gourmet series
Copyright 1996 by Oxmoor House, Inc.
Book Division of Southern Progress Corporation
P.O. Box 2463, Birmingham, Alabama 35201

Library of Congress Catalog Number: 95-73077
ISBN: 0-8487-1497-0

Manufactured in the United States of America
First Printing 1996

Be sure to check with your health-care provider before making any changes in your diet.

Editor-in-Chief: Nancy Fitzpatrick Wyatt
Senior Foods Editor: Katherine M. Eakin
Senior Editor, Editorial Services: Olivia Kindig Wells
Art Director: James Boone

Healthy Heart One-Dish Meals

Editor: Anne Chappell Cain, M.S., M.P.H., R.D.
Foods Editor: Deborah Garrison Lowery
Associate Art Director: Cynthia R. Cooper
Copy Editor: Jacqueline Giovanelli
Editorial Assistants: Lisa C. Bailey, Julie A. Cole
Director, Test Kitchens: Kathleen Royal Phillips
Assistant Director, Test Kitchens: Gayle Hays Sadler
Test Kitchen Home Economists: Molly Baldwin, Susan Hall Bellows,
    Julie Christopher, Michele Brown Fuller, Natalie E. King,
    Elizabeth Tyler Luckett, Iris Crawley O'Brien, Jan A. Smith
Recipe Developers: Pat Coker; Linda Leahy; Karen Levin;
    Karen Mangum, M.S., R.D.; Debby Maugans; Susan Reeves, R.D., L.D.;
    Elizabeth J. Taliaferro
Text Consultant: Deborah S. Hartz
Photographer: Ralph Anderson
Photo Stylist: Virginia R. Cravens
Publishing Systems Administrator: Rick Tucker
Director, Production and Distribution: Phillip Lee
Associate Production Manager: Theresa L. Beste
Production Coordinator: Marianne Jordan Wilson
Production Assistant: Valerie Heard

Cover: *Penne with Grilled Chicken and Eggplant* (page 117)
Back cover: *Taco Salad Supreme* (page 170), *Roasted Vegetable Pizza* (page 135),
    Wagon Wheel Beef Soup (page 199)
Page 1: *Horseradish Cheese Toast with Tomatoes* (page 32)
Right: *Wilted Greens and Black-Eyed Pea Salad* (page 175)

Healthy
Heart
One-Dish Meals

Shrimp and Black
Bean Salad
(page 180)

Contents

Healthy Heart Nutrition

Healthy Heart One-Dish Meals answers the question, "What easy recipe can I make tonight that my family will love and that will be good for them?"

Each Recipe Is a Meal-In-One

Several-course menus just don't fit into busy lives on most weeknights—or even on weekends any-more. That's one of the reasons why we—the home economists and registered dietitians at Oxmoor House—are excited about this new cookbook.

With every recipe we create a well-balanced meal that includes:
- **protein:** at least 10 grams from meat, poultry, fish, or meat alternatives (cheese, eggs, or beans)
- **a grain or starchy food:** rice, pasta, or potatoes
- **vegetables or fruit**

No Time to Cook? Here's Help

We know what it's like to need to cook in a hurry. So we thought you'd like to know the recipes that will help you beat the kitchen clock. Look for these symbols for super-quick and make-ahead recipes:

SUPER•QUICK You can make these recipes in 35 minutes or less. We timed them from the moment we picked up the first ingredient until the meal was on the table.

MAKE•AHEAD You can make these recipes a day ahead and cook them just before you serve them.

Italian Sausage with Peppers and Onions (page 161)

Mediterranean Spinach Lasagna (page 111)

Basics

Each Recipe Is Good for Your Heart

Every recipe in *Healthy Heart One-Dish Meals* helps you meet the American Heart Association (AHA) Guidelines for healthy eating. We've analyzed the recipes for the nutrients that are important in the prevention of heart disease. Look at the nutrient analysis example below, and note our suggestions for using the analysis to monitor your own dietary needs.

Island Chicken (page 150)

This figure tells you what **percent of the calories are from fat**. No more than 30% of the calories you eat *each day* should come from fat.

Total **calories** for each serving.

Total grams of **fat** per serving. If you eat 1500 calories a day, keep your daily fat gram intake at 50 grams or less.

Try to eat less than 300 milligrams of **cholesterol** a day.

Per Serving: Calories 436 (7% calories from fat)
Fat 3.4g (Sat 0.6g Mono 1.2g Poly 0.6g) Chol 66mg
Protein 31.6g Carbohydrate 67.9g Sodium 284mg
Exchanges: 3 Very Lean Meat, 4 Starch, 1 Fruit

If you use **exchange list values** to plan meals, you'll find these handy. We based our values on the *Exchange Lists for Meal Planning* developed by the American Diabetes Association and The American Dietetic Association. The values also are similar to the exchange lists used by many weight control programs.

At least 50% of your daily calories should be from **carbohydrate**. For a 1500 calorie-a-day diet, that's about 188 grams per day.

The AHA recommends a limit of 3000 milligrams of **sodium** each day.

One-Dish Meal Food Pyramid

pyramid (PEER-a-mid): an ancient structure usually seen in Egypt; now seen everywhere as a guide for healthy eating.

Pyramid Power

The Food Guide Pyramid is your blueprint for healthy eating. It outlines the number of servings you need each day from each food group. Every recipe in *Healthy Heart One-Dish Meals* helps you eat for your heart, pyramid-style—that is, lots of grains, pasta, fruit, and vegetables, topped with small servings of meat or meat alternatives, and a small amount of fats and oils.

Start Building

The foundation of the food pyramid is breads and grains. For some quick and easy ways to get your 6 to 11 servings a day, turn to *Super Simple Bread Ideas* on page 14.

And when you need a quick-fix salad to reach your five-a-day goal for vegetables and fruits, see *7 Salads in Seconds* on page 16.

Food Guide Pyramid
A Guide to Daily Food Choices

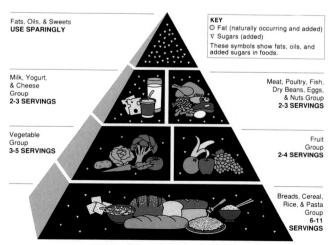

Exchange Values

The exchange values provided at the end of each recipe show you how the recipe meets your nutrient needs based upon the Food Guide Pyramid.

Caribbean Tuna provides three servings from the Meat, Poultry, Fish Group, which is the same as "3 Lean Meat" exchanges. Three servings from the Bread, Cereal, Rice, and Pasta Group is "3 Starch" exchanges. One serving from the Vegetable Group equals "1 Vegetable" exchange.

Caribbean Tuna (page 59)

Per Serving: Calories 410 (17% calories from fat) Fat 7.9g (Sat 1.7g Mono 2.5g Poly 2.2g) Chol 43mg Protein 33.5g Carbohydrate 51.7g Sodium 202mg

Exchanges: 3 Lean Meat, 3 Starch, 1 Vegetable

Caribbean Tuna

Here's how Caribbean Tuna fits into an eating plan based upon the Food Guide Pyramid.
- 3 servings from the Meat, Poultry, Fish Group
- 3 servings from the Breads, Cereal, Rice, and Pasta Group
- 1 serving from the Vegetable Group
- a small amount of oil

Fats and Oils:Use sparingly

Milk, Yogurt, & Cheese Group: 2-3 servings*

Meat, Poultry, Fish Group: 2-3 servings*

Vegetable Group: 3-5 servings*

Fruit Group: 2-4 servings*

Breads, Cereal, Rice, & Pasta Group (Starch): 6-11 servings*

*Recommended daily servings.

Dietary Guidelines (DIE-uh-terry GIDE-lines): a list of seven things that we can do to have a healthy heart; discussed often and enthusiastically by dietitians and other health experts.

Seven Simple Guidelines for Your Heart

If you remember just seven points (and follow them!) you're well on your way to having a healthy heart. That's because the United States Department of Agriculture (USDA) has distilled all the nutrition information you've heard about over the past few years into seven simple guidelines that define healthy eating.

These guidelines are intended for healthy people who want to stay healthy, and apply to anyone over two years of age. If you have a specific health concern like heart disease or diabetes, these guidelines still apply, but you may need to follow some of them more strictly. (The U.S. Dietary Guidelines mirror those of the American Heart Association.)

You'll be glad to know that you won't need to remember these seven points as long as you're cooking from *Healthy Heart One-Dish Meals.* Simply by using these recipes, you're helping your heart stay healthy. For more details about how to make the Dietary Guidelines a part of your life, see the next three pages.

Ham- and Cheese- Stuffed Potatoes (page 103)

U.S. DIETARY GUIDELINES

1. Eat a variety of foods.
2. Maintain or improve your weight.
3. Choose a diet low in fat, saturated fat, and cholesterol.
4. Choose a diet with plenty of grain products, vegetables, and fruits.
5. Choose a diet moderate in sugars.
6. Choose a diet moderate in salt and sodium.
7. If you drink alcoholic beverages, do so in moderation.

U.S. Department of Agriculture
U.S. Department of Health and Human Services, 1995

1. Eat a Variety of Foods

Life would be easier if there were one perfect food that provided all the nutrients you need with no excess calories. You could eat it, be slim, and probably be disease-free. But chances are, your taste buds would get bored.

Nature provides different nutrients in different foods, so eating a variety of foods is essential. It's up to us to mix and match the foods we eat throughout the day to make sure we get all the nutrients we need. The Food Guide Pyramid (page 8) can help you choose a diet that meets the Dietary Guidelines. And our one-dish meals make the process even simpler since *Healthy Heart One-Dish Meals* combines the food groups for you in each recipe.

2. Maintain or Improve Your Weight

How do you determine the best healthy weight for you? For starters, you can check the weight chart from the U.S. Dietary Guidelines on the right. You'll see a range of suggested ideal weights for both men and women based upon height. These ranges allow heavier weights for more muscular and larger boned bodies.

Another way to determine if you are at your ideal weight is to measure your waist and hips. Your waist should measure less than your hips.

Having too much fat around your waist is a greater health risk than having excess fat on your hips and thighs—it's better to be shaped like a pear than like an apple.

If you need to lose weight, set reasonable goals, and develop good eating and exercising habits that will last a lifetime.

Healthy Weight Ranges for Men and Women

Height (without shoes)	Weight in Pounds (without clothes)
5'0"	97-128
5'1"	101-132
5'2"	104-137
5'3"	107-141
5'4"	111-146
5'5"	114-150
5'6"	118-155
5'7"	121-160
5'8"	125-164
5'9"	129-169
5'10"	132-174
5'11"	136-179
6'0"	140-184
6'1"	144-189
6'2"	148-195
6'3"	152-200
6'4"	156-205
6'5"	160-211
6'6"	164-216

3. Choose a Diet Low in Fat, Saturated Fat, and Cholesterol

No more than 30 percent of your daily total of calories should come from fat. Although this doesn't mean that every food you eat has to be under 30 percent, *most* of the foods you eat during the day should contain no more than 30 percent calories from fat. Here's how this translates to grams of fat per day:

If you eat...	You can have...
1600 calories/day	Up to 53 grams of fat/day
2200 calories/day	Up to 73 grams of fat/day

But not all fat is created equal. In fact, fat is made of units called fatty acids. These are classified by their chemical structures as **saturated**, **monounsaturated**, or **polyunsaturated**. The fats in most foods are a mixture of these fatty acids, but are classified by the one that predominates.

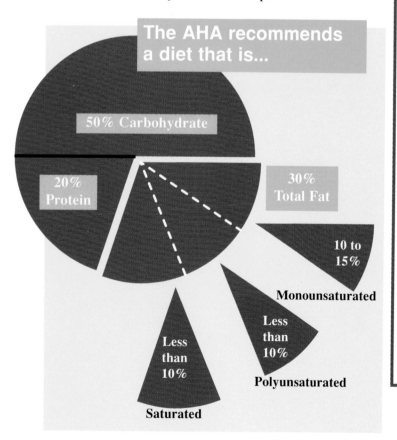

The AHA recommends a diet that is...

50% Carbohydrate
20% Protein
30% Total Fat
10 to 15% Monounsaturated
Less than 10% Polyunsaturated
Less than 10% Saturated

Besides decreasing your fat intake, you need to limit **cholesterol**, which is a fat-like substance found only in animal products. The AHA recommends limiting your intake of dietary cholesterol to 300 milligrams per day.

Just by eating fewer foods from animal sources and fewer high-fat and high-cholesterol foods, you automatically limit your saturated fat and your cholesterol intake.

HOW TO CUT THE FAT

- **Use** only 5 to 8 teaspoons of fat and oil a day (including what you use in cooking and put on salads). Use only small amounts of salad dressings, butter, margarine, and mayonnaise, and try reduced-fat or nonfat substitutes.
- **Choose** liquid vegetable oils instead of vegetable shortenings, butter, and other solid fats.
- **Check** food labels to see how much total fat and saturated fat are in a serving, and select foods accordingly.
- **Boil,** broil, bake, roast, poach, microwave, sauté, or steam foods. These are ways to cook with little or no fat.
- **Eat** no more than 6 ounces of cooked lean meat, fish, and/or poultry a day.
- **Focus** on grains and vegetables. Make meat the side dish.
- **Serve** beans and legumes like black beans or lentils instead of meat.
- **Eat** fewer organ meats (livers, brains, chitterlings, kidneys, hearts, gizzards, and sweetbreads).
- **Remove** skin from poultry either before or after cooking it.
- **Choose** low-fat dairy products like skim milk and nonfat or low-fat yogurts and cheeses.
- **Eat** no more than 3 or 4 egg yolks per week, including those used in cooking and in commercial products. Egg whites contain no fat, so you can eat all you wish.

4. Choose a Diet with Plenty of Grain Products, Vegetables, and Fruits

Carbohydrate foods are so important that heart experts recommend you get more than half of your calories from fruits, vegetables, and grains.

For fruits and vegetables, this amount translates to five servings a day, the minimum number of servings suggested in the Dietary Guidelines.

Your diet also should include at least six servings of starch (grain products like breads, cereals, pastas, and rice). These foods are generally low-fat, and provide vitamins, minerals, fiber, and complex carbohydrates. See page 14 for ways to add more bread to your diet.

5. Choose a Diet Moderate in Sugars

Sugar itself is not such a bad guy; it has 50 calories per tablespoon and no fat. But some of the foods that contain sugar—cookies, cakes, candies, soft drinks—supply a lot of calories and few nutrients.

When you read food labels, you'll see that sugar comes in many forms:

brown sugar	lactose
corn sweetener	maltose
fructose	molasses
glucose (dextrose)	syrup
honey	table sugar (sucrose)

Watch for sugars on low-fat food labels because excess sugar can make a low-fat food high in calories. If you have diabetes or high levels of blood fats, you may need to pay close attention to how much sugar you eat.

6. Choose a Diet Moderate in Salt and Sodium

The average American eats 4,000 to 6,000 milligrams of sodium (equivalent to 2 to 3 teaspoons of salt) a day. The AHA recommends that you decrease your daily sodium intake to less than 3,000 milligrams. Reducing your sodium intake may help you avoid high blood pressure or normalize your blood pressure.

HOW TO SHAKE THE SALT HABIT

•**Put** the saltshaker away. Add salt sparingly while cooking; don't add salt at the table.
•**Use** herbs and spices for flavor.
•**Avoid** buying high-sodium foods. Look for low-sodium varieties of cheese, processed meats, packaged mixes, canned soups and vegetables, and condiments.
•**Learn** the label lingo for sodium content.
very low sodium: 35 milligrams or less per serving
low sodium: 140 milligrams or less
reduced or less sodium products: contain at least 25 percent less sodium per serving than traditional versions
•**Cut** back on salted snacks. Look for reduced-sodium chips and crackers.

7. If You Drink Alcoholic Beverages, Do So in Moderation

Although studies have shown that drinking moderate amounts of alcohol may lower your risk of heart disease, alcohol supplies plenty of calories but few other nutrients. Also, drinking too much can lead to various health problems and accidents.

Moderate drinking is considered to be 12 ounces of regular beer, 4 to 5 ounces of wine, or 1½ ounces (80 proof) distilled spirits per day. As the AHA suggests: If you don't drink, don't start.

Super Simple Bread Ideas

Serving bread with a one-dish meal is as simple as going to the bakery or to the grocery store. Here are some ways to add shape, variety, and flavor to your meals.

Start with bagels

and make...

a sandwich,

chips,

croutons

Start with flour tortillas

and make...

burritos,

a bowl,

chips

Start with pita bread

and make...

a sandwich,

chips,

strips

Start with a sourdough loaf

and make...

a bread bowl,

slices,

croutons

7 Salads in Seconds

Buy seven easy-to-find ingredients and turn them into seven simple salads—one for each day of the week. The shopping list below tells you what to buy to serve four people a salad each day.

Start with these 7 ingredients:

- 3 heads curly leaf lettuce
- 1 head red cabbage
- 6 large tomatoes
- 1 pound carrots
- 4 cucumbers
- 5 medium onions
- Low-fat vinaigrette of choice

A SALAD A DAY

These salads are nutritious and colorful accompaniments to a week's worth of one-dish meals. And they'll add at least one serving of vegetables a day to your diet.

1 Zesty Greens: Combine 4 cups lettuce and ½ cup vinaigrette. Yield: 4 servings.

2 Marinated Tomatoes: Combine 2 large tomatoes (sliced), ¼ cup chopped onion, and ¼ cup vinaigrette. Cover and chill. Yield: 4 servings.

3 Zesty Greens and Tomato: Toss 6 cups torn lettuce, 1 cup chopped tomato, and ¼ cup vinaigrette. Yield: 4 servings.

4 **Mediterranean Salad:** Combine 1 medium onion (cut into rings), 2 tomatoes (quartered), and 1 cucumber (peeled and sliced). Marinate in ½ cup vinaigrette. Yield: 4 servings.

5 **Coleslaw:** Combine 4 cups shredded cabbage, 1 cup shredded carrot, ¾ cup chopped onion, and ½ cup vinaigrette. Yield: 4 servings.

6 **Marinated Cucumbers:** Combine 2 cucumbers (peeled and sliced), 1 onion (sliced), and ½ cup vinaigrette. Cover and chill. Yield: 4 servings.

7 **Tossed Salad:** Toss 6 cups torn lettuce, 1 cup chopped tomato, ½ cup chopped onion, 1 cup sliced cucumber, 1 cup shredded cabbage, 1 cup chopped carrot, and ½ cup vinaigrette. Yield: 4 servings.

Herbed Vinaigrette

Here's a low-fat vinaigrette you can use with the seven salads on the left.

Herbed Vinaigrette

2½ cups canned no-salt-added
    chicken broth, undiluted
1½ cups cider vinegar
1½ tablespoons vegetable oil
  2 teaspoons fresh herb of choice

Combine all ingredients in a jar; cover tightly, and shake vigorously to blend. Chill mixture thoroughly. Yield: 4 cups.

Per Tablespoon: Calories 5 (72% from fat)
Fat 0.4g (Sat 0.0g Mono 0.1g Poly 0.2g) Chol 0mg
Protein 0.1g Carbohydrate 0.4g Sodium 5mg
Exchanges: Free

Chili

Chunky
Beef Chili
in Tortilla
Bowls
(page 26)

chili (CHI-lee): a Texas creation that consists of a spicy stew most often made with ground meat and chili powder. Whether it contains beans or not is a sometimes hotly debated topic that has fired up many feuds and ended a few friendships.

Easy Sausage Chili (page 23)   Cincinnati Five-Way Chili (page 24)

Chunky Vegetable Chili

4½ cups canned no-salt-added chicken broth,
    undiluted and divided
¾ cup bulgur, uncooked
    Vegetable cooking spray
2 teaspoons olive oil
1 cup chopped onion
½ cup chopped green pepper
2 jalapeño peppers, seeded and minced
2 cloves garlic, minced
1½ cups water
2 (14½-ounce) cans no-salt-added stewed
    tomatoes
1 (15-ounce) can no-salt-added pinto beans,
    drained
¼ cup no-salt-added tomato paste
2 tablespoons chili powder
2 teaspoons ground cumin
½ teaspoon salt
½ teaspoon dried oregano
¼ teaspoon pepper
2 cups peeled, diced potato

Bring 1 cup chicken broth to a boil in a medium
saucepan; add bulgur. Cover and let stand 10 minutes
or until liquid is absorbed.

    Coat a Dutch oven with cooking spray; add oil.
Place over medium-high heat until hot. Add onion and
next 3 ingredients; sauté until tender. Add bulgur,
remaining 3½ cups chicken broth, water, and remaining ingredients; bring to a boil. Reduce heat; simmer,
uncovered, 1 hour and 10 minutes or until thickened.
Yield: 7 (1½-cup) servings.

Per Serving: Calories 268 (8% calories from fat)
Fat 2.5g (Sat 0.4g Mono 1.2g Poly 0.7g) Chol 0mg
Protein 12.0g Carbohydrate 51.1g Sodium 225mg
Exchanges: 3 Starch, 1 Vegetable, ½ Fat

White Bean Chili

¼ pound dried Great Northern beans
2 (14¼-ounce) cans no-salt-added chicken broth
    Vegetable cooking spray
2 teaspoons vegetable oil
1 cup chopped onion
½ cup sliced green onions
2 cloves garlic, minced
1 pound freshly ground raw chicken breast
1 cup fresh or frozen whole-kernel corn
1 tablespoon chili powder
½ teaspoon salt
¼ teaspoon ground cumin
1 (4½-ounce) can chopped green chiles
2 tablespoons yellow cornmeal
    Chopped green onions (optional)

Sort and wash beans; place beans in a large Dutch
oven. Cover with water to a depth of 2 inches above
beans. Bring to a boil; cover, remove from heat, and
let stand for 1 hour. Drain beans, and return to Dutch
oven. Add chicken broth; bring to a boil. Cover,
reduce heat, and simmer 1 hour or until beans are
tender. Remove ¼ cup cooked beans, and mash with
a fork. Return mashed beans to Dutch oven.

    Coat a large nonstick skillet with cooking spray; add
oil. Place over medium-high heat until hot; add
chopped onion, sliced green onions, and garlic; sauté
until tender. Add chicken; cook until chicken is no
longer pink, stirring until it crumbles. Add chicken
mixture to beans in Dutch oven; stir well. Add corn and
next 4 ingredients; bring to a boil. Reduce heat, and
simmer, uncovered, 20 minutes. Sprinkle cornmeal over
chili; cook until thickened, stirring often. To serve,
ladle into individual bowls, and top with chopped green
onions, if desired. Yield: 4 (1½-cup) servings.

Per Serving: Calories 344 (13% calories from fat)
Fat 4.8g (Sat 1.0g Mono 1.2g Poly 1.8g) Chol 66mg
Protein 35.6g Carbohydrate 38.6g Sodium 400mg
Exchanges: 4 Very Lean Meat, 2 Starch, 2 Vegetable

---

bulgur (BULL-guhr): whole wheat kernels that are boiled, dried, cracked, and sifted.

Chicken Chili

Vegetable cooking spray
1 teaspoon vegetable oil
1 pound freshly ground raw chicken breast
1½ cups chopped onion
1½ cups chopped green pepper
1 cup thinly sliced celery
1 tablespoon minced garlic
2 (15-ounce) cans no-salt-added kidney beans, drained
2 (14½-ounce) cans no-salt-added whole tomatoes, undrained and chopped
1 (14¼-ounce) can no-salt-added chicken broth
2 tablespoons chili powder
1½ tablespoons unsweetened cocoa
1½ tablespoons cider vinegar
2 teaspoons ground cumin
1 teaspoon salt
1 teaspoon ground red pepper
2 teaspoons honey

Coat a Dutch oven with cooking spray; add oil. Place over medium heat until hot. Add chicken and next 4 ingredients; cook 8 to 10 minutes or until chicken is no longer pink, stirring until it crumbles. Add kidney beans and remaining ingredients; stir well. Bring to a boil; reduce heat, and simmer, uncovered, 35 minutes. Yield: 6 (1½-cup) servings.

Per Serving: Calories 284 (15% calories from fat) Fat 4.6g (Sat 1.1g Mono 1.2g Poly 1.5g) Chol 53mg Protein 26.1g Carbohydrate 35.7g Sodium 512mg
Exchanges: 2 Lean Meat, 2 Starch, 1 Vegetable

Three-Bean Chicken Chili

Vegetable cooking spray
2 teaspoons vegetable oil
1 cup chopped onion
1 cup chopped zucchini
1 cup chopped celery
3 tablespoons seeded, chopped jalapeño pepper
2 tablespoons minced garlic
1 tablespoon dried oregano
1 tablespoon ground cumin
1 tablespoon chili powder
1 teaspoon dried crushed red pepper
3 cups canned low-sodium chicken broth, undiluted
1¾ cups chopped cooked chicken breast (skinned before cooking and cooked without salt)
1 (15-ounce) can no-salt-added pinto beans, drained
1 (15-ounce) can no-salt-added garbanzo beans, drained
1 (15-ounce) can cannellini beans, drained
1 (8-ounce) can no-salt-added tomato sauce
2 tablespoons balsamic vinegar
¼ cup chopped fresh cilantro
¼ cup nonfat sour cream
¼ cup (1 ounce) shredded, reduced-fat sharp Cheddar cheese
¼ cup chopped green onions

Coat a large nonstick skillet with cooking spray; add oil. Place over medium-high heat until hot. Add onion and next 4 ingredients; sauté until crisp-tender. Add oregano and next 3 ingredients; sauté 1 minute.

Add chicken broth and next 6 ingredients, stirring well. Bring to a boil; cover, reduce heat, and simmer 20 minutes. Add cilantro; cover and cook 5 additional minutes. To serve, ladle into bowls; top evenly with sour cream, cheese, and green onions. Yield: 5 (2-cup) servings.

Per Serving: Calories 425 (18% calories from fat) Fat 8.7g (Sat 2.1g Mono 2.5g Poly 2.6g) Chol 53mg Protein 33.3g Carbohydrate 45.2g Sodium 494mg
Exchanges: 3 Lean Meat, 3 Starch

Easy
Sausage
Chili

Easy Sausage Chili

¾ pound ground turkey sausage
1 cup chopped onion
1 cup chopped green pepper
1 cup chopped celery
2 (14½-ounce) cans no-salt-added whole
    tomatoes, undrained and chopped
1 (15-ounce) can no-salt-added kidney beans,
    drained
¼ cup no-salt-added tomato paste
½ teaspoon dried thyme
¼ teaspoon pepper
¼ cup nonfat sour cream
    Diced fresh tomato (optional)
    Fresh thyme sprigs (optional)

Cook first 4 ingredients in a Dutch oven over medium heat until sausage is browned and vegetables are tender, stirring until sausage crumbles. Drain mixture, and pat dry with paper towels. Wipe drippings from Dutch oven with a paper towel.

Return sausage mixture to Dutch oven; add canned tomato and next 4 ingredients. Bring to a boil; cover, reduce heat, and simmer 35 minutes.

To serve, ladle chili into individual bowls; top each serving with 1 tablespoon sour cream. If desired, garnish with diced tomato and fresh thyme. Yield: 4 (1½-cup) servings.

Per Serving: Calories 304 (28% calories from fat)
Fat 9.3g (Sat 2.6g Mono 0.1g Poly 2.4g) Chol 52mg
Protein 23.4g Carbohydrate 34.4g Sodium 528mg
Exchanges: 2 Medium-Fat Meat, 2 Starch, 1 Vegetable

Salsa Chili and Cornbread

1 pound ground round
1 cup chopped onion
1 cup no-salt-added salsa
½ cup beer
⅓ cup finely chopped fresh cilantro
¼ cup no-salt-added tomato paste
1 tablespoon chili powder
¼ teaspoon salt
1 (15-ounce) can no-salt-added kidney beans,
    drained
¼ cup yellow cornmeal
¼ cup all-purpose flour
1 teaspoon baking powder
⅛ teaspoon salt
2 teaspoons sugar
¼ teaspoon coarsely ground pepper
¼ cup frozen egg substitute, thawed
¼ cup evaporated skimmed milk
1 tablespoon vegetable oil
½ cup (2 ounces) shredded reduced-fat
    Cheddar cheese

Place meat and onion in a 10½-inch ovenproof skillet. Cook over medium-high heat until meat is browned, stirring until it crumbles. Drain mixture, and pat dry with paper towels. Wipe drippings from skillet with a paper towel.

Return meat mixture to skillet. Add salsa and next 6 ingredients. Bring to a boil; cover, reduce heat, and simmer 30 minutes.

Combine cornmeal and next 5 ingredients in a bowl; make a well in center of mixture. Combine egg substitute, milk, and oil; add to dry ingredients, stirring just until dry ingredients are moistened.

Pour batter over meat mixture in skillet. Bake, uncovered, at 400° for 10 minutes or until cornbread is golden. Sprinkle with cheese, and let stand 5 minutes or until cheese melts. Yield: 6 servings.

Per Serving: Calories 312 (27% calories from fat)
Fat 9.4g (Sat 3.2g Mono 2.7g Poly 1.7g) Chol 53mg
Protein 27.3g Carbohydrate 29.9g Sodium 397mg
Exchanges: 3 Lean Meat, 2 Starch

Cincinnati Five-Way Chili

Vegetable cooking spray
1 pound ground round
2 cups chopped onion
1 cup chopped green pepper
2 tablespoons chili powder
1 teaspoon sugar
1 teaspoon paprika
½ teaspoon salt
½ teaspoon garlic powder
¼ teaspoon ground red pepper
¼ teaspoon ground cinnamon
¼ teaspoon ground cumin
1 teaspoon cider vinegar
1 (15-ounce) can no-salt-added kidney beans, drained
1 (14½-ounce) can no-salt-added whole tomatoes, undrained and coarsely chopped
1 (8-ounce) can no-salt-added tomato sauce
1 bay leaf
4½ cups cooked spaghetti (cooked without salt or fat)
½ cup (2 ounces) shredded reduced-fat Cheddar cheese
Oyster crackers (optional)

Coat a Dutch oven with cooking spray. Add meat, onion, and green pepper; cook over medium heat until meat is browned, stirring until it crumbles. Drain mixture, and pat dry with paper towels. Wipe drippings from Dutch oven with a paper towel.

Return meat mixture to Dutch oven. Add chili powder and next 12 ingredients. Bring to a boil; cover, reduce heat, and simmer 1 hour or until mixture is very thick, stirring often. Remove and discard bay leaf.

To serve, place ¾ cup spaghetti on each of 6 plates; spoon ¾ cup chili over each serving. Top chili evenly with cheese. Add oyster crackers, if desired. Yield: 6 servings.

Per Serving: Calories 412 (18% calories from fat) Fat 8.1g (Sat 3.0g Mono 2.7g Poly 1.0g) Chol 53mg Protein 30.1g Carbohydrate 55.1g Sodium 347mg **Exchanges:** 2½ Lean Meat, 3 Starch, 2 Vegetable

---

ON TOP OF SPAGHETTI...

That's one way to serve traditional cinnamon-spiced chili in the Queen City. If you want this two-way version plus extra toppings, just keep counting—
•**Three-way** = plus shredded cheese
•**Four-way** = plus onions
•**Five-way** = plus beans
•**All-the-way** = plus oyster crackers

Cincinnati
Five-Way
Chili

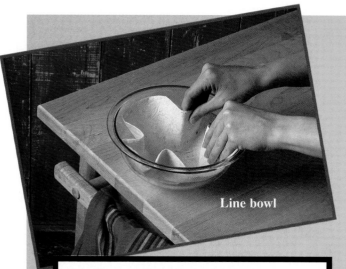

Line bowl

EASY EDIBLE BOWLS

•**Line** a 1½-quart glass bowl with a 10-inch flour tortilla. Prick holes in the bottom of the tortilla with a fork (this allows steam to escape as the tortilla cooks so it won't cause a bubble in the bottom of your tortilla bowl).

Microwave for 1½ to 2 minutes or until the tortilla is crisp. Take it out of the oven, and let it cool a little.

Remove from glass bowl

•**Remove** the tortilla from the glass bowl, and repeat the process until you have enough tortilla bowls for all your fiesta guests.

Chunky Beef Chili in Tortilla Bowls

6 (10-inch) flour tortillas
1 cup water
3 ancho chiles, seeded
1 pound lean boneless top sirloin steak, trimmed and cut into ½-inch pieces
¼ teaspoon salt
¼ teaspoon pepper
2 tablespoons all-purpose flour
Vegetable cooking spray
1 teaspoon vegetable oil
1 (14½-ounce) can no-salt-added beef broth, divided
1½ cups chopped onion
1 tablespoon paprika
¾ teaspoon ground oregano
3 cloves garlic, minced
1 cup canned no-salt-added whole-kernel corn, drained
Fresh oregano sprigs (optional)

Line a medium glass bowl with 1 tortilla. Prick bottom of tortilla with a fork. Microwave at HIGH 1½ minutes or until crisp. Repeat with remaining tortillas.

Bring water to a boil in a saucepan. Add chiles; cover, remove from heat, and let stand 30 minutes. Place chile mixture in container of an electric blender; cover and process until smooth. Set aside.

Sprinkle meat with salt and pepper. Place flour in a zip-top plastic bag; add meat. Seal bag; shake to coat.

Coat a Dutch oven with cooking spray; add oil. Place over medium-high heat until hot. Add meat; cook until browned. Remove meat from Dutch oven; set aside. Add ½ cup broth to Dutch oven; cook over high heat, deglazing Dutch oven by scraping particles that cling to bottom. Add chile mixture, meat, remaining broth, onion, and next 3 ingredients. Bring to a boil; cover, reduce heat, and simmer 1 hour or until meat is tender. Add corn; simmer 3 minutes. To serve, spoon chili into tortilla bowls. Garnish with fresh oregano, if desired. Yield 5 (1¼-cup) servings.

Per Serving: Calories 403 (23% calories from fat)
Fat 10.5g (Sat 2.6g Mono 3.9g Poly 2.5g) Chol 55mg
Protein 26.7g Carbohydrate 48.1g Sodium 461mg
Exchanges: 2 Medium-Fat Meat, 3 Starch, 1 Vegetable

Chunky
Beef
Chili in
Tortilla
Bowls

Chili Mac

1 pound ground round
1 cup coarsely chopped onion
½ cup coarsely chopped celery
3 cloves garlic, minced
1 cup canned no-salt-added beef broth,
   undiluted
1 cup water
1 (12-ounce) can beer
1 (8-ounce) can no-salt-added tomato sauce
3 tablespoons chili powder
1 tablespoon brown sugar
1 teaspoon paprika
½ teaspoon salt
½ teaspoon ground cumin
1½ cups elbow macaroni, uncooked
¼ cup (1 ounce) shredded reduced-fat Cheddar
   cheese

Cook first 4 ingredients in a Dutch oven over medium heat until meat is browned and vegetables are tender, stirring until meat crumbles. Drain and pat dry with paper towels. Wipe drippings from Dutch oven with a paper towel.

Return meat mixture to Dutch oven; add broth and next 8 ingredients. Bring to a boil; cover, reduce heat, and simmer 30 minutes. Uncover and stir in macaroni. Cook, uncovered, 10 minutes or until macaroni is done, stirring often.

To serve, ladle chili into individual bowls, and top each serving with 1 tablespoon cheese. Yield: 4 (1½-cup) servings.

Note: We used beer for extra flavor in the Chili Mac. If you'd rather not use beer, just use an additional 1½ cups no-salt-added beef broth instead.

Per Serving: Calories 427 (21% calories from fat)
Fat 9.9g (Sat 3.6g Mono 3.2g Poly 1.1g) Chol 74mg
Protein 33.3g Carbohydrate 45.2g Sodium 494mg
Exchanges: 3 Lean Meat, 3 Starch

Pork and Green Chile Chili

1½ pounds lean boneless pork loin
   Vegetable cooking spray
1 cup thinly sliced celery
3 cups diced round red potato
3 cups coarsely chopped tomato
4 (10¾-ounce) cans low-sodium chicken broth
2 (4½-ounce) cans chopped green chiles
1 (10-ounce) package frozen whole-kernel corn,
   thawed
2 tablespoons chili powder
1 teaspoon ground cumin
1 teaspoon dried oregano
½ teaspoon salt
1 (15-ounce) can no-salt-added black beans,
   drained and divided

Trim fat from pork; cut pork into 1-inch cubes. Coat a large Dutch oven with cooking spray, and place over medium-high heat until hot. Add pork and celery; cook, stirring constantly, until pork is browned and celery is tender. Remove from Dutch oven; wipe drippings from Dutch oven with a paper towel.

Return pork mixture to Dutch oven; add potato and next 8 ingredients, stirring well. Bring to a boil; cover, reduce heat, and simmer 1 hour or until pork is tender.

Place half of beans in a shallow dish; mash with a fork to form a paste. Add bean paste and remaining beans to pork mixture, stirring well; bring to a boil. Cook, uncovered, 10 minutes or until mixture is thickened. Yield: 7 (1½-cup) servings.

Per Serving: Calories 362 (30% calories from fat)
Fat 11.9g (Sat 3.8g Mono 5.0g Poly 1.8g) Chol 63 mg
Protein 27.3g Carbohydrate 38.9g Sodium 321mg
Exchanges: 2 Medium-Fat Meat, 2 Starch, 2 Vegetable

cilantro (sih-LAHN-troh): an herb in the parsley family; also known as coriander leaves or Chinese parsley. A typical ingredient in Mexican, Caribbean, Indian, and Asian dishes.

Pork Chili with Pintos

1 (2-pound) lean boneless pork loin roast
¼ teaspoon pepper
¼ teaspoon paprika
  Vegetable cooking spray
1 teaspoon vegetable oil
1 cup chopped onion
2 cloves garlic, minced
2 cups canned no-salt-added chicken broth,
  undiluted
1 tablespoon dried oregano
2 tablespoons chili paste
2 large poblano peppers, seeded and chopped
1 small jalapeño pepper, seeded and chopped
1 (15-ounce) can no-salt-added pinto beans
8 fat-free flour tortillas
½ cup mashed ripe avocado
¼ cup minced fresh cilantro
1 (12½-ounce) jar tomatillo salsa
½ cup diced jicama
  Fresh cilantro sprigs (optional)

Trim fat from pork; sprinkle roast with pepper and paprika.

Coat a large Dutch oven with cooking spray; add oil. Place over medium-high heat until hot. Add pork, and cook until browned on all sides. Drain and pat dry with paper towels. Wipe drippings from Dutch oven with a paper towel.

Coat Dutch oven with cooking spray. Place over medium-high heat until hot. Add onion and garlic; sauté until tender. Return pork to Dutch oven. Add chicken broth and next 4 ingredients. Bring to a boil; cover, reduce heat, and simmer 1½ hours or until pork is tender. Remove pork from broth.

Shred pork using two forks. Return pork to Dutch oven. Place beans in a bowl, and mash with a fork until smooth; add to Dutch oven, stirring well. Cook over medium-high heat until thoroughly heated.

Cut tortillas into wedges; place on a baking sheet coated with cooking spray. Bake at 400° for 5 minutes or until crisp and lightly browned.

Combine avocado, minced cilantro, and salsa in a small bowl, stirring well.

To serve, ladle chili into 8 serving bowls; top each serving with ¼ cup avocado mixture and 1 tablespoon jicama. Serve with tortilla wedges. Garnish with fresh cilantro sprigs, if desired. Yield: 8 (1-cup) servings.

Per Serving: Calories 408 (30% calories from fat)
Fat 13.5g (Sat 4.3g Mono 6.0g Poly 1.9g) Chol 72mg
Protein 28.8g Carbohydrate 40.1g Sodium 663mg
Exchanges: 3 Medium-Fat Meat, 2 Starch, 2 Vegetable

HOT AND HOTTER

Some chile peppers wear two sombreros: They have one name when fresh and another when dried. For example, the ancho chile is actually a dried poblano chile. With its dark red color, the ancho is one of Mexico's most popular peppers. The ancho is a relatively sweet-tasting pepper that ranges in spiciness from mild to medium.

The poblano is a fresh chile pepper that is dark green—almost black—and ranges from medium to hot.

If you have a hot chile pepper, you can make it milder by removing its ribs and seeds—that's where the heat is.

Eggs and

Vegetable-
Gruyère
Quiche
(page 43)

Cheese

eggs and cheese (eggz-'n'-cheez): a culinary duo as classic as salt 'n' pepper, meat 'n' potatoes, or peaches 'n' cream. Blended together, they're often served as sandwiches, stratas, quiches, and omelets.

Creole Omelet (page 39)

Horseradish Cheese Toast with Tomatoes (page 32)

Apple-Cheese Breakfast Sandwiches

⅓ cup vanilla low-fat yogurt
1 tablespoon honey
⅛ teaspoon ground cinnamon
2 English muffins, split
1 medium Granny Smith apple, cored and peeled
¼ cup (1 ounce) shredded reduced-fat sharp Cheddar cheese
2 (½-ounce) slices Canadian bacon
  Butter-flavored vegetable cooking spray

Spoon yogurt onto several layers of heavy-duty paper towels; spread to ½-inch thickness. Cover with additional paper towels; let stand 15 minutes. Scrape yogurt into a small bowl, using a rubber spatula. Add honey and cinnamon; stir well. Spread yogurt mixture evenly over 2 muffin halves.

Slice apple crosswise into thin rings; place 1 ring over yogurt mixture on each muffin half, reserving remaining apple.

Sprinkle cheese over apple on muffins; top with bacon and remaining 2 muffin halves.

Coat a nonstick skillet with cooking spray; place over medium heat until hot. Add sandwiches; cook 2 minutes on each side or until golden. Serve with remaining apple slices. Yield: 2 servings.

Per Serving: Calories 325 (16% calories from fat)
Fat 5.8g (Sat 2.2g Poly 0.3g Mono 1.3g) Chol 18mg
Protein 13.7g Carbohydrate 55.9g Sodium 619mg
Exchanges: 1 Medium-Fat Meat, 3 Starch, 1 Fruit

Horseradish Cheese Toast with Tomatoes

8 slices turkey bacon, cut in half crosswise
1 small onion, quartered
¾ cup (3 ounces) shredded reduced-fat sharp Cheddar cheese
1 tablespoon prepared horseradish
1 tablespoon plain nonfat yogurt
  Dash of pepper
8 (1-ounce) slices French bread (¾ inch thick), lightly toasted
2 small tomatoes
¼ cup thinly sliced green onions
  Cherry tomatoes (optional)
  Fresh oregano (optional)

Partially cook bacon 3 minutes in a nonstick skillet; drain and set aside.

Position knife blade in food processor bowl; add quartered onion. Process until finely chopped. Add cheese and next 3 ingredients; process until onion is minced, scraping sides of processor bowl occasionally. Set aside.

Place toasted bread slices on a baking sheet; spread cheese mixture evenly over slices, spreading to edges of bread. Cut each small tomato into 4 slices. Top each slice of bread with a tomato slice and 2 bacon pieces. Broil 5½ inches from heat (with electric oven door partially opened) 2 to 2½ minutes or until cheese melts and bacon is crisp. Sprinkle with green onions. If desired, garnish with cherry tomatoes and fresh oregano. Yield: 4 servings.

Per Serving: Calories 335 (26% calories from fat)
Fat 9.8g (Sat 3.7g Poly 1.8g Mono 2.4g) Chol 33mg
Protein 16.9g Carbohydrate 43.0g Sodium 907mg
Exchanges: 1 High-Fat Meat, 2 Starch, 2 Vegetable

Horseradish
Cheese Toast
with Tomatoes

Swiss Cheese Fondue

3 tablespoons reduced-calorie margarine
2 tablespoons all-purpose flour
¼ teaspoon garlic powder
  Dash of ground white pepper
2½ cups evaporated skimmed milk
3 cups (12 ounces) shredded reduced-fat
  Swiss cheese
½ cup dry white wine
1 teaspoon low-sodium Worcestershire sauce
  Dash of hot sauce
1 (8-ounce) loaf French bread, cut into
  1-inch cubes
4 medium Red Delicious apples, cut into wedges
4 Granny Smith apples, cut into wedges

Melt margarine in a medium saucepan over medium heat; add flour, garlic powder, and pepper. Cook 1 minute, stirring constantly with a wire whisk. Gradually add milk, stirring constantly. Cook, stirring constantly, 12 to 14 minutes or until thickened and bubbly. Add cheese and wine, stirring well. Cook over low heat until cheese melts. Add Worcestershire sauce and hot sauce, stirring occasionally.

Transfer cheese mixture to a fondue pot, and keep warm. Serve with bread cubes and apple wedges. Yield: 8 servings (serving size: ½ cup fondue, 8 bread cubes, and 8 apple wedges).

Note: This recipe can also be served with fresh raw vegetables like carrot sticks, celery sticks, and broccoli flowerets.

Per Serving: Calories 385 (27% calories from fat) Fat 11.4g (Sat 4.9g Mono 1.4g Poly 1.9g) Chol 30mg Protein 23.5g Carbohydrate 48.4g Sodium 382mg
Exchanges: 3 Lean Meat, 1 Starch, 2 Fruit

Tex-Mex Grits Casserole

4 cups water
¼ teaspoon salt
1 cup quick-cooking grits, uncooked
3 eggs, lightly beaten
½ cup minced reduced-fat, low-salt ham
¼ cup sliced green onions
1 cup no-salt-added pinto beans, drained
1 cup no-salt-added salsa, divided
  Vegetable cooking spray
2 tablespoons minced fresh cilantro
¼ teaspoon pepper
1 cup (4 ounces) shredded reduced-fat Monterey
  Jack cheese
  Tomato slices (optional)
  Fresh cilantro sprigs (optional)

Combine water and salt in a medium saucepan; bring to a boil. Stir in grits; cover, reduce heat, and simmer 5 minutes or until grits are thickened, stirring often. Gradually stir about one-fourth of hot grits mixture into eggs; add to remaining hot mixture, stirring constantly. Stir in ham and green onions. Set aside.

Position knife blade in food processor bowl; add beans and ¼ cup salsa. Process until smooth.

Spoon ⅓ cup grits mixture into each of 6 (10-ounce) ramekins or custard cups coated with cooking spray. Spoon bean mixture evenly over grits; sprinkle with minced cilantro and pepper. Spoon remaining ¾ cup salsa evenly over servings; sprinkle cheese over salsa. Spoon remaining grits mixture evenly over cheese. Bake at 350° for 30 minutes or until lightly browned. Let stand 15 minutes before serving. If desired, garnish with tomato slices and cilantro sprigs. Yield: 6 servings.

Per Serving: Calories 255 (26% calories from fat) Fat 7.5g (Sat 3.2g Mono 1.3g Poly 0.6g) Chol 130mg Protein 16.9g Carbohydrate 30.5g Sodium 460mg
Exchanges: 1 High-Fat Meat, 1½ Starch, 2 Vegetable

Peppered Grits Terrine

Vegetable cooking spray
1 teaspoon cracked pepper, divided
3¾ cups water
2¼ cups canned no-salt-added chicken broth, undiluted
¼ teaspoon salt
¼ teaspoon garlic powder
1¼ cups regular grits, uncooked
¾ cup (3 ounces) shredded reduced-fat sharp Cheddar cheese
¼ teaspoon hot sauce
4 slices turkey bacon, cooked
3 cups seeded, chopped tomato
3 cups seeded, chopped yellow tomato
¼ cup chopped green onions
2 tablespoons chopped fresh thyme
2 teaspoons lime juice

Coat a 9-inch loafpan with cooking spray. Line with heavy-duty plastic wrap, allowing plastic to extend over edges. Coat plastic wrap with cooking spray. Sprinkle ¼ teaspoon pepper on plastic wrap.

Combine ½ teaspoon pepper, water, and next 3 ingredients in a saucepan; bring to a boil. Add grits, stirring constantly. Cover, reduce heat, and simmer 15 minutes or until thickened, stirring occasionally. Remove from heat; stir in cheese and hot sauce.

Spread half of grits mixture in pan; place bacon lengthwise on top of grits. Spoon remaining grits over bacon. Sprinkle with remaining ¼ teaspoon pepper. Fold plastic wrap over grits; chill 8 hours.

Combine tomatoes and remaining 3 ingredients; cover and chill.

Invert grits loaf onto a cutting board; remove and discard plastic wrap. Cut loaf crosswise into 4 slices. Place on a baking sheet coated with cooking spray. Broil 3 inches from heat (with electric oven door partially opened) 10 minutes on each side or until golden. Top evenly with tomato mixture. Yield: 4 servings.

Per Serving: Calories 203 (31% calories from fat) Fat 6.9g (Sat 2.9g Mono 2.2g Poly 1.0g) Chol 23mg Protein 11.5g Carbohydrate 23.6g Sodium 503mg
Exchanges: 1 High-Fat Meat, 1 Starch, 1 Vegetable

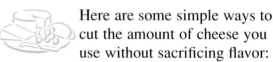

SAY CHEESE

Here are some simple ways to cut the amount of cheese you use without sacrificing flavor:
• If a recipe calls for 4 slices of cheese, add ½ cup (2 ounces) shredded cheese instead.
• Substitute a strong cheese (like sharp Cheddar) for a mild one (like colby). Reduce the amount by a third to a half.
• Or, easier yet, try one of the many low-fat cheeses now on the market. Just remember, low-fat cheeses take a little longer to melt and aren't as smooth and satiny as regular cheeses.

Scrambled Eggs and Vegetable Burritos

Vegetable cooking spray
2 small onions, thinly sliced and separated
   into rings
1 small green pepper, thinly sliced
2 cups seeded, chopped tomato
1¼ cups no-salt-added salsa, divided
1 cup canned no-salt-added whole-kernel corn
½ teaspoon cracked black pepper
¾ cup canned no-salt-added pinto beans,
   drained
1 tablespoon taco seasoning mix
8 (8-inch) flour tortillas
¾ cup (3 ounces) shredded reduced-fat Cheddar
   cheese
4 eggs
4 egg whites

Coat a nonstick skillet with cooking spray; place over
medium-high heat until hot. Add onion and green pepper; sauté until tender. Add tomato, 1 cup salsa, corn,
and black pepper; cook over medium heat until thoroughly heated. Set aside.

Position knife blade in food processor bowl; add
beans, seasoning mix, and remaining ¼ cup salsa.
Process until smooth, scraping sides of processor bowl
once. Spread about 2 tablespoons bean mixture across
center of each tortilla; sprinkle tortillas evenly with
cheese.

Combine eggs and egg whites; beat well. Coat a
nonstick skillet with cooking spray; place over medium heat until hot. Add egg mixture; cook, stirring
often, until mixture is firm but still moist. Spoon egg
mixture evenly over tortillas. Roll up tortillas; place,
seam side down, in an 11- x 7- x 1½-inch baking dish.
Cover with heavy-duty plastic wrap, and vent.

Microwave tortillas at HIGH 45 seconds or until
thoroughly heated. Spoon vegetable mixture evenly
over burritos. Serve immediately. Yield: 8 servings.

Per Serving: Calories 249 (27% calories from fat)
Fat 7.4g (Sat 2.4g Mono 1.9g Poly 1.4g) Chol 117mg
Protein 14.0g Carbohydrate 32.3g Sodium 405mg
Exchanges: 1 High-Fat Meat, 1½ Starch, 2 Vegetable

Peachy French Toast

1 cup skim milk
¼ cup sugar
1 tablespoon plus 1 teaspoon reduced-calorie
   margarine, melted
2 eggs
4 egg whites
   Vegetable cooking spray
12 (1-ounce) slices French bread (1 inch thick)
6 fresh peaches, peeled and quartered
3 tablespoons brown sugar
¼ teaspoon ground cinnamon
¾ cup low-fat sour cream
3 tablespoons reduced-calorie maple syrup
¼ teaspoon vanilla extract

Combine first 5 ingredients in a shallow dish, stirring
mixture well.

Coat a large nonstick skillet with cooking spray;
place over medium heat until hot. Dip bread slices,
one at a time, into egg mixture, coating well.

Place 4 bread slices in skillet, and cook 6 to 8 minutes on each side or until browned. Remove from skillet, and keep warm. Repeat with remaining bread and
egg mixture.

Place peaches on a baking sheet coated with cooking spray. Combine brown sugar and cinnamon; sprinkle over peaches. Broil 5½ inches from heat (with
electric oven door partially opened) 4 to 5 minutes or
until sugar mixture is bubbly.

Combine sour cream, maple syrup, and vanilla in a
small bowl; stir well.

To serve, place 2 slices French toast and 4 peach
quarters on each serving plate. Top peaches with sour
cream mixture. Yield: 6 servings.

Per Serving: Calories 360 (20% calories from fat)
Fat 8.3g (Sat 3.4g Mono 2.9g Poly 1.6g) Chol 88mg
Protein 12.4g Carbohydrate 58.4g Sodium 447mg
Exchanges: 1 High-Fat Meat, 2 Starch, 2 Fruit

Spanish Omelet Turnovers

1 (11-ounce) package refrigerated crusty French
   loaf dough
1 cup frozen egg substitute, thawed
2 tablespoons 1% low-fat milk
⅛ teaspoon onion powder
⅛ teaspoon salt
   Olive oil-flavored vegetable cooking spray
½ cup sliced fresh mushrooms
¼ cup chopped green pepper
¼ cup (1 ounce) shredded reduced-fat sharp
   Cheddar cheese
½ teaspoon cracked black pepper
4 (⅛-inch-thick) slices tomato, cut in half

Unroll dough into a 13- x 12-inch rectangle; cut into
4 rectangles. Set aside.

Combine egg substitute and next 3 ingredients; stir
well with a wire whisk.

Coat a small nonstick skillet with cooking spray;
place over medium-high heat until hot. Add mushrooms and green pepper; sauté until tender. Add egg
substitute mixture; cook over medium heat until mixture is firm but still moist, stirring occasionally.

Spoon one-fourth of egg substitute mixture
evenly over half of each rectangle; sprinkle evenly
with cheese and cracked pepper. Top each with a
tomato slice. Fold rectangles in half over mixture;
press edges together with a fork. Coat with cooking
spray. Place turnovers on a baking sheet coated with
cooking spray. Bake at 375° for 15 minutes or until
golden. Serve immediately. Yield: 4 servings.

Per Serving: Calories 255 (11% calories from fat)
Fat 3.1g (Sat 1.2g Mono 0.9g Poly 0.6g) Chol 5mg
Protein 16.4g Carbohydrate 39.0g Sodium 684mg
Exchanges: 1 Lean Meat, 2 Starch, 2 Vegetable

Cut into rectangles

Top with tomato

Press edges

EASY TURNOVERS

Making turnovers is easy when you
start with a package of refrigerated
bread dough.
•**Cut** it into 4 smaller rectangles.
Spoon the egg mixture over half of
each rectangle, and sprinkle with
cheese and cracked pepper.
•**Top** mixture with tomato slices, and
fold the dough over the mixture.
•**Press** the edges together with a fork.

Creole
Omelet

Creole Omelet

1 teaspoon vegetable oil
1 teaspoon all-purpose flour
½ cup thinly sliced onion
½ cup thinly sliced green pepper
½ cup thinly sliced celery
½ teaspoon dried thyme
1 clove garlic, minced
¼ cup canned no-salt-added chicken broth,
  undiluted
1 (14½-ounce) can no-salt-added whole
  tomatoes, drained and chopped
¼ teaspoon salt
2 eggs, separated
1 tablespoon skim milk
1 tablespoon all-purpose flour
  Dash of pepper
  Vegetable cooking spray

Place oil in a medium nonstick skillet; add 1 teaspoon flour, and stir until smooth. Cook over medium heat until mixture is caramel colored, stirring often. Add onion and next 4 ingredients; sauté over medium-high heat 4 minutes. Add chicken broth; cook until thickened and bubbly, stirring often. Stir in tomato and salt. Set aside, and keep warm.

Beat egg yolks in a small bowl at high speed of an electric mixer until thick and pale. Add milk, and beat until blended; set aside.

Beat egg whites at high speed of electric mixer until soft peaks form. Gradually add 1 tablespoon flour and dash of pepper, beating until stiff peaks form. Fold egg white mixture into egg yolk mixture.

Coat a nonstick skillet with cooking spray; place over medium heat until hot. Pour egg mixture into skillet, spreading evenly. Cover, reduce heat to medium-low, and cook 15 minutes or until just set. Loosen omelet with a spatula, and fold in half. Slide onto a serving platter. Spoon tomato mixture over omelet, cut in half, and serve immediately. Yield: 2 servings.

Per Serving: Calories 191 (40% calories from fat) Fat 8.5g (Sat 2.1g Mono 2.7g Poly 2.0g) Chol 221mg Protein 10.0g Carbohydrate 19.7g Sodium 436mg **Exchanges:** 1 High-Fat Meat, 1 Starch, 1 Vegetable

Potato-Vegetable Omelets

  Vegetable cooking spray
1 cup unpeeled, shredded round red potato
½ cup chopped zucchini
½ cup chopped sweet red pepper
¼ cup sliced green onions
¼ teaspoon hot sauce
1½ cups frozen egg substitute, thawed
¼ cup skim milk
½ teaspoon minced fresh oregano
¼ teaspoon pepper
⅛ teaspoon salt
4 slices turkey bacon, cooked and crumbled
½ cup (2 ounces) shredded reduced-fat Cheddar
  cheese

Coat a nonstick skillet with cooking spray; place over medium-high heat until hot. Add potato and next 4 ingredients; sauté 7 to 9 minutes or until tender.

Combine egg substitute and next 4 ingredients. Stir well with a wire whisk.

Coat a 10-inch skillet with cooking spray; place over medium-high heat until hot. Pour half of egg substitute mixture into skillet. As mixture begins to cook, gently lift edges of omelet with a spatula, and tilt pan to allow uncooked portion to flow underneath. When set, spoon half of vegetable mixture over half of omelet. Sprinkle vegetable mixture with half of bacon and half of cheese. Loosen omelet with a spatula; carefully fold in half. Cook 1 to 2 additional minutes or until cheese begins to melt. Slide omelet onto a serving plate, cut in half, and keep warm. Repeat procedure with remaining egg mixture, vegetable mixture, bacon, and cheese. Yield: 4 servings.

Per Serving: Calories 163 (27% calories from fat) Fat 4.8g (Sat 2.1g Mono 0.9g Poly 0.6g) Chol 18mg Protein 17.0g Carbohydrate 11.9g Sodium 505mg **Exchanges:** 2 Lean Meat, 1 Starch

Summer Garden Pudding

1½ medium zucchini, unpeeled and grated
    Vegetable cooking spray
 ½ cup minced onion
  1 clove garlic, minced
  3 cups fresh corn cut from the cob (about 6 ears)
1¼ cups shredded carrot
  1 cup evaporated skimmed milk, divided
  1 tablespoon all-purpose flour
1½ tablespoons yellow cornmeal
  1 cup 1% low-fat cottage cheese
  2 eggs
  1 tablespoon chopped fresh thyme
 ¼ teaspoon salt
 ¼ teaspoon freshly ground pepper
  1 tablespoon fine, dry breadcrumbs

Press zucchini between paper towels to remove excess moisture. Set aside.

Coat a large nonstick skillet with cooking spray; place over medium-high heat until hot. Add onion and garlic; sauté 5 minutes or until tender. Add corn and carrot, and sauté 5 minutes or until tender.

Combine ¼ cup milk, flour, and cornmeal; stir well, and add to corn mixture in skillet. Cook, stirring constantly, until thickened and bubbly. Remove from heat.

Combine ½ cup milk, cottage cheese, and next 4 ingredients in container of an electric blender; cover and process until smooth. Add cottage cheese mixture to corn mixture; stir well. Stir in zucchini. Coat an 11- x 7- x 1½-inch baking dish with cooking spray, and sprinkle with breadcrumbs. Spoon mixture into dish. Pour remaining ¼ cup milk over mixture. Bake, uncovered, at 325° for 1 hour. Let stand 5 minutes before serving. Yield: 4 servings.

Per Serving: Calories 282 (16% calories from fat)
Fat 5.1g (Sat 1.5g Mono 1.7g Poly 1.2g) Chol 115mg
Protein 20.7g Carbohydrate 42.6g Sodium 527mg
Exchanges: 1½ Lean Meat, 2½ Starch, 1 Vegetable

Potato Frittata

9 small round red potatoes, thinly sliced
    Vegetable cooking spray
  1 teaspoon olive oil
  1 cup thinly sliced leeks
  1 cup thinly sliced zucchini
  1 clove garlic, minced
  2 tablespoons coarsely chopped fresh basil
  1 teaspoon balsamic vinegar
 ¼ teaspoon salt
  1 teaspoon olive oil
 ¼ cup grated Parmesan cheese
 ¼ teaspoon cracked pepper
1½ cups frozen egg substitute, thawed
    Nonfat sour cream (optional)
    Fresh basil sprigs (optional)

Place potato slices on a baking sheet coated with cooking spray. Bake at 400° for 15 minutes or until tender.

Coat a large nonstick skillet with cooking spray; add 1 teaspoon oil, and place over medium-high heat until hot. Add leeks, zucchini, and garlic; sauté until tender. Combine sautéed vegetables, chopped basil, vinegar, and salt; toss lightly.

Wipe drippings from skillet with a paper towel. Add 1 teaspoon oil to skillet; place over medium heat until hot. Arrange potato slices in bottom of skillet. Cook over medium heat, without turning, 10 minutes or until potato is lightly browned. Spoon vegetable mixture over potato; sprinkle with cheese and pepper. Pour egg substitute over vegetable mixture. Cover and cook 15 minutes or until set. Cut into 4 wedges, and serve immediately. If desired, garnish with sour cream and basil sprigs. Yield: 4 servings.

Per Serving: Calories 224 (12% calories from fat)
Fat 3.1g (Sat 1.2g Mono 1.3g Poly 0.3g) Chol 4mg
Protein 15.6g Carbohydrate 34.2g Sodium 392mg
Exchanges: 1 Lean Meat, 2 Starch, 1 Vegetable

Tomato-Artichoke Quiche

1 cup sun-dried tomato halves
1 cup boiling water
1 (7-ounce) can refrigerated breadstick dough
   Vegetable cooking spray
1 tablespoon cornmeal
1 (4-ounce) jar marinated artichoke hearts
2 cloves garlic, minced
1 medium onion, halved and thinly sliced
2 tablespoons minced green onions
¼ cup shredded fresh basil
1 tablespoon minced fresh oregano
½ cup (2 ounces) shredded part-skim mozzarella
   cheese
¼ cup grated Parmesan cheese
1 cup evaporated skimmed milk
1½ teaspoons cornstarch
2 eggs
1 egg white

Combine tomato and water; let stand 15 minutes.
Drain and cut into thin slices.

Separate breadstick dough into strips. Coil 1 strip
of dough. Add second strip to end of first, pinching
ends together; continue coiling. Repeat procedure
with remaining strips to make an 8-inch-round coil.
Press coiled dough into a 13-inch circle, and place in
a 9-inch pieplate coated with cooking spray. Fold
edges under, and flute; sprinkle with cornmeal.

Drain artichokes in a wire-mesh strainer, reserving
liquid; chop artichokes. Pour liquid into a nonstick
skillet; place over medium-high heat until hot. Add
garlic and onions; sauté 5 minutes. Stir in basil and
oregano; remove from heat.

Arrange tomato, artichokes, and onion mixture
over dough; sprinkle with cheeses.

Combine milk and remaining 3 ingredients in container of an electric blender; cover and process until
smooth. Pour over cheese. Bake at 375° for 35 minutes. Let stand 10 minutes. Yield: 6 servings.

Per Serving: Calories 261 (29% calories from fat)
Fat 8.5g (Sat 2.9g Mono 3.3g Poly 1.2g) Chol 83mg
Protein 14.5g Carbohydrate 32.4g Sodium 664mg
Exchanges: 1 High-Fat Meat, 2 Starch, 1 Vegetable

QUICK CRUST

Here's how we use commercial breadstick dough to make a quiche crust:
•**Unroll** the breadstick dough, and
separate it into strips.
•**Coil** 1 strip of dough, and connect a
second strip to the end. Keep coiling;
then connect a third strip.
•**Connect** and coil the rest of the strips
until you have an 8-inch-round coil.

Unroll strips

Coil and connect strips

8-inch-round coil

Vegetable-
Gruyère
Quiche

Vegetable-Gruyère Quiche

1 cup julienne-sliced leeks
2 cups julienne-sliced zucchini
2 cups julienne-sliced yellow squash
1 cup julienne-sliced sweet red pepper
1⅓ cups all-purpose flour
¼ cup margarine
2 to 3 tablespoons cold water
2 eggs
1 egg white
2 tablespoons 1% low-fat milk
1 teaspoon dried Italian seasoning
½ teaspoon salt
¼ teaspoon pepper
¼ cup (1 ounce) finely grated reduced-fat
  Gruyère cheese

Add water to a Dutch oven to a depth of 2 inches; bring to a boil. Add leeks; cover and simmer 5 minutes. Add zucchini, squash, and sweet red pepper; cover and simmer 5 minutes. Drain well; pat dry with paper towels.

Place flour in a bowl; cut in margarine with a pastry blender until mixture resembles coarse meal. Sprinkle cold water, 1 tablespoon at a time, evenly over surface of mixture; stir with a fork until dry ingredients are moistened. Shape into a ball.

Place dough between 2 sheets of heavy-duty plastic wrap, and gently press into a 4-inch circle. Chill 20 minutes. Roll into a 12-inch circle. Freeze 5 minutes. Remove top sheet of plastic wrap. Invert and fit pastry into a 9-inch quiche dish or pieplate; remove remaining sheet of plastic. Fold edges of pastry under, and flute; seal to edge of pieplate. Bake pastry shell at 450° for 5 minutes. Spoon vegetable mixture into pastry.

Combine eggs and next 5 ingredients; stir well with a wire whisk. Pour over vegetable mixture. Bake at 375° for 30 minutes; sprinkle with cheese. Bake 5 additional minutes or until cheese melts. Let stand 5 minutes before serving. Yield: 4 servings.

Per Serving: Calories 384 (38% calories from fat)
Fat 16.3g (Sat 4.0g Mono 6.1g Poly 4.4g) Chol 115mg
Protein 14.0g Carbohydrate 46.8g Sodium 501mg
Exchanges: 1 High-Fat Meat, 3 Starch, 1½ Fat

Farmhouse Strata

8 ounces Italian turkey sausage
2 cups frozen egg substitute, thawed
1 cup skim milk
½ cup (2 ounces) shredded reduced-fat Cheddar
  cheese
½ teaspoon dry mustard
¼ teaspoon rubbed sage
  Dash of salt
  Dash of ground red pepper
¼ cup chopped green onions
6 (1-ounce) slices white bread, cut into ½-inch
  cubes
  Vegetable cooking spray
2 medium tomatoes, cut into ¼-inch-thick slices

Cook sausage in a nonstick skillet over medium-high heat until browned, stirring until it crumbles.

Combine egg substitute and next 6 ingredients in a medium bowl; stir well with a wire whisk. Stir in sausage, green onions, and bread cubes. Pour mixture into an 11- x 7- x 1½-inch baking dish coated with cooking spray; cover and chill at least 8 hours.

Bake, uncovered, at 350° for 45 minutes or until set and lightly browned. Cut into squares, and serve with sliced tomato. Yield: 6 servings.

Per Serving: Calories 246 (33% calories from fat)
Fat 9.0g (Sat 3.6g Mono 0.4g Poly 2.4g) Chol 24mg
Protein 19.5g Carbohydrate 21.1g Sodium 603mg
Exchanges: 2 Medium-Fat Meat, 1 Starch, 1 Vegetable

Eggs Sardou

Vegetable cooking spray
½ cup chopped onion
1 (9-ounce) package frozen artichoke hearts, thawed
8 cups tightly packed torn fresh spinach
¼ cup water
3 tablespoons grated Parmesan cheese, divided
4 eggs
1½ teaspoons cornstarch
⅔ cup 1% low-fat milk
2 tablespoons fresh lemon juice
2 teaspoons Dijon mustard
2 teaspoons margarine
⅛ teaspoon salt
8 (1-ounce) slices whole wheat bread

Coat a skillet with cooking spray. Place over medium-high heat until hot. Add onion and artichokes; sauté until tender. Add spinach and ¼ cup water; toss mixture lightly. Cover and cook 5 minutes or until spinach wilts. Uncover and cook until liquid evaporates. Add 2 tablespoons cheese; stir well.

Add water to a large saucepan to a depth of 2 inches. Bring to a boil; reduce heat, and maintain at a simmer. Break eggs, one at a time, into water. Simmer 7 to 9 minutes or until internal temperature of eggs reaches 160°. Remove eggs with a slotted spoon, and keep warm.

Place cornstarch in a saucepan; add milk, stirring with a wire whisk. Cook mixture over medium heat, stirring constantly, until thickened. Remove from heat; add lemon juice and next 3 ingredients. Stir with a wire whisk until smooth.

Remove crusts from bread; cut each bread slice in half diagonally, and toast. Place 4 bread triangles on each serving plate, and mound one-fourth of spinach mixture in center of toast, making an indentation in each mound of spinach with the back of a spoon. Place eggs in indentations. Top with sauce; sprinkle with remaining 1 tablespoon cheese. Yield: 4 servings.

Per Serving: Calories 290 (34% calories from fat) Fat 10.8g (Sat 3.3g Mono 3.6g Poly 2.1g) Chol 227mg Protein 17.7g Carbohydrate 34.1g Sodium 628mg
Exchanges: 1½ High-Fat Meat, 2 Starch, 1 Vegetable

EGGING YOU ON

The American Heart Association says it's okay to eat up to four egg yolks a week and as many egg whites as you wish (they're fat- and cholesterol-free).

Another option is to eat lower-cholesterol eggs. To be labeled "lower cholesterol," an egg can have no more than 159 milligrams of cholesterol. (A regular egg has 213 milligrams). These eggs come from chickens that are on a low-fat diet. The kind of eggs you put in your basket is up to you.

eggs Sardou (sahr-DOO): a specialty of Antoine's restaurant in New Orleans. We added spinach to the artichoke mixture and lightened the dish with a low-fat Hollandaise sauce.

Scotch Eggs

2 large baking potatoes, peeled and cut into
    1-inch cubes
¼ cup nonfat cream cheese
2 teaspoons minced fresh chives
2 tablespoons minced green onions
¼ teaspoon salt
    Dash of pepper
3 hard-cooked eggs
1 egg white, lightly beaten
½ cup reduced-fat round buttery cracker crumbs
    Vegetable cooking spray
12 fresh asparagus spears
½ cup nonfat sour cream
¼ cup reduced-calorie mayonnaise
2 tablespoons prepared horseradish
3 tablespoons skim milk
8 romaine lettuce leaves
    Chopped fresh chives (optional)

Cook potato in boiling water to cover 15 minutes or until tender; drain. Transfer to a bowl; beat potato at medium speed of an electric mixer until smooth. Add cream cheese and next 4 ingredients; beat well.

Cut hard-cooked eggs into quarters. Shape ¼ cup potato mixture around each egg quarter to form an egg shape. Brush each with egg white; roll in cracker crumbs. Place on a baking sheet coated with cooking spray. Bake at 400° for 5 minutes or until browned.

Snap off tough ends of asparagus. Remove scales from stalks with a knife or vegetable peeler, if desired. Arrange asparagus in a steamer basket over boiling water. Cover; steam 7 minutes or until crisp-tender. Drain.

Combine sour cream and next 3 ingredients; stir. To serve, arrange 3 asparagus spears and 3 baked egg quarters on each of 4 lettuce-lined serving plates. Top each serving with 3 tablespoons sour cream mixture. Garnish with chopped fresh chives, if desired. Yield: 4 servings.

Per Serving: Calories 319 (28% calories from fat) Fat 10.1g (Sat 1.6g Mono 2.1g Poly 0.7g) Chol 173mg Protein 16.2g Carbohydrate 41.4g Sodium 538mg
Exchanges: 1 High-Fat Meat, 2 Starch, 2 Vegetable

Rustic Potato Torte

    Olive oil-flavored vegetable cooking spray
2 tablespoons fine, dry breadcrumbs
2 cups peeled, diced eggplant
1½ cups diced onion
1 cup diced fresh mushrooms
1 cup diced zucchini
1 cup diced sweet red pepper
2 large baking potatoes, thinly sliced
1 tablespoon olive oil
½ teaspoon pepper
¼ teaspoon salt
2 cups 1% low-fat cottage cheese
¾ cup (3 ounces) shredded reduced-fat Gouda
    cheese
⅓ cup all-purpose flour
¼ teaspoon salt
2 eggs
1 egg white

Coat a 9-inch springform pan with cooking spray; sprinkle breadcrumbs evenly over bottom of pan.

Combine eggplant and next 5 ingredients. Drizzle with olive oil; sprinkle with pepper and ¼ teaspoon salt. Toss.

Coat a 15- x 10- x 1-inch jellyroll pan with cooking spray. Arrange vegetables in an even layer in pan, placing potato slices together at one end of pan. Bake at 400° for 45 minutes, stirring every 15 minutes.

Position knife blade in food processor bowl; add cottage cheese and remaining 5 ingredients. Process until smooth.

Arrange roasted potato slices around bottom of prepared springform pan in overlapping rows to form a crust. Reserve any remaining potato.

Pour one-third of cheese mixture over potato layer. Arrange half of vegetable mixture over cheese mixture. Top with half of remaining cheese mixture. Repeat layers, using remaining vegetable and cheese mixtures. Place reserved potato slices on top of cheese mixture, arranging slices around edge of pan. Bake at 325° for 1 hour or until firm. Serve warm. Yield: 6 servings.

Per Serving: Calories 291 (24% calories from fat) Fat 7.9g (Sat 2.9g Mono 2.6g Poly 0.7g) Chol 87mg Protein 20.9g Carbohydrate 34.6g Sodium 679mg
Exchanges: 2 Medium-Fat Meat, 2 Starch, 1 Vegetable

Fish and

Tropical
Seafood
Curry
(page 69)

Shellfish

fish and shellfish (fish and SHEL-fish): creatures that live in the sea and are enjoyed as fillets, steaks, kabobs, and in stir-fries by those who live on the land.

Grouper Dagwoods with Melon Salsa (page 53)

Scallop-Cashew Stir-Fry (page 64)

Amberjack with Gingered Vegetables

3 tablespoons low-sodium soy sauce, divided
2 tablespoons dry sherry, divided
2 teaspoons sesame oil, divided
3 tablespoons peeled, minced gingerroot, divided
1 pound amberjack steaks (¾ inch thick), cut into 1-inch pieces
½ cup canned low-sodium chicken broth, undiluted
2 tablespoons balsamic vinegar
1½ teaspoons cornstarch
1 teaspoon sugar
Vegetable cooking spray
2 medium carrots, scraped and cut into 2- x ¼-inch strips
2 cups sliced fresh shiitake mushrooms
6 green onions, sliced
3 cups cooked long-grain rice (cooked without salt or fat)

Combine 1½ tablespoons soy sauce, 1 tablespoon sherry, ½ teaspoon oil, and 2 tablespoons gingerroot; place in a heavy-duty, zip-top plastic bag. Add fish; seal bag, and shake gently until well coated. Marinate in the refrigerator 1 hour, turning occasionally.

Combine remaining 1½ tablespoons soy sauce, 1 tablespoon sherry, 1½ teaspoons oil, broth, and next 3 ingredients. Stir well, and set aside.

Coat a large wok or nonstick skillet with cooking spray; heat at medium-high (375°) until hot. Add carrot; stir-fry 5 minutes. Add remaining 1 tablespoon gingerroot; stir-fry 1 minute. Add mushrooms; stir-fry 2 minutes. Add green onions; stir-fry 1 minute. Remove vegetables from wok, and keep warm. Add fish mixture to wok; stir-fry 6 minutes or until fish flakes easily when tested with a fork.

Stir broth mixture; add to wok. Cook, stirring constantly, until thickened. Add vegetables, and cook until thoroughly heated. Serve over rice. Yield: 4 servings.

Per Serving: Calories 362 (13% calories from fat) Fat 5.4g (Sat 0.9g Mono 1.4g Poly 1.8g) Chol 49mg Protein 29.0g Carbohydrate 47.2g Sodium 362mg
Exchanges: 2½ Lean Meat, 2½ Starch, 2 Vegetable

Orange-Glazed Amberjack Kabobs

⅔ cup unsweetened orange juice
⅓ cup low-sugar orange marmalade
2 tablespoons honey mustard
1½ teaspoons peeled, minced gingerroot
½ teaspoon dried crushed red pepper
2 cloves garlic
1 pound amberjack steaks (1 inch thick), cut into 16 pieces
8 asparagus spears
1 large firm, ripe papaya, peeled, seeded, and cut into 16 pieces
1 large sweet red pepper, cut into 1½-inch pieces
1 medium orange, halved crosswise, and cut into 8 wedges
1 small purple onion, cut into 8 wedges
Vegetable cooking spray
4 cups cooked long-grain rice (cooked without salt or fat)
Orange zest (optional)

Combine first 6 ingredients in container of an electric blender; cover and process until smooth, stopping once to scrape down sides. Set aside half of juice mixture; pour remaining juice mixture into a heavy-duty, zip-top plastic bag. Add fish; seal bag, and shake until fish is well coated. Marinate in refrigerator 1 hour, turning bag occasionally.

Remove fish from marinade, discarding marinade. Snap off tough ends of asparagus. Remove scales from spears with a knife or vegetable peeler, if desired. Cut each spear diagonally into 4 slices.

Thread fish, asparagus, papaya, and next 3 ingredients onto 8 (12-inch) skewers. Coat grill rack with cooking spray; place on grill over medium-hot coals (350° to 400°). Place kabobs on rack; grill, covered, 5 minutes or until fish flakes easily when tested with a fork, turning once, and basting with reserved juice mixture. To serve, place 1 cup rice on each plate; sprinkle with orange zest, if desired. Top rice with kabobs. Yield: 4 servings.

Per Serving: Calories 450 (5% calories from fat) Fat 2.5g (Sat 0.5g Mono 0.4g Poly 0.6g) Chol 61mg Protein 29.7g Carbohydrate 77.5g Sodium 116mg
Exchanges: 3 Very Lean Meat, 4 Starch, 1 Fruit

Orange-
Glazed
Amberjack
Kabobs

Grilled Amberjack Tacos

1½ pounds amberjack fillets (¾ inch thick)
⅓ cup lime juice
1 tablespoon tequila
1 teaspoon olive oil
3 large sweet red peppers
    Vegetable cooking spray
6 (½-inch-thick) slices purple onion
12 (8-inch) flour tortillas
3 cups shredded romaine lettuce
¾ cup no-salt-added salsa
¾ cup nonfat sour cream

Place fish in a heavy-duty, zip-top plastic bag. Combine lime juice, tequila, and olive oil. Pour juice mixture over fish; seal bag, and shake until fish is well coated. Marinate in refrigerator 30 minutes. Remove fish from marinade, reserving marinade. Place marinade in a small saucepan; bring to a boil. Remove from heat, and set aside.

Cut peppers in half lengthwise; remove and discard stems, seeds, and membranes.

Coat grill rack with cooking spray; place on grill over medium-hot coals (350° to 400°). Place peppers and onion slices on rack; grill, covered, 7 to 8 minutes on each side or until tender, basting occasionally with reserved marinade. Cut peppers into thin strips, and cut onion slices in half. Set aside; keep warm.

Place fish on rack; grill, covered, 4 minutes on each side or until fish flakes easily when tested with a fork. Cut fish into large chunks.

Spoon fish and vegetables evenly down center of each tortilla; top with lettuce, salsa, and sour cream. Roll up tortillas, and serve immediately. Yield: 6 servings.

Note: This recipe works just as well with other white firm-fleshed fish like swordfish or mahimahi.

Per Serving: Calories 485 (18% calories from fat) Fat 9.7g (Sat 1.6g Mono 3.5g Poly 3.4g) Chol 49mg Protein 35.5g Carbohydrate 61.1g Sodium 492mg
Exchanges: 3 Lean Meat, 3 Starch, 3 Vegetable

Sea Bass with Black-Eyed Peas

1½ cups water
1 (10-ounce) package frozen black-eyed peas, thawed
    Olive oil-flavored vegetable cooking spray
1 teaspoon olive oil
1 cup diagonally sliced fresh green beans
½ cup diced carrot
½ cup diced celery
½ cup diced onion
1 tablespoon minced fresh thyme
1 cup canned low-sodium chicken broth, undiluted
½ teaspoon freshly ground pepper
¼ teaspoon salt
1 pound sea bass fillets (1½ inches thick), cut into 1½-inch pieces
3 cups cooked long-grain rice (cooked without salt or fat)

Bring water to a boil in a large nonstick skillet. Add peas; reduce heat to medium, and cook 35 minutes or until peas are tender. Remove peas from skillet; drain well, and set aside.

Wipe skillet dry with a paper towel. Coat skillet with cooking spray; add oil. Place over medium heat until hot. Add beans and next 4 ingredients; cover and cook 3 minutes or until vegetables are crisp-tender. Add broth, pepper, and salt. Bring to a boil. Add fish; cook, stirring occasionally, 6 minutes or until fish flakes easily when tested with a fork. Stir in black-eyed peas. To serve, spoon fish mixture over rice. Yield: 4 servings.

Per Serving: Calories 435 (14% calories from fat) Fat 6.6g (Sat 1.2g Mono 2.5g Poly 1.4g) Chol 77mg Protein 32.4g Carbohydrate 60.4g Sodium 271mg
Exchanges: 2½ Lean Meat, 3 Starch, 3 Vegetable

Baked Fish and Chips

¾ **pound baking potatoes, very thinly sliced**
¾ **pound sweet potatoes, very thinly sliced**
   Vegetable cooking spray
1 **tablespoon olive oil**
1 **teaspoon dried rosemary, crushed**
¼ **teaspoon dried thyme**
¼ **teaspoon salt**
⅛ **teaspoon coarsely ground pepper**
3 **tablespoons reduced-calorie mayonnaise**
1 **tablespoon water**
¾ **teaspoon grated lemon rind**
1 **tablespoon fresh lemon juice**
1 **pound flounder fillets**
1 **cup soft whole wheat breadcrumbs, toasted**
1 **teaspoon coarsely ground pepper**
¾ **teaspoon garlic powder**
   Radish Tartar Sauce

Place potatoes in a single layer on a large baking sheet coated with cooking spray. Brush evenly with oil. Sprinkle rosemary and next 3 ingredients over potatoes. Bake at 425° for 30 to 35 minutes or until potatoes are lightly browned, turning once.

Combine mayonnaise and next 3 ingredients. Brush both sides of fish fillets with mixture. Combine breadcrumbs, 1 teaspoon pepper, and garlic powder; dredge fish in breadcrumb mixture. Place on a baking sheet coated with cooking spray. Bake at 425° for 25 minutes. Serve fish and potato with Radish Tartar Sauce. Yield: 4 servings.

Radish Tartar Sauce

½ **cup nonfat sour cream**
¼ **cup reduced-calorie mayonnaise**
¾ **cup finely chopped radish**
⅓ **cup minced green onions**
1 **tablespoon capers, drained**
1 **tablespoon prepared horseradish**
⅛ **teaspoon salt**

Combine all ingredients; stir well. Cover and chill. Stir well before serving. Yield: 1½ cups.

Per Serving: Calories 430 (27% calories from fat)
Fat 13.1g (Sat 2.3g Mono 4.7g Poly 5.2g) Chol 63mg
Protein 29.1g Carbohydrate 49.2g Sodium 661mg
Exchanges: 3 Lean Meat, 3 Starch, 1 Vegetable

FIVE FABULOUS REASONS TO EAT MORE FISH

 Fish offers a bounty of health benefits; it's low in saturated fat, cholesterol, calories, and sodium. So by eating fish more often you can—
1. Reduce your chance of developing heart disease
2. Reduce your risk of having a stroke
3. Lower your blood fat level
4. Lose weight
5. Lower your blood pressure

Grouper
Dagwoods
with Melon
Salsa

Grouper Dagwoods with Melon Salsa

4 (4-ounce) grouper fillets
¼ cup plus 2 tablespoons fresh lime juice, divided
2 teaspoons honey
2 teaspoons minced garlic
1 teaspoon peeled, minced gingerroot
1 cup diced fresh pineapple
½ cup diced cantaloupe
½ cup diced honeydew melon
¼ cup chopped purple onion
3 tablespoons minced jalapeño pepper
3 tablespoons reduced-calorie margarine, melted
1½ tablespoons chopped fresh basil
1½ tablespoons chopped fresh marjoram
1 tablespoon chopped fresh chives
1 teaspoon sugar
4 (1½-ounce) French rolls, split
    Vegetable cooking spray
1 cup shredded Bibb lettuce

Place fish in a small bowl. Combine 3 tablespoons lime juice and next 3 ingredients. Pour over fish; toss lightly to coat. Cover and marinate in refrigerator 1 hour.

Combine remaining 3 tablespoons lime juice, pineapple, and next 4 ingredients in a small bowl; cover and chill.

Combine margarine and next 4 ingredients. Brush mixture evenly on both sides of French roll halves.

Coat grill rack with cooking spray; place on grill over medium-hot coals (350° to 400°). Remove fish from marinade, discarding marinade. Place fish on rack, and cook, covered, 8 minutes on each side or until fish flakes easily when tested with a fork. Remove fish from grill; set aside, and keep warm. Place rolls on rack. Grill, uncovered, 3 minutes on each side or until toasted.

To serve, arrange ¼ cup lettuce on bottom half of each roll. Place grilled fish on lettuce, and top with ½ cup of fruit salsa. Top with remaining roll halves. Yield: 4 servings.

Per Serving: Calories 341 (21% calories from fat) Fat 8.0g (Sat 1.4g Mono 2.7g Poly 3.2g) Chol 43mg Protein 27.0g Carbohydrate 40.6g Sodium 396mg
Exchanges: 3 Lean Meat, 2 Starch, 1 Fruit

Fish Market Tostadas

½ cup chopped onion
¼ cup plus 2 tablespoons minced fresh cilantro, divided
1¼ cups green salsa
½ cup canned no-salt-added chicken broth, undiluted
1 clove garlic, minced
2 cups water
1 pound grouper fillets
¾ pound small round red potatoes, cut into ½-inch cubes
6 (6-inch) corn tortillas
3 cups shredded lettuce
2 medium tomatoes, seeded and chopped
¾ cup (3 ounces) shredded reduced-fat Monterey Jack cheese
¼ cup plus 2 tablespoons nonfat sour cream

Combine onion and 2 tablespoons cilantro; set aside.

Combine salsa, broth, garlic, and 2 tablespoons cilantro in container of an electric blender; cover and process until smooth. Transfer mixture to a saucepan; bring to a boil. Reduce heat, and simmer, uncovered, 5 minutes or until slightly thickened, stirring occasionally. Remove from heat, and set aside.

Place water in a saucepan; bring to a boil. Place fish in boiling water; cover, reduce heat, and simmer 8 minutes or until fish flakes easily when tested with a fork. Remove fish with a slotted spoon; remove and discard skin. Add potato to water in saucepan; cook 5 minutes or until tender. Drain well. Flake fish with a fork. Combine fish, potato, and ½ cup salsa mixture; stir well.

Place tortillas on ungreased baking sheets. Bake at 350° for 15 to 20 minutes or until crisp. Place 1 tortilla on each serving plate. Top tortillas evenly with shredded lettuce, fish mixture, tomato, cheese, sour cream, and reserved onion mixture. Sprinkle evenly with remaining 2 tablespoons cilantro, and serve with remaining salsa mixture. Yield: 6 servings.

Per Serving: Calories 254 (16% calories from fat) Fat 4.5g (Sat 1.9g Mono 0.4g Poly 0.8g) Chol 37mg Protein 24.2g Carbohydrate 29.7g Sodium 335mg
Exchanges: 2 Lean Meat, 2 Starch

Oriental Halibut Stir-Fry

½ cup rice wine vinegar
⅓ cup low-sodium soy sauce
 2 teaspoons sugar
 2 teaspoons sesame oil
 2 (3-ounce) packages dry ramen noodles, broken
   Vegetable cooking spray
 2 teaspoons vegetable oil, divided
 2 pounds halibut steak (1 inch thick), cut into
   2-inch pieces
 2 tablespoons peeled, minced gingerroot
 2 (6-ounce) packages frozen snow pea pods
 2 cups thinly sliced sweet red pepper
 2 large stalks celery, sliced diagonally into
   ¼-inch pieces
¼ cup fresh cilantro leaves

Combine first 4 ingredients; stir well, and set aside.

Cook ramen noodles according to package directions, omitting seasoning packets. Drain and set aside.

Coat a wok or large nonstick skillet with cooking spray; drizzle 1 teaspoon oil around top of wok, coating sides. Heat at medium-high (375°) until hot. Add fish and gingerroot; stir-fry 4 to 6 minutes or until fish flakes easily when tested with a fork. Remove fish from wok, and set aside.

Drizzle remaining 1 teaspoon oil around top of wok; add snow peas, pepper, and celery. Stir-fry 2 to 3 minutes or until crisp-tender; reduce heat. Add vinegar mixture, noodles, and fish to wok. Cook, stirring constantly, until thoroughly heated. Sprinkle with cilantro. Yield: 5 (2-cup) servings.

Per Serving: Calories 357 (22% calories from fat)
Fat 8.7g (Sat 1.3g Mono 2.5g Poly 3.4g) Chol 85mg
Protein 42.4g Carbohydrate 23.0g Sodium 612mg
Exchanges: 5 Very Lean Meat, 1 Starch, 2 Vegetable

Scandinavian Baked Halibut

12 small round red potatoes (about 1 pound)
¼ cup all-purpose flour
¼ teaspoon salt
¼ teaspoon pepper
 1 (16-ounce) halibut steak (1 inch thick)
   Vegetable cooking spray
 1 teaspoon vegetable oil
16 cherry tomatoes
¼ cup dry white wine
¼ cup chopped fresh dillweed
 2 tablespoons reduced-calorie margarine, melted
 8 lemon wedges

Cut each potato in half, and place in a large ovenproof skillet; add water to depth of 1 inch. Bring to a boil; cover, reduce heat, and simmer 8 to 10 minutes or until potato is tender. Drain and set aside.

Combine flour, salt, and pepper; sprinkle evenly on both sides of fish. Coat skillet with cooking spray; add oil. Place over high heat until hot. Add fish; cook 2 minutes on each side. Remove skillet from heat; add potato, tomatoes, and wine. Sprinkle with dillweed. Bake, uncovered, at 425° for 8 minutes or until fish flakes easily when tested with a fork. Remove from oven, and drizzle with margarine. To serve, cut fish into 4 pieces. Serve with lemon wedges. Yield: 4 servings.

Per Serving: Calories 326 (23% calories from fat)
Fat 8.2g (Sat 1.1g Mono 2.5g Poly 3.4g) Chol 53mg
Protein 28.8g Carbohydrate 36.0g Sodium 287mg
Exchanges: 3 Lean Meat, 2 Starch, 1 Vegetable

Orange Roughy with Greens and White Beans

1½ pounds fresh turnip greens
    Vegetable cooking spray
2 teaspoons olive oil
¼ teaspoon dried crushed red pepper
2 cloves garlic, minced
2 tablespoons water
1 (15.8-ounce) can great Northern beans,
    drained
1 teaspoon sugar
¼ teaspoon salt
2 teaspoons hot pepper vinegar sauce
4 (4-ounce) orange roughy fillets (½ inch thick)
½ teaspoon salt-free lemon-pepper seasoning
8 tomato slices (¼ inch thick)

Remove and discard stems from turnip greens. Wash greens, and drain well. Set aside.

Coat a large Dutch oven with cooking spray; add oil. Place over medium heat until hot. Add crushed red pepper and garlic; sauté 1 minute. Add greens and water; cover and cook until greens wilt, stirring occasionally. Drain well. Return to Dutch oven, and stir in beans, sugar, and salt. Toss lightly, and set aside.

Cut 4 (15-inch) squares of parchment paper; fold each square in half, and trim each into a large heart shape. Place parchment hearts on a large baking sheet, and open out flat.

Spoon one-fourth of greens mixture onto half of each parchment heart near the crease; sprinkle greens mixture evenly with vinegar sauce. Sprinkle fish evenly with lemon-pepper seasoning; place 1 fillet on each portion of greens mixture. Place 2 tomato slices over each fillet.

Fold paper edges over to seal securely. Starting with rounded edges of hearts, pleat and crimp edges of parchment to make an airtight seal. Bake at 450° for 15 minutes or until packets are puffed and lightly browned.

To serve, place packets on individual serving plates; cut an opening in the top of each packet, and fold paper back. Serve immediately. Yield: 4 servings.

Per Serving: Calories 239 (15% calories from fat) Fat 4.1g (Sat 0.5g Mono 2.3g Poly 0.6g) Chol 23mg Protein 25.5g Carbohydrate 27.1g Sodium 492mg
Exchanges: 3 Very Lean Meat, 1 Starch, 2 Vegetable

PUT IT IN THE PAPER

Cooking "in paper" (or "en papillote") is good for your heart because the food cooks in its own juices without any added fat. For the best results, use parchment paper, a heavy, grease-resistant, moisture-resistant paper that puffs up into a dome as the food inside bakes and releases moisture. You can find parchment paper at some grocery stores, bakery shops, or specialty kitchen shops. If you can't find it, use aluminum foil instead.

Mustard-Baked Salmon and Asparagus

¼ cup minced fresh dillweed
¼ cup Dijon mustard
3 tablespoons brown sugar
3 tablespoons water
1 tablespoon commercial reduced-fat
   olive oil vinaigrette
1 pound small round red potatoes, cut into
   ¼-inch-thick slices
  Vegetable cooking spray
4 (4-ounce) salmon fillets
1 pound fresh asparagus

Combine first 5 ingredients in a small bowl; stir well. Combine 2 tablespoons dillweed mixture and potato in a 13- x 9- x 2-inch baking dish coated with cooking spray; toss well. Spread potato in baking dish in a single layer. Bake, uncovered, at 350° for 20 minutes, stirring once.

Push potato to sides of baking dish, and arrange fish in center of dish. Drizzle ¼ cup plus 2 tablespoons dillweed mixture over fish.

Snap off tough ends of asparagus spears. Remove scales from spears with a knife or vegetable peeler, if desired. Arrange asparagus over potato; drizzle with remaining dillweed mixture. Cover and bake at 350° 30 minutes or until fish flakes easily when tested with a fork. To serve, arrange fish, potato, and asparagus on individual plates. Yield: 4 servings.

Per Serving: Calories 323 (25% calories from fat) Fat 9.1g (Sat 1.4g Mono 3.7g Poly 2.4g) Chol 44mg Protein 29.1g Carbohydrate 30.5g Sodium 548mg
Exchanges: 3 Lean Meat, 2 Starch, 1 Vegetable

French Onion Snapper

1 tablespoon olive oil
2 tablespoons grated Parmesan cheese
½ teaspoon garlic powder
3 cups cubed French bread
   Vegetable cooking spray
3 cups sliced onion
1 teaspoon sugar
½ teaspoon paprika
4 (4-ounce) red snapper fillets
2 tablespoons lemon juice
¼ teaspoon salt
¼ teaspoon ground red pepper
1 cup chopped green pepper
1 (8-ounce) package presliced fresh mushrooms
2 cups seeded, chopped tomato
¼ cup dry sherry

Combine first 3 ingredients in a large heavy-duty, zip-top plastic bag. Add bread cubes; seal bag, and shake until cubes are well coated. Arrange bread cubes in a single layer on a 15- x 10- x 1-inch jellyroll pan coated with cooking spray. Bake at 350° for 15 minutes or until golden, stirring occasionally. Remove from oven, and let cool completely.

Coat a large nonstick skillet with cooking spray; place over medium-high heat until hot. Add onion, sugar, and paprika; sauté 10 to 12 minutes or until onion is tender and lightly browned. Transfer onion mixture to an 11- x 7- x 1½-inch baking dish coated with cooking spray. Place fish over onion, and sprinkle with lemon juice, salt, and red pepper.

Wipe skillet dry with a paper towel. Coat skillet with cooking spray; place over medium-high heat until hot. Add green pepper and mushrooms, and sauté until tender. Stir in tomato. Spoon mushroom mixture over fish; drizzle with sherry. Cover and bake at 400° for 15 minutes. Uncover; top with bread cubes. Bake, uncovered, 5 additional minutes or until fish flakes easily when tested with a fork. Yield: 4 servings.

Per Serving: Calories 330 (21% calories from fat) Fat 7.6g (Sat 1.6g Mono 3.5g Poly 1.7g) Chol 45mg Protein 30.4g Carbohydrate 35.8g Sodium 420mg
Exchanges: 3 Lean Meat, 2 Starch, 1 Vegetable

Salsa Snapper

3 medium ears fresh corn
Vegetable cooking spray
1 cup seeded, chopped tomato
½ cup chopped purple onion
¾ cup minced fresh cilantro, divided
1 tablespoon lime juice
½ teaspoon hot sauce
1 (4-ounce) can chopped green chiles
4 (4-ounce) red snapper fillets
½ cup plain nonfat yogurt
½ teaspoon garlic powder
¼ teaspoon salt
Lime slices (optional)

Remove husks and silks from corn. Coat 3 large pieces of heavy-duty aluminum foil with cooking spray. Wrap each ear in a piece of foil. Twist foil at each end. Bake at 500° for 20 minutes. Remove from oven and let cool slightly. Cut corn from cob, and place in a medium bowl. Add tomato, onion, ½ cup cilantro, and next 3 ingredients; stir well.

Place 1 fish fillet on each of 4 additional large pieces of heavy-duty aluminum foil coated with cooking spray. Combine yogurt, garlic powder, and salt; spread evenly on both sides of fillets. Let stand 15 minutes.

Spoon corn mixture evenly onto fillets. Wrap each fillet securely, sealing edges. Bake at 450° for 20 to 25 minutes. Unwrap fillets; sprinkle with remaining ¼ cup cilantro. Serve with lime slices, if desired. Yield: 4 servings.

Per Serving: Calories 240 (11% calories from fat) Fat 3.0g (Sat 0.6g Mono 0.6g Poly 1.1g) Chol 54mg Protein 34.6g Carbohydrate 19.8g Sodium 366mg **Exchanges:** 4 Very Lean Meat, 1 Starch, 1 Vegetable

Roasted Sole Ratatouille

4 cups cubed eggplant
2 cups fresh or frozen whole-kernel corn, thawed
1½ cups sliced zucchini
1 medium onion, peeled and sliced
1 large sweet red pepper, cut into very thin strips
1 tablespoon dried basil
1 teaspoon dried oregano
1 teaspoon olive oil
½ teaspoon freshly ground pepper
¼ teaspoon salt
Vegetable cooking spray
4 (4-ounce) sole fillets
¼ cup plus 2 tablespoons freshly grated Parmesan cheese

Combine first 10 ingredients in a large bowl; toss well. Place in a roasting pan coated with cooking spray. Cover and bake at 425° for 45 minutes.

Arrange fish over vegetable mixture, and sprinkle with cheese. Broil 5½ inches from heat (with electric oven door partially opened) 8 to 10 minutes or until fish flakes easily when tested with a fork. Yield: 4 servings.

Per Serving: Calories 275 (19% calories from fat) Fat 5.9g (Sat 2.1g Mono 2.0g Poly 1.0g) Chol 67mg Protein 29.5g Carbohydrate 29.1g Sodium 391mg **Exchanges:** 3 Lean Meat, 1 Starch, 3 Vegetable

ratatouille (ra-tuh-TOO-ee): a combination of eggplant, tomato, onion, green pepper, and herbs cooked in olive oil; often served as a side dish—we added fish to make it an entrée.

Caribbean
Tuna

Caribbean Tuna

1½ cups chopped fresh pineapple
1 cup quartered cherry tomatoes
½ cup finely chopped green pepper
2 tablespoons rice vinegar
½ teaspoon curry powder
¼ teaspoon ground red pepper
½ cup frozen orange juice concentrate, thawed
  and undiluted
½ cup water
2 tablespoons minced fresh thyme
2 teaspoons olive oil
1 teaspoon freshly ground pepper
4 cloves garlic, minced
4 (4-ounce) tuna steaks (1 inch thick)
  Vegetable cooking spray
1½ cups water
¼ teaspoon salt
1 cup couscous, uncooked

Combine first 6 ingredients in a medium bowl, stirring well. Cover and set aside.

Combine concentrate and next 5 ingredients; reserve one-half of mixture. Pour remaining mixture into a heavy-duty, zip-top plastic bag; add fish. Seal bag, and shake lightly until fish is well coated. Marinate in refrigerator up to 3 hours, turning bag occasionally.

Remove fish from marinade, discarding marinade. Coat a nonstick skillet with cooking spray; place over medium-high heat until hot. Add fish; cook 2 to 3 minutes on each side or until browned. Add reserved juice mixture to skillet. Bring to a boil; reduce heat, and simmer 10 to 12 minutes or until fish flakes easily when tested with a fork.

Bring 1½ cups water and salt to a boil in a small saucepan; stir in couscous. Remove from heat; cover and let stand 5 minutes. Fluff with a fork.

To serve, place couscous evenly on 4 plates; top couscous with fish. Spoon any remaining pan juices over fish and couscous. Top evenly with reserved pineapple mixture. Yield: 4 servings.

Per Serving: Calories 410 (17% calories from fat)
Fat 7.9g (Sat 1.7g Mono 2.5g Poly 2.2g) Chol 43mg
Protein 33.5g Carbohydrate 51.7g Sodium 202mg
Exchanges: 3 Lean Meat, 3 Starch, 1 Vegetable

Curried Skillet Tuna

1 pound sweet potatoes, peeled and cut into
  2- x ½-inch strips
1 large sweet red pepper, seeded and cut into
  2- x ½-inch strips
1 large green pepper, seeded and cut into
  2- x ½-inch strips
  Vegetable cooking spray
3 tablespoons reduced-calorie margarine, melted
1 teaspoon curry powder
¼ teaspoon ground red pepper
4 (4-ounce) tuna steaks (1 inch thick)

Combine first 3 ingredients in a 10-inch cast-iron skillet coated with cooking spray. Combine margarine, curry powder, and ground red pepper. Add half of margarine mixture to vegetable mixture; toss lightly.

Bake, uncovered, at 450° for 15 to 20 minutes or until vegetables are tender and lightly browned, stirring occasionally. Remove vegetables from skillet; set aside, and keep warm.

Brush remaining margarine mixture over fish. Coat skillet with cooking spray; place over medium-high heat until hot. Add fish, and cook 1 minute on each side or until browned. Reduce oven temperature to 400°. Place skillet in oven, and bake, uncovered, 8 to 10 minutes or until fish flakes easily when tested with a fork. Serve with vegetable mixture. Yield: 4 servings.

Per Serving: Calories 337 (32% calories from fat)
Fat 12.0g (Sat 2.3g Mono 3.6g Poly 4.6g) Chol 43mg
Protein 28.8g Carbohydrate 28.8g Sodium 142mg
Exchanges: 3 Medium-Fat Meat, 1½ Starch, 1 Vegetable

Italian Seafood Casserole

Vegetable cooking spray
1 teaspoon olive oil
¾ pound fresh mushrooms, halved
2 cups chopped green pepper
1 cup chopped onion
1 teaspoon dried oregano
4 cloves garlic, minced
1 cup low-fat spaghetti sauce
½ cup canned low-sodium chicken broth, undiluted
½ cup dry Marsala wine
⅔ pound large sea scallops, cut in half crosswise
½ pound swordfish steak (1 inch thick), cubed
3 cups cooked long-grain rice (cooked without salt or fat)
⅓ cup grated Parmesan cheese

Coat a large Dutch oven with cooking spray; add oil. Place over medium-high heat until hot. Add mushrooms and next 4 ingredients; sauté 10 minutes or until onion is tender. Stir in spaghetti sauce, broth, and wine; bring to a boil. Stir in scallops and fish. Remove from heat, and stir in rice.

Spoon seafood mixture into a 13- x 9- x 2-inch baking dish coated with cooking spray. Bake, uncovered, at 350° for 30 minutes. Stir seafood mixture, and sprinkle with cheese. Bake, uncovered, 10 additional minutes or until cheese melts. Yield: 4 servings.

Per Serving: Calories 418 (16% calories from fat) Fat 7.4g (Sat 2.2g Mono 2.3g Poly 1.2g) Chol 48mg Protein 31.9g Carbohydrate 55.6g Sodium 491mg **Exchanges:** 3 Lean Meat, 3 Starch, 2 Vegetable

Seafood Risotto

1½ cups water
1 cup dry white wine
½ cup clam juice
2 tablespoons no-salt-added tomato paste
3 (10½-ounce) cans low-sodium chicken broth
Vegetable cooking spray
2 cloves garlic, minced
1½ cups Arborio rice, uncooked
1 pound medium-size fresh shrimp, peeled and deveined
½ pound bay scallops
½ cup chopped sun-dried tomato (packed without oil)
8 ounces fresh lump crabmeat, drained
3 ounces goat cheese, crumbled
¼ cup minced fresh basil

Combine first 5 ingredients in a large saucepan; place over medium heat. Cover and bring just to a simmer; reduce heat to low, and keep warm. (Do not boil.)

Coat a large nonstick skillet with cooking spray; place over medium-high heat until hot. Add garlic, and sauté 1 minute. Stir in rice; cook, stirring constantly, 2 minutes. Reduce heat to medium-low.

Add 1 cup of simmering broth mixture to rice mixture, stirring constantly until most of liquid is absorbed. Add remaining broth, ½ cup at a time, cooking and stirring constantly until each ½ cup addition is absorbed, about 50 minutes. (Rice will be tender and will have a creamy consistency.) Stir in shrimp, scallops, and tomato after 30 minutes of cooking. Stir in crabmeat after 40 minutes of cooking.

Remove from heat; stir in goat cheese and basil. Serve immediately. Yield: 6 servings.

Per Serving: Calories 429 (18% calories from fat) Fat 8.6g (Sat 4.2g Mono 2.0g Poly 1.2g) Chol 151mg Protein 36.1g Carbohydrate 50.1g Sodium 547mg **Exchanges:** 3½ Lean Meat, 3 Starch, 1 Vegetable

Arborio (ar-BOH-ree-oh): a short-grain rice with a high starch content. Because other varieties of rice don't get creamy when cooked, Arborio is the rice of choice for risotto.

Crabmeat Quiche

3 cups cooked brown rice (cooked without salt
   or fat)
1 cup (4 ounces) shredded reduced-fat Swiss
   cheese, divided
1 egg white, lightly beaten
¼ teaspoon salt
   Vegetable cooking spray
1 cup chopped fresh broccoli
½ cup chopped sweet red pepper
¼ cup chopped green onions
¼ cup canned no-salt-added chicken broth,
   undiluted
½ pound fresh lump crabmeat, drained
½ cup skim milk
1 tablespoon chopped fresh basil
¼ teaspoon salt
¼ teaspoon dry mustard
¼ teaspoon ground red pepper
1 (8-ounce) carton frozen egg substitute, thawed
   Cherry tomatoes (optional)
   Fresh basil sprigs (optional)

Combine rice, ½ cup Swiss cheese, egg white, and
¼ teaspoon salt; stir well. Press mixture evenly into
bottom and up sides of a 10-inch deep-dish pieplate
coated with cooking spray. Bake at 350° for 10 minutes; set aside.

Coat a large nonstick skillet with cooking spray;
place over medium-high heat until hot. Add broccoli
and next 3 ingredients. Cook, stirring constantly, until
vegetables are crisp-tender. Drain, if necessary.

Combine remaining ½ cup Swiss cheese, vegetable mixture, crabmeat, and next 6 ingredients in a
large bowl. Spoon mixture into prepared crust. Bake
at 350° for 40 minutes or until set. Let stand 10 minutes before serving. If desired, garnish with cherry
tomatoes and basil sprigs. Yield: 6 servings.

Per Serving: Calories 241 (19% calories from fat)
Fat 5.1g (Sat 2.2g Mono 0.5g Poly 0.7g) Chol 50mg
Protein 22.2g Carbohydrate 25.9g Sodium 416mg
Exchanges: 2 Lean Meat, 1 Starch, 2 Vegetable

Crabmeat Imperial

   Vegetable cooking spray
¼ cup chopped green pepper
¼ cup chopped sweet red pepper
¼ cup chopped celery
1 tablespoon minced onion
1 tablespoon chopped fresh parsley
1½ tablespoons all-purpose flour
1 cup skim milk, divided
1 cup instant nonfat dry milk powder
1 tablespoon reduced-calorie margarine
2 tablespoons dry sherry
⅛ teaspoon salt
⅛ teaspoon hot sauce
1 pound fresh lump crabmeat, drained
4 (1-ounce) slices white bread
   Fresh parsley sprigs (optional)

Coat a small nonstick skillet with cooking spray;
place over medium-high heat until hot. Add chopped
peppers, celery, and onion; sauté until tender. Remove
from heat, and stir in chopped parsley.

Combine flour and ¼ cup milk; stir until smooth.
Combine flour mixture, remaining ¾ cup milk, milk
powder, and margarine in a large saucepan; stir well.
Cook over medium heat, stirring constantly, until mixture is thickened and bubbly. Remove from heat; stir
in sherry, salt, and hot sauce.

Add vegetable mixture to sauce; stir well. Add
crabmeat, stirring lightly. Spoon crabmeat mixture
evenly into 4 gratin dishes coated with cooking spray.

Remove crusts from bread; cut each slice into 4
triangles. Lightly toast bread triangles.

Arrange gratin dishes on a baking sheet. Bake crabmeat mixture at 375° for 15 minutes; arrange toast
around edges of dishes. Bake 15 additional minutes or
until crabmeat mixture is golden. Garnish with parsley
sprigs, if desired. Yield: 4 servings.

Per Serving: Calories 332 (14% calories from fat)
Fat 5.0g (Sat 0.9g Mono 1.3g Poly 1.8g) Chol 114mg
Protein 36.8g Carbohydrate 33.4g Sodium 685mg
Exchanges: 4 Very Lean Meat, 2 Starch, 1 Vegetable

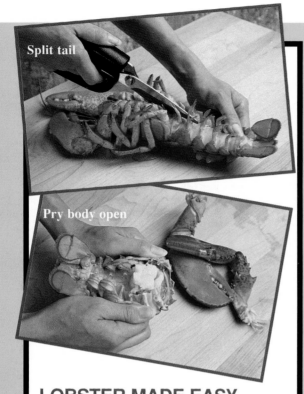

Split tail

Pry body open

LOBSTER MADE EASY

Love fresh lobster but never thought of serving it at home? It's really not complicated. Serve it in the shell, or pull out the meat before you serve.

If you choose to serve the boiled lobster out of the shell, drain it well, and turn it on its back.

•**Split** the tail lengthwise. Then use a fork to lift the tail meat out in one piece. Insert a knife between the body and the tail to cut the two apart.

•**Pry** open the remaining part of the body, and pick the meat out with a fork. Crack the shell of the claws and legs with a seafood cracker, and pull out the meat.

Lobster Pot

  1 teaspoon white peppercorns
  1 teaspoon black peppercorns
  1 teaspoon dried thyme
  1 teaspoon celery seeds
  ½ teaspoon mustard seeds
  3 bay leaves, crumbled
24 small round red potatoes
  6 ears fresh corn, cut into thirds
  6 (1-pound) live lobsters
1½ cups dry white wine
  ¼ cup plus 2 tablespoons reduced-calorie
     margarine
  2 tablespoons lemon juice
  2 tablespoons Dijon mustard
  1 teaspoon hot sauce
    Fresh thyme sprigs (optional)

Combine first 6 ingredients in a spice mill or small food processor; process until finely ground.

Add 4 inches water to a large stock pot; bring to a boil. Stir in spice mixture. Cover, reduce heat, and simmer 15 minutes. Add potatoes and corn; cover and simmer 25 minutes. Plunge lobsters headfirst into boiling water. Return water to a boil; cover, reduce heat, and simmer 10 minutes.

Place wine in a small nonaluminum saucepan; bring to a boil. Reduce heat, and simmer, uncovered, 15 minutes or until wine is reduced to ½ cup. Add margarine and next 3 ingredients; stir until margarine melts.

Remove lobsters from pot; drain well. To serve in the shells, place each lobster on its back. Cut the shell of the tail segment lengthwise. Insert a sharp knife between the body shell and tail shell, cutting the two apart. Crack claws.

Remove corn and potato with a slotted spoon. Place lobster, corn, and potato on a platter, and serve with margarine mixture. Garnish with fresh thyme sprigs, if desired. Yield: 6 servings.

Per Serving: Calories 344 (25% calories from fat) Fat 9.5g (Sat 1.3g Mono 1.9g Poly 3.7g) Chol 61mg Protein 23.3g Carbohydrate 45.5g Sodium 615mg
Exchanges: 2 Lean Meat, 3 Starch, 1 Fat

Lobster Pot

Mussels on Mexican Rice

3½ dozen mussels (about 2 pounds)
2 teaspoons olive oil
1 cup finely chopped green onions
1 cup finely chopped green pepper
4 cloves garlic, minced
2 jalapeño peppers, seeded and minced
1½ cups canned low-sodium chicken broth, undiluted
½ cup dry white wine
1 teaspoon paprika
¼ teaspoon salt
1 cup basmati rice, uncooked
½ cup minced fresh parsley

Remove beards on mussels, and scrub shells with a brush. Discard opened, cracked, or heavy mussels (they're filled with sand). Set aside.

Heat oil in a large Dutch oven over medium heat. Add green onions and next 3 ingredients; sauté until tender. Add chicken broth and next 3 ingredients; bring to a boil. Add rice; cover, reduce heat, and simmer 20 minutes. Stir in parsley; place mussels on rice. Cover and cook 8 minutes or until mussels are open. (Discard any mussels that do not open during cooking.) Yield: 4 servings.

Per Serving: Calories 333 (15% calories from fat)
Fat 5.7g (Sat 1.0g Mono 2.5g Poly 1.2g) Chol 28mg
Protein 17.4g Carbohydrate 47.5g Sodium 373mg
Exchanges: 1 Medium-Fat Meat, 3 Starch, 1 Vegetable

Scallop-Cashew Stir-Fry

2 tablespoons cornstarch
3 tablespoons dry sherry
¼ cup plus 2 tablespoons low-sodium teriyaki sauce
¼ teaspoon dried crushed red pepper
1 (10½-ounce) can low-sodium chicken broth
Vegetable cooking spray
1 pound sea scallops
2 cups broccoli flowerets
3 large carrots, scraped and cut diagonally into ¼-inch-thick pieces
2 cloves garlic, minced
1 cup fresh snow pea pods
2 tablespoons chopped unsalted cashews, toasted
4 cups cooked long-grain rice (cooked without salt or fat)

Combine first 5 ingredients; stir well. Set aside.

Coat a wok or large nonstick skillet with cooking spray; heat at medium-high (375°) until hot. Add scallops; stir-fry 5 to 7 minutes or until scallops are opaque. Remove from wok, and set aside. Add broccoli, carrot, and garlic; stir-fry 5 to 7 minutes or until crisp-tender. Add snow peas; stir-fry 1 minute. Return scallops to wok. Stir cornstarch mixture well with a wire whisk, and add to wok. Cook, stirring constantly, 3 minutes or until thickened and bubbly. Sprinkle with cashews, and serve over rice. Yield: 4 servings.

Per Serving: Calories 419 (9% calories from fat)
Fat 4.4g (Sat 0.8g Mono 1.7g Poly 0.9g) Chol 37mg
Protein 26.3g Carbohydrate 65.1g Sodium 823mg
Exchanges: 2 Lean Meat, 4 Starch, 1 Vegetable

Scallop-
Cashew
Stir-Fry

Spicy Scallop Stir-Fry

½ cup plus 2 tablespoons canned no-salt-added chicken broth, undiluted
1 tablespoon cornstarch
2 tablespoons rice wine vinegar
2 tablespoons low-sodium soy sauce
1 tablespoon low-sodium Worcestershire sauce
½ teaspoon sugar
  Vegetable cooking spray
2 teaspoons sesame oil, divided
2 tablespoons peeled, minced gingerroot
1 teaspoon dried crushed red pepper
2 cloves garlic, minced
1 (9-ounce) package frozen Sugar Snap peas, thawed
1 large sweet red pepper, cut into ½-inch pieces
1½ pounds sea scallops
4 cups cooked long-grain rice (cooked without salt or fat)
  Green onion strips (optional)

Combine first 6 ingredients; stir well. Set aside.

Coat a wok or large nonstick skillet with cooking spray; drizzle 1 teaspoon oil around top of wok, coating sides. Heat at medium-high (375°) until hot. Add gingerroot, crushed red pepper, and garlic; stir-fry 1 minute. Add peas and sweet red pepper; stir-fry 3 minutes. Remove vegetable mixture from wok; set aside. Wipe wok dry with a paper towel.

Coat wok with cooking spray; drizzle remaining 1 teaspoon oil around top of wok, coating sides. Heat at medium-high (375°) until hot. Add scallops; stir-fry 3 minutes or until scallops are opaque. Add chicken broth mixture to wok; cook, stirring constantly, 1 minute or until mixture is thickened. Return vegetable mixture to wok; cook, stirring constantly, until mixture is thoroughly heated. Serve over rice. Garnish with green onion strips, if desired. Yield: 4 servings.

Per Serving: Calories 450 (9% calories from fat)
Fat 4.6g (Sat 0.5g Mono 1.0g Poly 1.6g) Chol 56mg
Protein 35.1g Carbohydrate 63.0g Sodium 511mg
Exchanges: 3 Very Lean Meat, 4 Starch, 1 Vegetable

Mediterranean Scallops and Lentils

  Vegetable cooking spray
2 cloves garlic, minced
1¼ cups dried lentils
3 cups canned low-sodium chicken broth, undiluted
1 bay leaf
2 cups peeled, seeded, and chopped tomato
1 cup diced green pepper
⅓ cup diced purple onion
¼ cup minced fresh parsley
¼ cup balsamic vinegar
½ teaspoon freshly ground pepper
¼ teaspoon salt
1 tablespoon olive oil
1 pound sea scallops

Coat a large saucepan with cooking spray; place over medium-high heat until hot. Add garlic; sauté 1 minute. Add lentils, broth, and bay leaf; bring to a boil. Cover, reduce heat, and simmer 25 minutes or until lentils are tender. Remove and discard bay leaf. Transfer lentil mixture to a bowl; stir in tomato and next 6 ingredients. Set aside, and keep warm.

Add olive oil to saucepan; place over medium-high heat until hot. Add scallops; sauté 7 to 8 minutes or until scallops are opaque.

To serve, transfer lentil mixture to a serving platter, and top with scallops. Yield: 4 servings.

Per Serving: Calories 402 (15% calories from fat)
Fat 6.8g (Sat 0.7g Mono 2.7g Poly 1.1g) Chol 37mg
Protein 39.3g Carbohydrate 48.5g Sodium 408mg
Exchanges: 4 Lean Meat, 3 Starch, 1 Vegetable

Shrimp Enchiladas

1 pound unpeeled medium-size fresh shrimp
2 poblano chiles
10 tomatillos, husked
1 (14¼-ounce) can no-salt-added chicken broth
2 tablespoons chopped fresh cilantro, divided
¼ teaspoon salt
¼ teaspoon freshly ground pepper
    Vegetable cooking spray
2 teaspoons vegetable oil
¾ cup diced sweet red pepper
¾ cup diced green pepper
½ cup chopped onion
2 plum tomatoes, diced
2 cloves garlic, minced
1 tablespoon chopped fresh basil
½ teaspoon ground cumin
1 cup (4 ounces) shredded reduced-fat Monterey
    Jack cheese, divided
⅛ teaspoon freshly ground pepper
8 (6-inch) corn tortillas
    Nonfat sour cream (optional)
    Fresh cilantro sprigs (optional)

Peel and devein shrimp; set aside.

Dice 1 poblano chile, and set aside. Cut remaining poblano chile in half lengthwise; remove and discard seeds and membrane. Place seeded chile, skin side up, and tomatillos on a baking sheet; broil 5½ inches from heat (with electric oven door partially opened) 15 minutes or until charred. Place chile in ice water until cool; peel and discard skin. Seed tomatillos.

Combine peeled chile, tomatillos, broth, and 1 tablespoon chopped cilantro in a large saucepan. Bring to a boil; reduce heat, and simmer, uncovered, 15 minutes, stirring occasionally. Stir in salt and ¼ teaspoon pepper. Position knife blade in food processor bowl; add tomatillo mixture. Process until smooth; set aside.

Coat a nonstick skillet with cooking spray; add oil, and place over medium-high heat until hot. Add diced poblano chile, peppers, and onion; sauté 4 minutes or until crisp-tender. Add tomato and garlic; sauté 1 minute. Add shrimp, remaining 1 tablespoon chopped cilantro, basil, and cumin; sauté 3 minutes or until shrimp turn pink. Remove from heat; stir in ½ cup cheese and ⅛ teaspoon pepper.

Spoon shrimp mixture evenly down centers of tortillas. Roll up tortillas, and place, seam side down, in a 13- x 9- x 2-inch baking dish coated with cooking spray. Sprinkle with remaining ½ cup cheese. Spoon ½ cup tomatillo mixture over tortillas. Bake at 350° for 10 to 15 minutes or until thoroughly heated. Serve with remaining tomatillo mixture. If desired, garnish with sour cream and cilantro sprigs. Yield: 4 servings.

Per Serving: Calories 388 (28% calories from fat)
Fat 11.9g (Sat 4.0g Mono 1.2g Poly 2.9g) Chol 148mg
Protein 31.4g Carbohydrate 40.3g Sodium 545mg
Exchanges: 3 Lean Meat, 2 Starch, 2 Vegetable

SHY AWAY FROM SHRIMP?

 Go ahead, peel 'n' eat those shrimp. Although they contain higher levels of cholesterol than some other seafoods, they're low in saturated fats. So enjoy them, says the American Heart Association.

A quarter pound of boiled or steamed shrimp has just 1.2 grams of fat. The same amount of shrimp has 221 milligrams cholesterol, which is still under the 300 milligram-a-day AHA recommendation. So the next time you consider broiling a T-bone for dinner at 24 grams of fat per quarter pound, think shrimp instead.

Key West Shrimp Kabobs

1½ pounds unpeeled large fresh shrimp
½ cup low-fat coconut milk
½ cup fresh lime juice
½ cup unsweetened pineapple juice
3 tablespoons brown sugar
2 teaspoons Dijon mustard
2 cloves garlic, minced
⅓ cup nonfat mayonnaise
¼ teaspoon grated lime rind
2½ tablespoons fresh lime juice
1 teaspoon brown sugar
1 teaspoon Dijon mustard
⅛ teaspoon pepper
¾ cup fresh cubed pineapple
1 medium-size sweet red pepper, cut into 1-inch pieces
1 medium-size green pepper, cut into 1-inch pieces
8 pearl onions
Vegetable cooking spray
4 cups cooked long-grain rice (cooked without salt or fat)

Peel and devein shrimp, leaving tails intact. Place in a large heavy-duty, zip-top plastic bag.

Combine coconut milk and next 5 ingredients. Pour ¾ cup mixture over shrimp; set remaining mixture aside. Seal bag securely, and shake until shrimp are well coated. Marinate in refrigerator 3 hours, turning bag occasionally.

Combine mayonnaise and next 5 ingredients in a small bowl; stir well. Cover and chill thoroughly.

Remove shrimp from marinade; discard marinade. Thread shrimp, pineapple, peppers, and onion onto 4 (16-inch) skewers. Coat grill rack with cooking spray; place on grill over medium-hot coals (350° to 400°). Place kabobs on rack; grill, uncovered, 4 minutes on each side or until shrimp turn pink, basting frequently with reserved coconut milk mixture. Serve kabobs over rice; top with mayonnaise mixture. Yield: 4 servings.

Per Serving: Calories 401 (6% calories from fat)
Fat 2.7g (Sat 1.1g Mono 0.2g Poly 0.6g) Chol 166mg
Protein 22.8g Carbohydrate 70.7g Sodium 515mg
Exchanges: 1 Lean Meat, 4 Starch, 2 Vegetable, 1 Fruit

Nassau Shrimp and Grits

1½ pounds unpeeled medium-size fresh shrimp
Vegetable cooking spray
1 cup finely chopped onion
1 cup finely chopped green pepper
¾ cup minced turkey ham
2¾ cups canned low-sodium chicken broth, undiluted
1 (14½-ounce) can no-salt-added stewed tomatoes, undrained and chopped
¾ cup quick-cooking grits, uncooked
2 ounces Neufchâtel cheese, cubed
2 teaspoons olive oil
1 tablespoon lime juice

Peel and devein shrimp. Set aside.

Coat a large saucepan with cooking spray; place over medium-high heat until hot. Add onion, green pepper, and ham; sauté 7 minutes or until vegetables are tender. Add chicken broth and tomato; bring to a boil. Reduce heat, and simmer, uncovered, 10 minutes. Stir in grits; cover and simmer 5 minutes, stirring occasionally. Add cheese; stir until cheese melts. Remove from heat, and keep warm.

Heat oil in a large nonstick skillet over medium-high heat. Add shrimp; cook 3 minutes or until shrimp turn pink. Sprinkle with lime juice; remove from heat.

To serve, spoon grits mixture onto individual serving plates; arrange shrimp over grits mixture. Serve immediately. Yield: 4 servings.

Per Serving: Calories 355 (24% calories from fat)
Fat 9.6g (Sat 3.5g Mono 3.7g Poly 1.4g) Chol 193mg
Protein 30.4g Carbohydrate 37.4g Sodium 743mg
Exchanges: 3 Lean Meat, 2 Starch, 1 Vegetable

Tropical Seafood Curry

2 (5-ounce) fresh or frozen lobster tails, thawed
1 pound unpeeled large fresh shrimp
2 teaspoons vegetable oil, divided
¼ pound sea scallops
¼ cup minced shallots
1 teaspoon sugar
1 teaspoon curry powder
¼ teaspoon ground ginger
⅛ teaspoon dried crushed red pepper
½ cup canned no-salt-added chicken broth, undiluted
¼ cup unsweetened pineapple juice
¼ cup low-fat coconut milk
2 teaspoons cornstarch
2 tablespoons water
3 cups cooked long-grain rice (cooked without salt or fat)
Tropical Salsa
1 small cucumber, thinly sliced

Split lobster tails; remove meat, and slice. Discard shells. Peel and devein shrimp. Heat 1 teaspoon oil in a large nonstick skillet over medium heat. Add lobster, shrimp, and scallops; sauté 5 minutes or until seafood is done. Remove from skillet, and set aside.

Heat remaining 1 teaspoon oil in skillet over medium heat. Add shallots and next 4 ingredients; sauté 1 minute. Add chicken broth, pineapple juice, and coconut milk; bring to a boil. Cover, reduce heat, and simmer 5 minutes. Combine cornstarch and water; stir well. Add to broth mixture, stirring well.

Add seafood mixture; cook over medium heat until thoroughly heated, stirring lightly. Spoon seafood mixture over rice. Serve with Tropical Salsa and cucumber slices. Yield: 4 servings.

Tropical Salsa

1 cup peeled, diced ripe mango
½ cup finely chopped tomato
2 tablespoons minced onion
2 tablespoons minced cilantro
1 tablespoon lime juice

Combine all ingredients in a small bowl; stir well. Cover and chill. Yield: 1 cup.

Per Serving: Calories 423 (12% calories from fat)
Fat 5.7g (Sat 1.6g Mono 1.1g Poly 1.9g) Chol 189mg
Protein 36.2g Carbohydrate 54.8g Sodium 387mg
Exchanges: 4 Very Lean Meat, 3 Starch, 1 Fruit

MILKING THAT COCONUT

The low-fat coconut milk in our Tropical Seafood Curry contains 75 percent less fat than the sweet, creamy coconut milk you may have put in your last piña colada. But, like coconut, the fat it has is saturated—so don't go nuts.

Quick
Paella

Quick Paella

2 cups canned low-sodium chicken broth, undiluted
¼ teaspoon threads of saffron, crushed
2 teaspoons olive oil, divided
½ pound medium-size fresh shrimp, peeled and deveined
½ pound sea scallops, cut in half crosswise
½ teaspoon salt
½ teaspoon freshly ground black pepper
1 (7-ounce) jar roasted red peppers in water, drained and sliced
1 cup chopped onion
2 cloves garlic, minced
1 cup Arborio rice, uncooked
⅛ teaspoon ground red pepper
1 (14½-ounce) can no-salt-added whole tomatoes, undrained and chopped
1 cup frozen artichoke hearts, thawed
1 cup frozen English peas, thawed

Combine broth and saffron in a saucepan. Bring to a boil. Remove from heat; set aside.

Place 1 teaspoon oil in a nonstick skillet; place over medium-high heat until hot. Add shrimp; sauté 3 minutes or until shrimp turn pink. Remove from skillet, and keep warm. Place remaining 1 teaspoon oil in skillet; place over medium-high heat until hot. Add scallops; sauté 2 minutes or until scallops are opaque. Stir in shrimp, salt, black pepper, and roasted pepper. Remove from skillet, set aside, and keep warm.

Add onion and garlic to skillet; sauté 3 minutes. Stir in broth mixture, rice, ground red pepper, and tomato. Bring to a boil; cover, reduce heat, and simmer 20 minutes.

Stir in artichoke hearts, peas, and seafood mixture; cover and cook 5 minutes or until rice is tender and liquid is absorbed, stirring occasionally. Yield: 4 (2-cup) servings.

Per Serving: Calories 402 (11% calories from fat)
Fat 4.8g (Sat 0.9g Mono 2.3g Poly 1.0g) Chol 83mg
Protein 27.4g Carbohydrate 62.3g Sodium 585mg
Exchanges: 2 Lean Meat, 3 Starch, 3 Vegetable

Seafood-Sausage Jambalaya

8 ounces Italian turkey sausage
Vegetable cooking spray
2½ cups chopped green pepper
2 cups finely chopped onion
1½ cups finely chopped celery
2 tablespoons minced garlic
1 teaspoon dried thyme
1 teaspoon chili powder
1 teaspoon freshly ground pepper
½ teaspoon salt
1 (14½-ounce) can no-salt-added whole tomatoes, undrained and chopped
2 bay leaves
2 (12-ounce) containers fresh oysters, undrained
3 (14¼-ounce) cans no-salt-added chicken broth
2½ cups long-grain rice, uncooked
2½ pounds medium-size fresh shrimp, peeled and deveined
¾ pound bay scallops
½ cup chopped fresh parsley
Hot sauce (optional)

Remove casing from sausage; slice sausage into ½-inch pieces. Coat a Dutch oven with cooking spray; place over medium-high heat until hot. Add sausage, green pepper, and next 3 ingredients; cook, until sausage is browned and vegetables are tender, stirring often. Add thyme and next 5 ingredients.

Drain oysters, reserving liquid. Set oysters aside. Add water to liquid to make 1 cup. Add liquid mixture and broth to Dutch oven. Bring to a boil; reduce heat, and simmer, uncovered, 10 minutes, stirring occasionally.

Add rice; cover and cook over low heat 15 minutes. Stir in oysters, shrimp, and scallops. Cover and cook 10 minutes or until liquid is absorbed. Remove and discard bay leaves. Stir in parsley. Serve with hot sauce, if desired. Yield: 10 servings.

Per Serving: Calories 332 (26% calories from fat)
Fat 9.5g (Sat 2.9g Mono 0.9g Poly 3.0g) Chol 191mg
Protein 34.6g Carbohydrate 24.7g Sodium 647mg
Exchanges: 4 Lean Meat, 1½ Starch, 1 Vegetable

Shrimp and Rice Casserole

1½ pounds unpeeled medium-size fresh shrimp
1 pound fresh asparagus
   Vegetable cooking spray
1 tablespoon reduced-calorie margarine
1 cup sliced fresh mushrooms
½ cup sliced green onions
1½ tablespoons all-purpose flour
1 cup evaporated skimmed milk, divided
⅓ cup dry sherry
¼ teaspoon salt
¼ teaspoon pepper
1 (10¾-ounce) can 98% fat-free cream of
   chicken soup
1 cup (4 ounces) shredded reduced-fat sharp
   Cheddar cheese
1½ cups chopped cooked chicken breast (skinned
   before cooking and cooked without salt)
8 cups cooked long-grain and wild rice blend
   (cooked without salt or fat)
   Paprika (optional)

Peel and devein shrimp; set aside.

Snap off tough ends of asparagus. Remove scales from stalks with a knife or vegetable peeler, if desired. Cut asparagus into 1-inch pieces.

Coat a large saucepan with cooking spray; add margarine. Place over medium-high heat until margarine melts. Add asparagus, mushrooms, and green onions; sauté 3 to 4 minutes or until asparagus is crisp-tender. Add shrimp; sauté 2 to 3 minutes or until shrimp turn pink.

Combine flour and ¼ cup milk, stirring until smooth. Combine flour mixture, remaining milk, sherry, and next 3 ingredients; stir until smooth. Add to saucepan; cook over medium heat, stirring constantly, until thickened and bubbly. Add cheese, and stir until cheese melts. Remove from heat, and stir in chicken.

Spoon rice into a 13- x 9- x 2-inch baking dish coated with cooking spray. Pour shrimp mixture over rice; sprinkle with paprika, if desired. Cover loosely with aluminum foil, and bake at 350° for 30 to 35 minutes or until bubbly. Serve immediately. Yield: 8 servings.

Per Serving: Calories 376 (17% calories from fat)
Fat 7.0g (Sat 2.4g Mono 1.4g Poly 1.3g) Chol 124mg
Protein 30.4g Carbohydrate 48.3g Sodium 485mg
Exchanges: 3 Lean Meat, 3 Starch, 1 Vegetable

THE GOOD, THE BAD, THE CHOLESTEROL

You've heard the good news: The American Heart Association says it's okay to eat shrimp even though it contains a little more cholesterol than other shellfish and fish. Is this because it contains "good" cholesterol?

Not exactly—there's no such thing as "good" and "bad" cholesterol in *food*. It's when the cholesterol gets in your *body* that it becomes either good or bad. Your individual metabolism determines what happens to the little cholesterol packages that travel in your bloodstream.

Bad cholesterol (LDL) helps carry cholesterol to your blood vessels, so a high level of this kind of cholesterol is associated with heart disease. Good cholesterol (HDL) acts like a scavenger, removing cholesterol from your blood and lowering your risk of heart disease.

Shrimp Piquante

2 pounds unpeeled medium-size fresh shrimp
½ cup all-purpose flour
    Vegetable cooking spray
1 teaspoon vegetable oil
1 tablespoon minced garlic
1½ cups chopped onion
1 cup chopped celery
1 cup chopped green pepper
1 (14½-ounce) can no-salt-added whole
    tomatoes, undrained and chopped
1 (8-ounce) can no-salt-added tomato sauce
¼ cup dry red wine
½ teaspoon salt
½ teaspoon ground red pepper
½ teaspoon black pepper
1 teaspoon dried thyme
2 bay leaves
2 cups water
6 cups cooked long-grain rice (cooked without
    salt or fat)

Peel and devein shrimp; set aside.

Place a small nonstick skillet over medium heat;
add flour. Cook, uncovered, 8 to 10 minutes or until
browned, stirring often. Set aside.

Coat a Dutch oven with cooking spray; add oil,
and place over medium-high heat until hot. Add garlic, and sauté 1 minute. Add onion, celery, and green
pepper; sauté 5 to 7 minutes or until tender. Stir in
browned flour. Add tomato and next 7 ingredients; stir
well. Stir in water; bring to a boil. Cover, reduce heat,
and simmer 30 minutes. Remove and discard bay
leaves.

Stir in shrimp, and cook 8 minutes or until shrimp
turn pink. Serve over rice. Yield: 6 (1½-cup) servings.

Per Serving: Calories 434 (7% calories from fat)
Fat 3.4g (Sat 0.6g Mono 0.6g Poly 1.3g) Chol 172mg
Protein 29.9g Carbohydrate 69.0g Sodium 402mg
Exchanges: 2 Very Lean Meat, 3 Starch, 3 Vegetable

Sweet-and-Sour Shrimp

2 pounds unpeeled medium-size fresh shrimp
1 (20-ounce) can unsweetened pineapple chunks
¾ cup unsweetened pineapple juice
¼ cup firmly packed brown sugar
¼ cup white wine vinegar
2 tablespoons cornstarch
3 tablespoons low-sodium soy sauce
3 tablespoons reduced-calorie ketchup
1 tablespoon low-sodium Worcestershire sauce
1 teaspoon ground ginger
¼ teaspoon garlic powder
¼ teaspoon curry powder
    Vegetable cooking spray
1 cup thinly sliced carrot
1 small sweet red pepper, cut into very thin strips
3 cups cooked long-grain rice (cooked without
    salt or fat)

Peel and devein shrimp; set aside.

Drain pineapple, reserving juice; set pineapple
chunks aside. Combine reserved juice, ¾ cup
unsweetened pineapple juice, and next 9 ingredients in
a large nonstick skillet, stirring well. Bring to a boil;
reduce heat to medium, and cook, stirring constantly, 5
minutes or until mixture is thickened and bubbly.
Transfer mixture to a bowl; set aside, and keep warm.
Wipe skillet dry with paper towels.

Coat skillet with cooking spray; place over medium-
high heat until hot. Add carrot and red pepper; sauté 4
minutes. Add shrimp; sauté 3 minutes or until shrimp
turn pink. Add pineapple chunks and pineapple juice
mixture to shrimp mixture; cook until thoroughly heated, stirring often. Serve over rice. Yield: 6 servings.

Per Serving: Calories 372 (6% calories from fat)
Fat 2.4g (Sat 0.4g Mono 0.3g Poly 0.8g) Chol 172mg
Protein 26.0g Carbohydrate 59.8g Sodium 389mg
Exchanges: 3 Very Lean Meat, 2 Starch, 2 Fruit

Meats

Open-Face Italian Hamburgers (page 78)

meats (meets): lean cuts of beef, pork, and lamb. Once considered the heart of the meal, meats are combined here with pastas, grains, and vegetables for one-dish, good-for-your-heart meals.

Jamaican Jerk Pork with Black Beans (page 99)

Mediterranean Leg of Lamb (page 94)

Ancho-Beef Enchiladas

1 (3-ounce) package whole ancho chiles
1½ cups boiling water
½ cup no-salt-added tomato sauce
1 teaspoon dried oregano
½ teaspoon ground cumin
⅛ teaspoon salt
1 teaspoon vegetable oil
1 clove garlic, minced
  Vegetable cooking spray
½ pound ground round
1 cup chopped onion
1 cup chopped sweet red pepper
2 cloves garlic, minced
1 cup drained canned no-salt-added pinto beans
8 (8½-inch) fat-free flour tortillas
1 cup (4 ounces) shredded reduced-fat Cheddar
  cheese
4 cups shredded romaine lettuce
1 cup chopped tomato
  Nonfat sour cream (optional)

Place chiles on an ungreased baking sheet. Bake at 400° for 3 minutes. Cut chiles in half lengthwise; remove and discard seeds and membranes. Tear chiles into 2-inch pieces. Combine chile pieces and boiling water in a bowl; cover and let stand 45 minutes.

Place chiles and water in container of an electric blender; cover and process until smooth, stopping once to scrape down sides. Transfer mixture to a saucepan. Add tomato sauce and next 5 ingredients. Bring to a boil; reduce heat, and simmer, uncovered, 10 minutes, stirring often. Spoon ½ cup tomato mixture into a 13- x 9- x 2-inch baking dish coated with cooking spray. Set remaining tomato mixture aside.

Combine meat and next 3 ingredients in a nonstick skillet; cook over medium heat until meat is browned, stirring until it crumbles. Drain if necessary. Add ½ cup tomato mixture and beans; stir well.

Spoon about ⅓ cup meat mixture across center of each tortilla. Roll up tortillas; place, seam side down, over tomato mixture in baking dish. Brush remaining tomato mixture over tortillas. Cover and bake at 350° for 20 minutes. Uncover and sprinkle with cheese; bake 3 to 5 additional minutes or until cheese melts.

To serve, place ½ cup lettuce and 1 enchilada on each plate. Top each with 2 tablespoons tomato and, if desired, sour cream. Yield: 8 servings.

Per Serving: Calories 321 (18% calories from fat)
Fat 6.5g (Sat 2.3g Mono 1.4g Poly 0.7g) Chol 26mg
Protein 23.3g Carbohydrate 45.9g Sodium 600mg
Exchanges: 2 Lean Meat, 3 Starch

GETTING THE GROUND RULES

How do you know if you're buying the kind of ground beef with the least amount of fat? First, look for the cut of meat on the label—chuck, sirloin, or round. Ground chuck is the fattest; ground round is the leanest. Or look for the *percent lean*, for example, "70 percent lean ground beef." This means 70 percent lean and 30 percent fat. Under USDA regulations, ground beef cannot have more than 30 percent fat, so a product labeled 70 percent lean would be the highest fat ground beef that you could buy. Look for a package that is closer to 95 percent lean (5 percent fat).

Veggie-Beef Hobo Dinner

1 pound ground round
¾ cup soft whole wheat breadcrumbs
¼ cup finely chopped onion
¼ cup no-salt-added tomato sauce
¼ cup frozen egg substitute, thawed
½ teaspoon pepper
   Vegetable cooking spray
2 large baking potatoes, thinly sliced
1 medium onion, thinly sliced and separated
   into rings
3 large carrots, scraped and thinly sliced
2 tablespoons canned low-sodium chicken broth,
   undiluted
1 teaspoon chopped fresh basil
1 teaspoon chopped fresh thyme
1 teaspoon chopped fresh chives
2 teaspoons garlic-flavored vegetable oil
½ teaspoon chopped fresh rosemary
¼ teaspoon salt
¼ teaspoon pepper

Combine first 6 ingredients in a medium bowl, stirring well. Shape mixture into 4 (4-inch) patties.

Cut 4 (18- x 12-inch) pieces of heavy-duty aluminum foil; coat with cooking spray. Place a meat patty on one end of each piece of foil; place potato and onion evenly over patties. Top evenly with carrot.

Combine broth and remaining 7 ingredients, stirring well. Spoon broth mixture evenly over vegetables. For each packet, fold free end of foil over meat and vegetables; bring edges of foil together. Fold over to seal; pleat and crimp to make an airtight seal.

Place grill rack over medium coals (300° to 350°). Place packets on rack; grill 15 to 20 minutes or until packets are puffed. Remove packets from grill. Cut an opening in the top of each packet, and fold foil back. Remove patties and vegetables from foil, and transfer to serving plates. Top evenly with remaining juices. Yield: 4 servings.

Per Serving: Calories 321 (24% calories from fat)
Fat 8.7g (Sat 2.5g Mono 3.2g Poly 1.6g) Chol 66mg
Protein 30.8g Carbohydrate 29.7g Sodium 315mg
Exchanges: 3 Lean Meat, 2 Starch

Mexicali Stuffed Peppers

2 large sweet red peppers
2 large sweet yellow peppers
½ pound ground round
1 medium onion, chopped
2 cloves garlic, minced
2 cups cooked long-grain rice (cooked without
   salt or fat)
1¼ cups no-salt-added salsa
1 cup fresh or frozen whole-kernel corn, thawed
1½ teaspoons ground cumin
½ cup chopped fresh cilantro
1 cup (4 ounces) shredded reduced-fat Cheddar
   cheese

Cut tops off peppers; remove and discard seeds and membranes. Trim stems from tops, and discard stems. Chop pepper tops; set aside. Arrange pepper shells in an 11- x 7- x 1½-inch baking dish. Cover with heavy-duty plastic wrap, and vent. Microwave at HIGH 7 minutes, rotating dish a quarter-turn every 2 minutes. Set aside.

Combine meat, onion, garlic, and chopped pepper in a large nonstick skillet; cook over medium heat until meat is browned, stirring until it crumbles. Drain, if necessary.

Add rice and next 3 ingredients. Cook until thoroughly heated, stirring occasionally. Stir in cilantro. Spoon meat mixture evenly into pepper shells; place shells in an 8-inch square baking dish. Bake at 350° for 20 minutes; sprinkle evenly with cheese, and bake 5 additional minutes or until cheese melts. Yield: 4 servings.

Note: Pepper shells may be precooked in a steamer basket over boiling water. Cover and steam 5 minutes; drain well.

Per Serving: Calories 363 (23% calories from fat)
Fat 9.1g (Sat 4.2g Mono 1.4g Poly 0.5g) Chol 51mg
Protein 26.7g Carbohydrate 45.0g Sodium 434mg
Exchanges: 2 Medium-Fat Meat, 2 Starch, 3 Vegetable

Tuscan-Style Torta

¾ **pound ground round**
1 **cup chopped onion**
2 **cloves garlic, minced**
¾ **cup fat-free no-salt-added spaghetti sauce**
1 **cup part-skim ricotta cheese**
3 **tablespoons chopped fresh basil**
1 **egg white, lightly beaten**
8 **sheets frozen phyllo pastry, thawed**
   Vegetable cooking spray
¼ **cup plus 2 tablespoons grated Parmesan**
   cheese, divided
1 **(7-ounce) jar roasted red peppers in water,**
   drained and thinly sliced

Combine first 3 ingredients in a large nonstick skillet; cook over medium-high heat until meat is browned, stirring until it crumbles. Drain, if necessary.

Stir in spaghetti sauce. Bring to a boil; reduce heat, and simmer, uncovered, 5 minutes, stirring occasionally. Remove from heat; set aside. Combine ricotta cheese, basil, and egg white, stirring well.

Place 1 sheet of phyllo on a damp towel (keep remaining phyllo covered). Coat phyllo with cooking spray. Fold in half crosswise, bringing short ends together; coat with cooking spray. Place folded phyllo in a 9-inch pieplate coated with cooking spray, allowing one end to extend over edge of pieplate. Repeat with remaining phyllo, fanning each folded sheet to the right to form a circle around the pieplate.

Sprinkle 2 tablespoons Parmesan cheese over phyllo in bottom of pieplate; spoon meat mixture over Parmesan cheese. Spoon ricotta cheese mixture over meat mixture; top with red pepper and remaining Parmesan cheese. Bring phyllo ends up and over filling, gently twisting ends together; coat with cooking spray. Bake at 375° for 30 minutes. Let stand 5 minutes before serving. Yield: 6 servings.

Per Serving: Calories 265 (32% calories from fat)
Fat 9.3g (Sat 4.2g Mono 3.0g Poly 1.1g) Chol 50mg
Protein 22.4g Carbohydrate 21.2g Sodium 333mg
Exchanges: 2 Medium-Fat Meat, 1 Starch, 1 Vegetable

Open-Face Italian Hamburgers

1 **pound ground round**
1 **tablespoon chopped fresh basil**
¼ **teaspoon dried crushed red pepper**
¼ **teaspoon salt**
2 **small sweet red peppers**
¼ **cup fat-free Italian dressing**
2 **cloves garlic, minced**
4 **(¼-inch-thick) slices purple onion**
   Vegetable cooking spray
2 **(5½-inch) focaccia rounds (Italian flatbread),**
   cut in half horizontally
12 **large spinach leaves**
8 **large basil leaves**

Combine first 4 ingredients in a medium bowl; stir well. Shape mixture into 4 (½-inch-thick) patties.

Cut peppers in half lengthwise; remove and discard stems, seeds, and membranes.

Combine Italian dressing and garlic. Brush pepper halves and onion slices with dressing mixture.

Coat grill rack with cooking spray; place on grill over medium-hot coals (350° to 400°). Place meat patties, pepper halves, and onion slices on rack; grill, covered, 5 minutes on each side or until done, basting occasionally with dressing mixture. Brush focaccia rounds lightly with dressing mixture. Place on grill rack; grill 2 minutes on each side or until lightly toasted.

To serve, place focaccia rounds on serving plates; arrange 3 spinach leaves on each. Top each with a meat patty, onion slice, pepper half, and 2 basil leaves. Yield: 4 servings.

Per Serving: Calories 307 (28% calories from fat)
Fat 9.4g (Sat 3.5g Mono 3.0g Poly 0.5g) Chol 70mg
Protein 29.5g Carbohydrate 26.9g Sodium 569mg
Exchanges: 3 Lean Meat, 1½ Starch, 1 Vegetable

focaccia (foh-CAH-chee-ah): a flat Italian bread, usually flavored with olive oil and herbs. Sometimes featured as a pizza crust, but appearing here as a hamburger bun.

Open-Face
Italian
Hamburgers

Meatball Hoagie

1 pound ground round
2 cups fat-free, no-salt-added spaghetti sauce, divided
¼ cup fine, dry breadcrumbs
3 tablespoons grated onion
1 clove garlic, minced
  Vegetable cooking spray
1½ cups julienne-sliced sweet red pepper
1 small onion, thinly sliced
6 (3-ounce) submarine rolls

Combine meat, ¼ cup spaghetti sauce, and next 3 ingredients; stir well. Shape mixture into 48 (1-inch) meatballs. Place on a broiler pan coated with cooking spray. Broil 5½ inches from heat (with electric oven door partially opened) 10 minutes or until done.

Coat a large nonstick skillet with cooking spray; place over medium-high heat until hot. Add red pepper and sliced onion; sauté until tender. Add meatballs and remaining 1¾ cups spaghetti sauce; reduce heat, and cook, uncovered, 5 minutes, stirring often.

Cut a ¼-inch-thick slice off top of each roll; set tops aside. Cut a 2-inch-wide, V-shaped wedge down length of each roll. Reserve bread wedges for another use. Place rolls and tops on a baking sheet; broil 5½ inches from heat (with electric oven door partially opened) until lightly toasted.

Spoon meatball mixture evenly into bottom portions of toasted rolls; cover with roll tops. Serve warm. Yield: 6 servings.

Per Serving: Calories 413 (24% calories from fat)
Fat 11.2g (Sat 2.7g Mono 3.2g Poly 1.4g) Chol 70mg
Protein 23.7g Carbohydrate 51.4g Sodium 335mg
Exchanges: 2 Medium-Fat Meat, 3 Starch, 1 Vegetable

Summertime Roast Beef Subs

1¼ cups fresh or frozen whole-kernel corn, thawed
⅓ cup diced sweet red pepper
¼ cup diced purple onion
¼ cup reduced-calorie Caesar dressing
4 (3-ounce) submarine rolls
4 red leaf lettuce leaves
8 (¼-inch-thick) tomato slices
8 (1-ounce) slices lean cooked roast beef

Combine first 4 ingredients; set aside.

Cut a ¼-inch-thick slice off top of each roll; set tops aside. Hollow out centers of rolls, leaving ½-inch-thick shells; reserve inside of rolls for another use. Place 1 lettuce leaf in bottom portion of each roll. Spoon corn mixture evenly over lettuce; top each serving with 2 tomato slices and 2 slices roast beef. Cover with roll tops. Yield: 4 servings.

Per Serving: Calories 427 (27% calories from fat)
Fat 12.9g (Sat 2.6g Mono 2.8g Poly 1.3g) Chol 62mg
Protein 24.2g Carbohydrate 53.5g Sodium 534mg
Exchanges: 2 Medium-Fat Meat, 3 Starch, 1 Vegetable

Grilled Beef and Vegetable Fajitas

1½ cups no-salt-added salsa, divided
¼ cup fresh lime juice
1 teaspoon ground cumin
2 cloves garlic, minced
1 (1-pound) lean flank steak
1 large sweet red pepper, seeded and cut
　　lengthwise into quarters
1 large green pepper, seeded and cut
　　lengthwise into quarters
　Vegetable cooking spray
4 (¼-inch-thick) slices purple onion
8 (8½-inch) fat-free flour tortillas
⅓ cup chopped fresh cilantro
½ cup nonfat sour cream

Combine 1 cup salsa and next 3 ingredients in a
heavy-duty, zip-top plastic bag. Trim fat from steak.
Add steak and peppers to bag. Seal bag, and shake
until steak and peppers are well coated. Marinate in
refrigerator at least 8 hours, turning bag occasionally.

Remove steak and peppers from marinade, reserving marinade. Place marinade in a small saucepan;
bring to a boil. Remove from heat, and set aside.

Coat grill rack with cooking spray; place on grill
over medium-hot coals (350° to 400°). Place steak,
peppers, and onion on rack; brush with reserved marinade. Grill, covered, 7 minutes on each side or to
desired degree of doneness.

Wrap tortillas in heavy-duty aluminum foil. Place
on grill rack; grill 5 minutes or until heated.

Slice steak diagonally across grain into thin slices.
Slice peppers into thin strips, and separate onion into
rings. Arrange steak and vegetables evenly down centers of tortillas; sprinkle with chopped cilantro. Roll
up tortillas. Top each with 1 tablespoon salsa and
1 tablespoon sour cream. Yield: 8 servings.

Per Serving: Calories 268 (23% calories from fat)
Fat 6.9g (Sat 2.8g Mono 2.7g Poly 0.3g) Chol 30mg
Protein 16.5g Carbohydrate 34.6g Sodium 417mg
Exchanges: 1 High-Fat Meat, 2 Starch, 1 Vegetable

Grillade Casserole

1 pound lean boneless top sirloin steak
　Vegetable cooking spray
2 cloves garlic, minced
¼ teaspoon salt
½ cup julienne-sliced green pepper
½ cup julienne-sliced sweet red pepper
1 medium onion, cut into thin wedges
1 (6-ounce) can no-salt-added tomato paste
1½ teaspoons dried basil
2 cups water
⅔ cup quick-cooking grits, uncooked
½ cup (2 ounces) shredded part-skim mozzarella
　　cheese
2 egg whites
¼ cup grated Parmesan cheese

Trim fat from steak; slice steak in half lengthwise.
Slice halves into ¼-inch-wide strips. Coat a nonstick
skillet with cooking spray; place over medium-high
heat until hot. Add meat, and cook 3 minutes or until
browned on all sides, stirring often. Add garlic, and
sauté 30 seconds. Transfer meat mixture to a bowl;
sprinkle with salt, and set aside.

Coat skillet with cooking spray, and place over
medium-high heat until hot. Add peppers and onion;
sauté 5 minutes or until crisp-tender. Add tomato paste,
basil, and meat mixture; stir well. Transfer to an 11- x
7- x 1½-inch baking dish coated with cooking spray.

Bring water to a boil in a saucepan. Add grits;
cover, reduce heat, and simmer 5 minutes or until
thickened, stirring often. Remove from heat; stir in
mozzarella.

Beat egg whites at high speed of an electric mixer
until stiff peaks form. Stir one-fourth of beaten egg
whites into grits mixture. Fold remaining egg whites
into grits mixture. Spread grits mixture over meat
mixture; sprinkle with Parmesan cheese. Bake at 350°
for 35 minutes or until puffed and golden. Let stand
10 minutes before serving. Yield: 4 servings.

Per Serving: Calories 317 (30% calories from fat)
Fat 10.7g (Sat 5.0g Mono 3.7g Poly 0.5g) Chol 83mg
Protein 35.2g Carbohydrate 20.1g Sodium 458mg
Exchanges: 4 Lean Meat, 1 Starch, 1 Vegetable

Sirloin and Vegetable Kabobs

Sirloin and Vegetable Kabobs

1 pound lean boneless top sirloin steak
4 ears fresh corn
½ cup fat-free barbecue sauce
½ cup beer
2 cloves garlic, crushed
1½ pounds round red potatoes, quartered
   Vegetable cooking spray
12 large cherry tomatoes

Trim fat from steak; cut steak into 1-inch cubes. Remove and discard husks and silks from corn; cut corn into 1-inch pieces. Combine barbecue sauce, beer, and garlic in a heavy-duty, zip-top plastic bag. Add meat and corn; seal bag, and shake until meat and corn are well coated. Marinate in refrigerator up to 8 hours, turning occasionally.

Cook potato in boiling water to cover in a medium saucepan 12 to 15 minutes or until tender; drain.

Remove meat and corn from marinade, reserving marinade. Place marinade in a small saucepan; bring to a boil. Remove from heat, and set aside.

Thread meat, corn, and potato alternately onto 6 (15-inch) metal skewers. Coat grill rack with vegetable cooking spray; place on grill over medium-hot coals (350° to 400°). Place kabobs on rack; grill, covered, 10 minutes or until meat is done, turning and basting often with reserved marinade. Add cherry tomatoes to skewers during last 2 minutes of cooking time. Yield: 6 servings.

Per Serving: Calories 329 (14% calories from fat)
Fat 5.0g (Sat 1.4g Mono 1.8g Poly 1.1g) Chol 36mg
Protein 20.3g Carbohydrate 55.7g Sodium 316mg
Exchanges: 1 Medium-Fat Meat, 3 Starch, 2 Vegetable

Cowboy Steak and Beans

1 pound lean boneless top sirloin steak
2 teaspoons ground cumin
1 teaspoon chili powder
¼ teaspoon ground red pepper
   Vegetable cooking spray
1½ cups chopped onion
1¼ cups chopped green pepper
2 cloves garlic, minced
½ cup canned no-salt-added beef broth, undiluted
3 tablespoons brown sugar
1 (15-ounce) can no-salt-added pinto beans, drained
1½ cups quartered cherry tomatoes

Trim fat from steak; cut steak into 4 pieces. Combine cumin, chili powder, and red pepper. Sprinkle half of mixture over meat. Coat a nonstick skillet with cooking spray; place over medium heat. Add meat; cook 5 minutes on each side. Remove from skillet; keep warm.

Add onion, green pepper, and garlic to skillet; sauté until tender. Add remaining cumin mixture, broth, sugar, and beans. Bring to a boil; reduce heat, and simmer, uncovered, 5 minutes, stirring occasionally. Stir in tomato. Arrange meat over bean mixture. Cover and simmer 5 minutes. Yield: 4 servings.

Per Serving: Calories 333 (19% calories from fat)
Fat 7.2g (Sat 2.3g Mono 2.6g Poly 0.8g) Chol 69mg
Protein 32.5g Carbohydrate 35.0g Sodium 88mg
Exchanges: 3 Lean Meat, 2 Starch, 1 Vegetable

A STEAK IN YOUR HEALTH

You may have heard that you can't eat steak on a low-fat diet. But you *can* enjoy beef by eating small portions of lean cuts like sirloin and round steak. Just remember that 3 ounces of meat—about the size of a deck of cards—is the American Heart Association's recommendation for one serving. And the nutrition experts say that you don't need more than 6 ounces of lean meat a day.

Beef and Couscous Skillet Dinner

1 pound lean boneless top sirloin steak
¼ teaspoon salt
¼ teaspoon freshly ground pepper
   Vegetable cooking spray
1 teaspoon olive oil
2 cloves garlic, minced
2 cups frozen broccoli, carrot, and cauliflower
   mix, thawed
1 (14¼-ounce) can no-salt-added beef broth
1 cup couscous, uncooked
1½ cups seeded, coarsely chopped tomato
½ cup lightly packed sliced fresh basil
2 tablespoons balsamic vinegar

Trim fat from steak; slice steak in half lengthwise.
Slice halves into ¼-inch-wide strips. Sprinkle with
salt and pepper. Coat a large nonstick skillet with
cooking spray; place over medium-high heat until hot.
Add meat, and cook 5 to 7 minutes or until browned
on all sides. Remove meat from skillet; keep warm.

   Add oil to skillet. Place over medium-high heat
until hot. Add garlic; sauté 30 seconds. Add vegetable
mix and broth. Bring to a boil; cover, reduce heat, and
simmer 4 minutes or until vegetables are crisp-tender.
Stir in meat and couscous; cover and let stand 5 minutes or until liquid is absorbed. Add tomato, basil, and
vinegar; stir well. Yield: 4 servings.

Per Serving: Calories 407 (18% calories from fat)
Fat 8.1g (Sat 2.4g Mono 3.3g Poly 0.7g) Chol 69mg
Protein 33.6g Carbohydrate 48.5g Sodium 268mg
Exchanges: 3 Lean Meat, 3 Starch, 1 Vegetable

Teriyaki Beef with Broccoli

1 pound lean boneless top sirloin steak
¾ cup canned no-salt-added beef broth,
   undiluted
⅓ cup reduced-sodium teriyaki sauce
2 teaspoons cornstarch
¼ teaspoon dried crushed red pepper
2 cloves garlic, minced
   Vegetable cooking spray
1 teaspoon vegetable oil
4 cups fresh broccoli flowerets
1 medium-size sweet red pepper, cut into thin
   strips
4 cups cooked long-grain rice (cooked without
   salt or fat)

Trim fat from steak; slice steak diagonally into thin
strips. Combine broth and next 4 ingredients in a
heavy-duty, zip-top plastic bag. Add meat; seal bag,
and shake until meat is well coated. Marinate in
refrigerator at least 8 hours, turning bag occasionally.

   Drain meat, reserving marinade. Place marinade in
a small saucepan; bring to a boil. Remove from heat,
and set aside.

   Coat a wok or large nonstick skillet with cooking
spray; drizzle oil around top of wok, coating sides.
Heat at medium-high (375°) until hot. Add meat, and
stir-fry 5 minutes. Remove meat from wok.

   Add broccoli and sweet red pepper to wok; stir-fry
3 minutes. Add meat and reserved marinade; stir-fry 2
to 3 minutes or until mixture is thickened. Serve over
rice. Yield: 4 servings.

Per Serving: Calories 412 (14% calories from fat)
Fat 6.4g (Sat 1.9g Mono 2.2g Poly 0.9g) Chol 54mg
Protein 26.9g Carbohydrate 60.1g Sodium 469mg
Exchanges: 2 Lean Meat, 3 Starch, 2 Vegetable

Saucy Tenderloin with Polenta

1¾ cups water
¼ teaspoon salt
1 (14¼-ounce) can no-salt-added chicken broth
1 cup yellow cornmeal
¾ pound beef tenderloin
  Vegetable cooking spray
1 teaspoon olive oil
¼ teaspoon freshly ground pepper
3 cloves garlic, minced
1 (3½-ounce) package fresh shiitake
  mushrooms, sliced
1 (3½-ounce) package fresh oyster mushrooms,
  sliced
¼ cup minced shallots
¼ cup dry red wine
1 (14½-ounce) can no-salt-added stewed
  tomatoes, undrained
1 tablespoon no-salt-added tomato paste
1 tablespoon chopped fresh thyme

Combine first 3 ingredients in a medium saucepan; bring to a boil. Add cornmeal in a slow, steady stream, stirring constantly. Reduce heat to medium, and cook, stirring constantly, 20 minutes or until cornmeal mixture (polenta) pulls away from sides of pan.

Trim fat from tenderloin; cut tenderloin into ¾-inch pieces. Coat a nonstick skillet with cooking spray; add oil. Place over medium-high heat until hot. Add meat, pepper, and garlic; cook 4 minutes or until meat is browned on all sides, stirring often. Remove from skillet. Drain and pat dry. Wipe drippings from skillet.

Coat skillet with cooking spray; place over medium-high heat until hot. Add mushrooms and shallots; sauté 2 minutes. Add wine and tomatoes; bring to a boil. Reduce heat; simmer, uncovered, 5 minutes. Stir in tomato paste and thyme; simmer 3 minutes, stirring occasionally. Return meat mixture to skillet, and cook until thoroughly heated. To serve, spoon meat mixture over polenta. Yield: 4 servings.

Per Serving: Calories 335 (22% calories from fat)
Fat 8.2g (Sat 2.6g Mono 3.3g Poly 0.7g) Chol 54mg
Protein 23.9g Carbohydrate 40.2g Sodium 214mg
Exchanges: 2 Lean Meat, 2 Starch, 2 Vegetable

Combine cornmeal and liquids

Microwave and stir

PERFECT POLENTA

If stirring polenta constantly for 20 minutes isn't your idea of a good time, cook it in the microwave.
•**Combine** the cornmeal and liquids in a large glass bowl, and stir with a wire whisk. Cover with wax paper.
•**Microwave** at HIGH 6 minutes, and stir. The mixture will start to thicken. Microwave for 5 more minutes; the mixture should now be very thick. Stir it again with the whisk. Cover the polenta, and let it stand for 5 minutes.

Beef Tagine

Vegetable cooking spray
2 teaspoons olive oil
1½ pounds lean boneless shoulder roast,
    cut into 2-inch cubes
1½ tablespoons all-purpose flour
½ teaspoon salt
½ teaspoon freshly ground pepper
1 (14½-ounce) can no-salt-added stewed
    tomatoes, undrained
½ cup canned no-salt-added beef broth,
    undiluted
2 teaspoons peeled, minced gingerroot
1 teaspoon ground turmeric
¼ teaspoon ground cinnamon
2 cloves garlic, minced
2 cups sliced carrot
2 medium zucchini
¼ cup pitted, chopped kalamata olives
6 cups cooked couscous (cooked without salt
    or fat)

Coat a Dutch oven with cooking spray; add oil. Place over medium-high heat until hot. Add meat, and cook until browned on all sides, stirring often. Drain and pat dry with paper towels. Wipe drippings from Dutch oven with a paper towel.

Return meat to Dutch oven; sprinkle with flour, salt, and pepper, tossing well. Add tomatoes and next 5 ingredients; stir well. Add carrot; bring to a boil. Cover, reduce heat, and simmer 1 hour and 15 minutes.

Cut zucchini in half lengthwise; cut each half crosswise into thin slices. Add zucchini and olives to meat mixture; simmer 20 additional minutes or until meat and vegetables are tender. Serve over couscous. Yield: 6 servings.

Per Serving: Calories 416 (17% calories from fat)
Fat 7.8g (Sat 2.0g Mono 3.5g Poly 0.6g) Chol 64mg
Protein 33.4g Carbohydrate 53.5g Sodium 339mg
Exchanges: 3 Lean Meat, 3 Starch, 2 Vegetable

Beef Brisket with Sweet Potato Mélange

1 (3-pound) lean beef brisket
2 cups thinly sliced onion
1 orange, thinly sliced
1 cup unsweetened orange juice
2 tablespoons brown sugar
2 tablespoons no-salt-added tomato paste
2 teaspoons dried thyme
½ teaspoon ground cloves
2 (14½-ounce) cans low-sodium chicken broth
2 (3-inch) sticks cinnamon, broken in half
1 pound carrots, scraped and cut into
    ½-inch-thick slices
1 pound sweet potatoes, peeled and cut cross-
    wise into ½-inch-thick slices
1 medium Granny Smith apple, peeled and cut
    into 1-inch pieces
8 ounces dried pitted prunes
¼ cup all-purpose flour

Trim fat from brisket. Place onion in a large Dutch oven; top with meat. Arrange orange slices over meat. Combine juice and next 6 ingredients, stirring well. Pour mixture over meat. Bring to a boil; cover, reduce heat, and simmer 1½ hours.

Add carrot, potato, and apple to Dutch oven; cover and cook 30 minutes or until carrot and potato are tender. Add prunes; cook 15 additional minutes.

Transfer meat and vegetable mixture to a serving platter, using a slotted spoon; set aside, and keep warm.

Skim fat from broth in Dutch oven. Add flour to broth, stirring until smooth. Cook over medium heat, stirring constantly, until thickened.

Cut meat diagonally across grain into ¼-inch-thick slices. Serve meat and vegetable mixture with gravy. Yield: 12 servings.

Per Serving: Calories 307 (19% calories from fat)
Fat 6.4g (Sat 2.1g Mono 2.6g Poly 0.4g) Chol 67mg
Protein 27.3g Carbohydrate 36.1g Sodium 123mg
Exchanges: 3 Lean Meat, 1 Starch, 1 Vegetable, 1 Fruit

tagine (tah-GEEN): a Moroccan stew of slowly simmered meat, vegetables, and, often, both savory and sweet spices. Couscous or bread is a typical accompaniment.

German-Style Beef Brisket

1 (2½-pound) beef brisket
  Vegetable cooking spray
4½ cups sliced baking apple (about 2 large)
2¾ cups sauerkraut, drained
1 teaspoon caraway seeds
1 (14¼-ounce) can no-salt-added chicken broth
10 medium-size round red potatoes, quartered

Trim fat from brisket. Place meat on a rack in a roasting pan coated with cooking spray. Arrange apple slices over meat; spoon sauerkraut over apple, and sprinkle with caraway seeds. Drizzle broth over and around brisket. Cover and bake at 325° for 1½ hours.

Arrange potato around meat; baste potato and meat with pan juices. Cover and bake 2 hours or until potato is tender.

Transfer meat to a serving platter. Arrange apple, sauerkraut, and potato around meat; drizzle with 1 cup pan juices. Yield: 10 servings.

Per Serving: Calories 361 (16% calories from fat)
Fat 6.3g (Sat 2.0g Mono 2.5g Poly 0.4g) Chol 67mg
Protein 29.8g Carbohydrate 46.2g Sodium 431mg
Exchanges: 3 Lean Meat, 2 Starch, 1 Fruit

Homestyle Pot Roast

1 (3-pound) beef eye-of-round roast
2 large cloves garlic, thinly sliced
¼ cup all-purpose flour
½ teaspoon salt
½ teaspoon coarsely ground pepper
  Vegetable cooking spray
1 large onion, sliced
1 bay leaf
2 cups dry red wine, divided
1 (8-ounce) can no-salt-added tomato sauce
1 tablespoon brown sugar
1 tablespoon low-sodium Worcestershire sauce
1 teaspoon prepared mustard
1 teaspoon dried oregano
½ teaspoon pepper
12 small round red potatoes, halved
6 carrots, scraped and quartered
4 stalks celery, cut into 2-inch pieces

Trim fat from roast. Cut 1-inch slits in roast; insert a garlic slice into each slit. Combine flour, salt, and pepper; stir well. Lightly dredge meat in flour mixture; reserve remaining flour mixture.

Coat a Dutch oven with cooking spray; place over medium-high heat until hot. Add meat; cook until browned on all sides. Add onion and bay leaf.

Combine remaining flour mixture and ¼ cup wine; stir well. Add remaining 1¾ cups wine, tomato sauce, and next 5 ingredients, stirring well. Pour mixture over roast. Bring to a boil; cover, reduce heat, and simmer 2 hours. Add potato, carrot, and celery; bring to a boil. Cover, reduce heat, and simmer 1 hour or until meat and vegetables are tender. Remove and discard bay leaf.

Transfer meat to a serving platter; spoon vegetables around meat, using a slotted spoon. Serve with remaining sauce. Yield: 12 servings.

Per Serving: Calories 248 (18% calories from fat)
Fat 4.9g (Sat 1.7g Mono 1.9g Poly 0.3g) Chol 65mg
Protein 28.6g Carbohydrate 21.7g Sodium 205mg
Exchanges: 3 Very Lean Meat, 1 Starch, 1 Vegetable

Pot Roast
with Root
Vegetables

Pot Roast with Root Vegetables

1 (3-pound) boneless beef eye-of-round roast
   Vegetable cooking spray
2 cloves garlic, minced
1 teaspoon salt
½ teaspoon freshly ground pepper
1 cup canned no-salt-added beef broth,
   undiluted
8 medium carrots, scraped and cut in half
   crosswise
8 medium parsnips, scraped and cut in half
   crosswise
4 medium turnips, quartered
1 large onion, cut into wedges
1 cup nonfat sour cream
2 tablespoons prepared horseradish
   Fresh rosemary sprigs (optional)

Trim fat from roast. Coat a Dutch oven with cooking spray; place over medium-high heat until hot. Add meat, and cook until browned on all sides; sprinkle with garlic, salt, and pepper. Pour broth over meat; bring to a boil. Cover, reduce heat, and simmer 1 hour and 45 minutes. Add carrot and next 3 ingredients; bring to a boil. Cover, reduce heat, and simmer 45 minutes or until meat and vegetables are tender.

Combine sour cream and horseradish; set aside.

Transfer meat to a serving platter. Arrange vegetables around roast. Let meat stand 10 minutes before slicing. Serve with sour cream mixture. Garnish with rosemary sprigs, if desired. Yield: 12 servings.

Per Serving: Calories 213 (20% calories from fat)
Fat 4.7g (Sat 1.7g Mono 1.9g Poly 0.3g) Chol 65mg
Protein 28.3g Carbohydrate 12.3g Sodium 304mg
Exchanges: 3½ Lean Meat, ½ Starch, 1 Vegetable

Quick Veal Cassoulet

1 pound veal cutlets (¼ inch thick)
1 teaspoon dried thyme
½ teaspoon salt
¼ teaspoon freshly ground pepper
2 teaspoons olive oil
1½ cups sliced leeks
3 cloves garlic, minced
2 (14½-ounce) cans no-salt-added stewed
   tomatoes, undrained
2 (15-ounce) cans cannellini beans, drained
5 (1-ounce) slices Italian bread, toasted
1¼ teaspoons olive oil

Trim fat from veal. Cut veal into 1½- x ½-inch strips; sprinkle with thyme, salt, and pepper, and toss. Heat 2 teaspoons oil in a Dutch oven over medium-high heat. Add veal, and cook 3 minutes or until lightly browned. Remove veal from Dutch oven; set aside, and keep warm.

Add leeks and garlic to Dutch oven, and sauté until tender. Add tomatoes and beans. Bring to a boil; cover, reduce heat, and simmer 15 minutes. Stir in veal. Bring to a boil; cover, reduce heat, and simmer 5 minutes.

Brush each slice of bread with ¼ teaspoon olive oil, and serve with veal mixture. Yield: 5 servings.

Per Serving: Calories 358 (16% calories from fat)
Fat 6.3g (Sat 1.2g Mono 3.0g Poly 0.6g) Chol 76mg
Protein 28.1g Carbohydrate 46.3g Sodium 684mg
Exchanges: 2 Lean Meat, 2 Starch, 3 Vegetable

cassoulet (ka-soo-LAY): a classic French dish of white beans and meat, traditionally cooked very slowly. Our version gets you out of the kitchen in minutes.

WRAP IT UP

To cook in parchment paper—
en papillote—start with a 12- by 12-
inch piece of parchment paper, and
fold it in half.

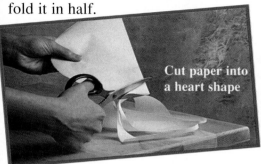

Cut paper into a heart shape

•**Cut** the parchment into a heart shape.
Open it, and place it flat on a baking
sheet. Put the food close to the center
crease, and fold the free side of the
paper over the food.

Pleat and crimp edges

•**Pleat and crimp** the two layers of
paper together. As the meat bakes, the
paper will puff up.

Slit the paper to display food

•**Slit** the paper with scissors or a knife,
and roll it back to display the food.

Veal and Vegetables en Papillote

Vegetable cooking spray
4 (4-ounce) veal cutlets
2 teaspoons minced garlic
¼ teaspoon salt
¼ teaspoon freshly ground pepper
2 large round red potatoes, thinly sliced
1 sweet red pepper, cut into thin strips
1 medium-size yellow squash, thinly sliced
1 medium zucchini, thinly sliced
1 tablespoon chopped fresh thyme
1 tablespoon chopped fresh basil
1 tablespoon chopped fresh chives
2 teaspoons olive oil

Cut 4 (12-inch) squares of parchment paper; fold
squares in half, and trim each into a large heart shape.
Place parchment hearts on a baking sheet, and open
out flat. Coat open side of parchment paper with
cooking spray.

Place a veal cutlet on half of each parchment heart
near the crease. Sprinkle veal evenly with garlic, salt,
and ground pepper. Arrange potato slices over veal.

Combine red pepper strips and remaining 6 ingredients in a large bowl; toss well. Spoon vegetable
mixture evenly over potato slices. Fold free halves of
hearts over veal and vegetables; bring edges together.
Starting with rounded edges of hearts, pleat and crimp
edges to make airtight seals. Bake at 350° for 25 minutes or until packets are puffed and lightly browned.

Place packets on individual serving plates; cut an
opening in the top of each packet, and fold paper
back. Serve immediately. Yield: 4 servings.

Per Serving: Calories 247 (22% calories from fat)
Fat 6.1g (Sat 1.4g Mono 2.7g Poly 0.7g) Chol 94mg
Protein 26.3g Carbohydrate 22.1g Sodium 253mg
Exchanges: 3 Very Lean Meat, 1 Starch, 1 Vegetable

Veal Risotto Milanese

1 ounce dried porcini mushrooms
1 cup boiling water
4½ cups canned no-salt-added chicken broth, undiluted
¾ pound veal cutlets (¼ inch thick)
1 teaspoon ground coriander
¼ teaspoon salt
¼ teaspoon ground white pepper
  Vegetable cooking spray
2 teaspoons olive oil
2 cloves garlic, minced
1 cup Arborio rice, uncooked
¼ cup dry white wine
1 (10-ounce) package frozen English peas, thawed
¼ cup freshly grated Parmesan cheese

Combine mushrooms and boiling water in a small bowl; let stand 30 minutes. Drain, reserving liquid. Coarsely chop mushrooms; set aside.

Combine mushroom liquid and broth in a saucepan; place over medium heat. Cover and bring to a simmer; reduce heat to low, and keep warm. (Do not boil.)

Cut veal into 1½-inch pieces. Combine veal and next 3 ingredients, tossing lightly. Coat a large non-stick skillet with cooking spray; add oil, and place over medium heat until hot. Add veal and garlic; cook 3 minutes or until browned, stirring occasionally. Remove from skillet, and keep warm.

Add rice and wine to skillet; cook, stirring constantly, 2 minutes. Reduce heat to medium-low. Add 1 cup simmering broth mixture to rice, stirring constantly until most of liquid is absorbed. Add remaining broth, ½ cup at a time, cooking and stirring constantly until each ½ cup addition is absorbed (about 40 minutes). (Rice will be tender and will have a creamy consistency.) Add mushrooms, veal, and peas; cook, stirring constantly, until mixture is thoroughly heated. Top with cheese. Yield: 4 servings.

Per Serving: Calories 434 (15% calories from fat) Fat 7.3g (Sat 2.3g Mono 3.1g Poly 0.7g) Chol 75mg Protein 28.0g Carbohydrate 57.8g Sodium 421mg
Exchanges: 2 Lean Meat, 3 Starch, 2 Vegetable

Italian Veal Kabobs

2 pounds medium-size round red potatoes, quartered
1 pound lean boneless veal, cut into 1-inch pieces
¼ cup plus 2 tablespoons dry white wine
¼ cup fresh lemon juice
1 tablespoon olive oil
5 cloves garlic, minced
2 large sweet red peppers, cut into 2-inch pieces
1 small purple onion, cut into ½-inch wedges
½ teaspoon salt
½ teaspoon freshly ground pepper
  Vegetable cooking spray
¼ cup finely chopped flat-leaf parsley
1 teaspoon lemon zest

Cook potato in boiling water to cover in a large saucepan 12 to 15 minutes or until tender. Drain and let cool.

Place veal and potato in a heavy-duty, zip-top plastic bag. Combine wine and next 3 ingredients, and stir well. Pour wine mixture over veal and potato; seal bag, and marinate in refrigerator at least 8 hours, turning occasionally.

Drain veal and potato, reserving marinade. Place marinade in a small saucepan; bring to a boil. Remove from heat, and set aside.

Thread veal, potato, red pepper, and onion onto 4 (12-inch) metal skewers. Brush with reserved marinade. Sprinkle with salt and ½ teaspoon pepper.

Coat grill rack with cooking spray; place on grill over medium-hot coals (350° to 400°). Place kabobs on rack; grill, covered, 6 to 7 minutes on each side, brushing occasionally with marinade.

Combine parsley and lemon zest; sprinkle over kabobs just before serving. Yield: 4 servings.

Per Serving: Calories 410 (22% calories from fat) Fat 9.8g (Sat 2.2g Mono 4.5g Poly 1.1g) Chol 100mg Protein 33.6g Carbohydrate 47.9g Sodium 391mg
Exchanges: 3 Lean Meat, 3 Starch, 1 Vegetable

Tuscan Ossobuco

4 (5-ounce) veal shanks
2 tablespoons all-purpose flour
¼ teaspoon salt
¼ teaspoon freshly ground pepper
2 teaspoons olive oil
Vegetable cooking spray
1 medium onion, thinly sliced and cut in half
3 cloves garlic
2 (14½-ounce) cans no-salt-added stewed
tomatoes, undrained
½ cup vermouth
1½ teaspoons dried rosemary, crushed
1 (15-ounce) can cannellini beans, drained
¼ cup chopped flat-leaf parsley
¼ teaspoon freshly ground pepper

Trim fat from veal shanks. Combine flour, salt, and ¼ teaspoon pepper; dredge veal shanks in flour mixture. Heat oil in a Dutch oven over medium-high heat; add veal shanks, and cook until browned on both sides. Drain and pat dry with paper towels; set aside, and keep warm. Wipe drippings from Dutch oven with a paper towel.

Coat Dutch oven with cooking spray. Place over medium-high heat until hot; add onion and garlic, and sauté until tender. Return veal to Dutch oven. Add tomatoes, vermouth, and rosemary; bring to a boil. Cover, reduce heat, and simmer 1 hour and 30 minutes or until veal is tender, turning once. Transfer veal to a serving platter; keep warm. Stir beans into tomato mixture; cook over medium heat until thoroughly heated. Spoon bean mixture over veal; sprinkle with parsley and ¼ teaspoon pepper. Yield: 4 servings.

Per Serving: Calories 326 (22% calories from fat)
Fat 8.0g (Sat 2.4g Mono 3.6g Poly 0.8g) Chol 66mg
Protein 24.8g Carbohydrate 40.2g Sodium 374mg
Exchanges: 2 Medium-Fat Meat, 2 Starch, 2 Vegetable

Shepherd's Pie

1 pound lean ground lamb
1 cup chopped onion
2 cloves garlic, minced
2 tablespoons reduced-calorie margarine
½ cup finely chopped carrot
½ cup finely chopped sweet red pepper
3 tablespoons all-purpose flour
1½ cups canned no-salt-added chicken broth,
undiluted
½ cup dry white wine
2 tablespoons no-salt-added tomato paste
1 tablespoon white wine Worcestershire sauce
½ teaspoon freshly ground pepper
1 cup frozen English peas, thawed
Vegetable cooking spray
2⅔ cups frozen mashed potato
1⅓ cups plus 1 tablespoon skim milk
¼ cup grated Parmesan cheese

Combine first 3 ingredients in a nonstick skillet; cook over medium-high heat until meat is browned, stirring until it crumbles. Drain and pat dry with paper towels. Wipe drippings from skillet with a paper towel.

Melt margarine in skillet over medium-high heat. Add carrot and red pepper, and sauté until crisp-tender. Add flour; cook, stirring constantly, 1 minute. Gradually add broth and next 4 ingredients. Bring to a boil; reduce heat, and simmer 10 minutes, stirring occasionally. Return meat mixture to skillet; stir well. Stir in peas. Spoon meat mixture into an 8-inch square baking dish coated with cooking spray.

Cook frozen potato in skim milk according to package directions. Spread potato over meat mixture. Top with cheese. Bake at 400° for 30 minutes or until golden and bubbly. Yield: 4 servings.

Per Serving: Calories 451 (33% calories from fat)
Fat 16.6g (Sat 5.6g Mono 4.1g Poly 0.7g) Chol 91mg
Protein 34.9g Carbohydrate 39.0g Sodium 459mg
Exchanges: 3 Medium-Fat Meat, 2 Starch, 2 Vegetable

ossobuco (AW-soh-BOO-koh): an Italian dish of veal shanks braised in olive oil, white wine, and tomatoes. We added cannellini beans (Italian kidney beans) to make it even heartier.

Moussaka

2 medium eggplants, peeled
Vegetable cooking spray
1 pound lean ground lamb
2 cups chopped onion
4 cloves garlic, minced
½ cup dry red wine
3 tablespoons no-salt-added tomato paste
½ teaspoon salt
½ teaspoon freshly ground pepper
¼ teaspoon ground cinnamon
½ cup chopped fresh parsley
2 tablespoons reduced-calorie margarine
2 tablespoons all-purpose flour
1½ cups skim milk
1 cup part-skim ricotta cheese
½ cup frozen egg substitute, thawed
¼ teaspoon grated nutmeg
¾ cup fine, dry breadcrumbs, divided
¼ cup grated Parmesan cheese

Slice eggplants crosswise into ¼-inch-thick slices. Coat a baking sheet with cooking spray. Place eggplant on baking sheet, and coat slices with cooking spray. Broil 5½ inches from heat (with electric oven door partially opened) 7 to 9 minutes on each side or until eggplant is browned. Set aside.

Coat a large nonstick skillet with cooking spray. Place over medium-high heat until hot. Add meat, onion, and garlic; cook until meat is browned, stirring until it crumbles. Drain meat mixture, and pat dry with paper towels. Wipe drippings from skillet with a paper towel.

Return meat mixture to skillet; add wine and next 4 ingredients. Bring to a boil; reduce heat, and simmer, uncovered, 10 minutes or until liquid evaporates. Stir in parsley; set aside.

Melt margarine in a medium saucepan over medium heat; add flour. Cook 1 minute, stirring constantly with a wire whisk. Gradually add milk, stirring constantly. Cook, stirring constantly, 3 minutes or until thickened and bubbly. Remove from heat, and stir in ricotta cheese, egg substitute, and nutmeg.

Coat a 13- x 9- x 2-inch baking dish with cooking spray. Sprinkle ¼ cup breadcrumbs over bottom of dish. Place half of eggplant in dish; top with half of meat mixture and ¼ cup breadcrumbs. Repeat layers with remaining eggplant, meat mixture, and breadcrumbs. Pour ricotta cheese mixture over meat mixture, and top with Parmesan cheese. Bake, uncovered, at 375° for 50 minutes or until golden. Let stand 15 minutes before serving. Yield: 8 servings.

Per Serving: Calories 286 (32% calories from fat) Fat 10.3g (Sat 4.1g Mono 3.1g Poly 0.6g) Chol 53mg Protein 24.1g Carbohydrate 25.0g Sodium 450mg
Exchanges: 2 Medium-Fat Meat, 1 Starch, 2 Vegetable

moussaka (moo-SAH-kah): a popular Greek dish consisting of layered eggplant and lamb. You can use ground beef instead of lamb, if you prefer.

Grilled Lamb Sandwiches

1 pound lean boneless lamb
⅓ cup red wine vinegar
1 tablespoon low-sodium Worcestershire sauce
1 teaspoon ground turmeric
1 teaspoon pepper
½ teaspoon ground ginger
2 teaspoons minced garlic
1½ teaspoons olive oil
1 green pepper, cut into ¾-inch pieces
1 medium onion, cut into 6 wedges
1 (8-ounce) carton plain nonfat yogurt
½ cup diced cucumber
2 teaspoons chopped fresh mint
1 teaspoon minced garlic
½ teaspoon prepared horseradish
  Vegetable cooking spray
4 (7-inch) whole wheat pita bread rounds
2 cups shredded romaine lettuce
1 large tomato, seeded and chopped

Trim fat from lamb; cut lamb into ¾-inch pieces. Combine vinegar and next 6 ingredients in a heavy-duty, zip-top plastic bag. Add meat, green pepper, and onion; seal bag, and shake until meat and vegetables are coated. Marinate in refrigerator 8 hours, turning bag occasionally. Combine yogurt and next 4 ingredients. Cover and chill.

Remove meat and vegetables from marinade, reserving marinade. Place marinade in a saucepan; bring to a boil. Remove from heat; set aside. Thread meat, pepper, and onion onto 4 (15-inch) skewers. Coat grill rack with cooking spray; place on grill over medium-hot coals (350° to 400°). Place kabobs on rack; grill, covered, 10 minutes or until meat is done, turning and basting often with marinade.

Cut ¼ inch off top of each pita round, reserving tops for another use. Fill pitas evenly with lettuce and tomato. Spoon meat and vegetables into pitas. Top with yogurt mixture. Yield: 4 servings.

Per Serving: Calories 388 (23% calories from fat)
Fat 10.1g (Sat 2.8g Mono 4.2g Poly 0.9g) Chol 77mg
Protein 31.9g Carbohydrate 39.8g Sodium 374mg
Exchanges: 3 Lean Meat, 2 Starch, 2 Vegetable

Mediterranean Leg of Lamb

1 (3½-pound) leg of lamb
5 cloves garlic, thinly sliced and divided
2 teaspoons dried rosemary, divided
1 teaspoon freshly ground black pepper, divided
  Vegetable cooking spray
1 pound small round red potatoes, cut in half
1 pound fresh mushrooms
12 plum tomatoes, halved
1 small eggplant, peeled and cut into 1-inch cubes
1 medium-size sweet red pepper, cut into 1-inch pieces
1 medium-size sweet yellow pepper, cut into 1-inch pieces
1 large purple onion, cut into wedges
¼ cup canned low-sodium chicken broth, undiluted
2 tablespoons balsamic vinegar
1 tablespoon olive oil
  Fresh rosemary sprigs (optional)

Trim fat from lamb. Cut 1-inch slits in meat; insert half of garlic slices into slits, reserving remaining garlic. Rub meat with 1 teaspoon dried rosemary and ½ teaspoon pepper; place on a rack in a large roasting pan coated with cooking spray. Insert meat thermometer into thickest part of meat, if desired. Add potato to pan. Bake at 325° for 1 hour.

Remove stems from mushrooms; reserve stems for another use. Combine mushroom caps, tomato, eggplant, red pepper, yellow pepper, and onion; add to roasting pan.

Combine remaining garlic, 1 teaspoon dried rosemary, ½ teaspoon pepper, broth, vinegar, and oil; stir well. Pour broth mixture over vegetables in roasting pan. Bake at 325° for 50 minutes or until thermometer registers 150°. Let stand 10 minutes before serving. Garnish with rosemary sprigs, if desired. Yield: 10 servings.

Per Serving: Calories 251 (30% calories from fat)
Fat 8.4g (Sat 2.5g Mono 3.8g Poly 0.8g) Chol 72mg
Protein 26.3g Carbohydrate 18.3g Sodium 71mg
Exchanges: 3 Lean Meat, 1 Starch, 1 Vegetable

Mediterranean
Leg of Lamb

Santa Fe Pork Burritos

8 ounces lean ground pork
1 cup chopped onion
¾ cup coarsely chopped sweet red pepper
2 cloves garlic, minced
1 cup no-salt-added salsa
1 teaspoon ground cumin
1 teaspoon chili powder
1 (16-ounce) can no-salt-added black beans,
    drained
⅓ cup chopped fresh cilantro
4 (8½-inch) fat-free flour tortillas
1 cup (4 ounces) shredded reduced-fat
    Cheddar cheese
¼ cup no-salt-added salsa
¼ cup nonfat sour cream

Combine first 4 ingredients in a large nonstick skillet; cook over medium-high heat until meat is browned and vegetables are tender, stirring until meat crumbles. Drain and pat dry with paper towels. Wipe drippings from skillet with a paper towel. Return meat mixture to skillet; add 1 cup salsa and next 3 ingredients. Cook over medium heat, uncovered, 10 minutes, stirring often. Stir in cilantro.

Wrap tortillas in heavy-duty aluminum foil. Bake at 350° for 5 minutes or until thoroughly heated.

Spoon meat mixture evenly down centers of tortillas; top with cheese. Roll up tortillas, and top each with 1 tablespoon salsa and 1 tablespoon sour cream. Yield: 4 servings.

Per Serving: Calories 443 (26% calories from fat)
Fat 12.6g (Sat 5.5g Mono 3.0g Poly 1.3g) Chol 57mg
Protein 31.7g Carbohydrate 51.3g Sodium 812mg
Exchanges: 3 Medium-Fat Meat, 3 Starch, 1 Vegetable

Pork Chops with Curried Barley Pilaf

4 (6-ounce) center-cut loin pork chops
1 tablespoon curry powder, divided
    Vegetable cooking spray
1¼ cups chopped onion
2 cloves garlic, minced
¼ cup water
2 tablespoons no-salt-added tomato paste
¼ teaspoon salt
3 (10½-ounce) cans low-sodium chicken broth
1 cup fine barley, uncooked
⅓ cup golden raisins
2 cups fresh broccoli flowerets
2 tablespoons chopped fresh cilantro
    Mango chutney (optional)

Trim fat from pork; sprinkle pork with 1 teaspoon curry powder. Coat a large nonstick skillet with cooking spray; place over medium heat until hot. Add pork chops; cook 3 minutes on each side or until browned. Remove pork from skillet.

Add onion and garlic to skillet; sauté until tender. Add remaining 2 teaspoons curry powder, water, and next 3 ingredients. Bring to a boil; stir in barley and raisins. Cover, reduce heat, and simmer 30 minutes. Arrange broccoli and pork chops over barley mixture. Cover and simmer 30 minutes or until pork and barley are tender. Let stand, covered, 10 minutes. Sprinkle with cilantro, and serve with mango chutney, if desired. Yield: 4 servings.

Per Serving: Calories 466 (20% calories from fat)
Fat 10.6g (Sat 3.4g Mono 3.8g Poly 1.2g) Chol 70mg
Protein 34.2g Carbohydrate 60.8g Sodium 318mg
Exchanges: 3½ Lean Meat, 3 Starch, 1 Fruit

Pork Medaillons with Cajun Rice

1 (¾-pound) pork tenderloin
1 teaspoon Creole seasoning, divided
   Vegetable cooking spray
½ cup finely chopped sweet red pepper
½ cup finely chopped green pepper
½ cup finely chopped carrot
½ cup finely chopped celery
½ cup finely chopped onion
2 cloves garlic, minced
1 cup long-grain rice, uncooked
2¼ cups canned no-salt-added beef broth,
   undiluted
1 bay leaf
   Chopped fresh parsley (optional)
   Hot sauce (optional)

Trim fat from tenderloin. Cut tenderloin crosswise into 1-inch-thick slices. Place between 2 sheets of heavy-duty plastic wrap; flatten to ½-inch thickness. Sprinkle with ½ teaspoon Creole seasoning.

Coat a large nonstick skillet with cooking spray. Add pork; cook over medium-high heat 3 minutes on each side or until browned. Remove from skillet, and keep warm.

Coat skillet with vegetable cooking spray; place over medium-high heat until hot. Add red pepper and next 5 ingredients; sauté 8 to 10 minutes or until tender. Add rice; stir well. Add beef broth, bay leaf, and remaining ½ teaspoon Creole seasoning; bring to a boil. Cover, reduce heat, and simmer 20 minutes or until rice is tender and liquid is absorbed.

Return pork to skillet; remove from heat. Cover and let stand 5 minutes before serving. Remove and discard bay leaf. If desired, sprinkle with parsley, and serve with hot sauce. Yield: 3 servings.

Per Serving: Calories 400 (9% calories from fat)
Fat 3.8g (Sat 1.2g Mono 1.4g Poly 0.6g) Chol 74mg
Protein 29.6g Carbohydrate 59.4g Sodium 483mg
Exchanges: 2 Very Lean Meat, 3 Starch, 3 Vegetable

THE SKINNY ON PORK

Think pork is fatty? Compared to a decade ago, today's pork is—
•31 percent leaner
•17 percent lower in calories
•10 percent lower in cholesterol
   In fact, roasted pork tenderloin has about the same amount of fat as the same size portion of skinless roasted chicken breast. To make sure you buy the leanest cuts of pork, look for "loin" or "leg" on the package label (pork tenderloin, top loin roast, top leg roast, loin chops, pork sirloin roast).
   And if you've been avoiding traditional pork sausage, ham, and bacon products, look for the reduced-fat and reduced-sodium versions that are now available.

Jamaican
Jerk Pork
with Black
Beans

Jamaican Jerk Pork with Black Beans

1 (1-pound) pork tenderloin
2 teaspoons dried thyme
½ teaspoon ground allspice
¼ teaspoon ground red pepper
   Vegetable cooking spray
1 cup chopped onion
1 cup chopped sweet red pepper
1 cup thinly sliced carrot
2 cloves garlic, minced
½ cup canned no-salt-added chicken broth,
   undiluted
⅓ cup spicy pepper sauce (like Pickapeppa)
¼ teaspoon salt
1 (15-ounce) can no-salt-added black beans,
   drained
1 tablespoon fresh lime juice
¼ cup finely chopped green onions
3 cups cooked long-grain rice (cooked without
   salt or fat)
¼ teaspoon ground turmeric

Trim fat from tenderloin; cut tenderloin into ½-inch-thick slices.

Combine thyme, allspice, and ground red pepper. Sprinkle half of spice mixture over pork slices. Coat a large nonstick skillet with cooking spray; place over medium heat until hot. Add pork; cook 3 minutes on each side or until browned. Remove from skillet, and keep warm.

Increase heat to medium-high; add 1 cup onion and next 3 ingredients, and sauté until crisp-tender. Add remaining spice mixture, broth, and next 3 ingredients. Arrange pork over bean mixture. Bring to a boil; cover, reduce heat, and simmer 10 minutes or until pork is tender. Stir in lime juice; sprinkle with green onions.

Combine rice and turmeric; toss well. Serve pork mixture over rice. Yield: 4 servings.

Per Serving: Calories 452 (8% calories from fat)
Fat 4.1g (Sat 1.2g Mono 1.3g Poly 0.6g) Chol 74mg
Protein 35.0g Carbohydrate 67.6g Sodium 414mg
Exchanges: 3 Very Lean Meat, 4 Starch, 1 Vegetable

Moo Shu Pork

8 (8-inch) flour tortillas
1 (½-pound) pork tenderloin
2 tablespoons low-sodium soy sauce, divided
2 cloves garlic, minced
   Vegetable cooking spray
1 teaspoon vegetable oil
2 cups shredded Chinese cabbage
1 cup sliced fresh mushroom caps
1 medium-size sweet red pepper, seeded and cut
   into thin strips
1 cup fresh bean sprouts
3 green onions, thinly sliced into 2-inch strips
1 tablespoon hoisin sauce
¼ cup plum sauce

Wrap tortillas in heavy-duty aluminum foil; bake at 325° for 12 minutes or until thoroughly heated.

Trim fat from tenderloin; slice tenderloin into 2- x ¼-inch strips.

Combine pork, 1 tablespoon soy sauce, and garlic, tossing well. Coat a wok or large nonstick skillet with cooking spray; drizzle 1 teaspoon oil around top of wok, coating sides. Heat at medium-high (375°) until hot. Add pork mixture; stir-fry 3 minutes or until browned. Transfer to a bowl, and set aside.

Add cabbage, mushrooms, and pepper to wok; stir-fry 3 minutes. Add bean sprouts and onions; stir-fry 2 minutes. Return pork mixture to wok. Add remaining 1 tablespoon soy sauce and hoisin sauce; stir-fry 2 minutes or until thickened.

Spread 1½ teaspoons plum sauce over one side of each tortilla; top evenly with pork mixture. Roll up tortillas, and serve immediately. Yield: 4 servings.

Per Serving: Calories 407 (20% calories from fat)
Fat 9.1g (Sat 1.7g Mono 3.4g Poly 3.2g) Chol 37mg
Protein 21.8g Carbohydrate 58.6g Sodium 773mg
Exchanges: 1 Medium-Fat Meat, 3 Starch, 2 Vegetable

Shanghai Pork and Mushrooms

1 (1-pound) pork tenderloin
¼ cup low-sodium soy sauce
2 tablespoons rice vinegar
3 cloves garlic, minced
1 (3½-ounce) package shiitake mushrooms
8 cups canned no-salt-added chicken broth, undiluted
8 ounces vermicelli, uncooked
1 tablespoon cornstarch
   Vegetable cooking spray
2 teaspoons vegetable oil
1 (3½-ounce) package oyster mushrooms, halved
4 green onions, cut into 1-inch pieces
1 (8-ounce) can sliced water chestnuts, drained

Trim fat from tenderloin; cut tenderloin into ½-inch strips. Combine soy sauce, vinegar, and garlic in a large heavy-duty, zip-top plastic bag. Add pork; seal bag, and shake until pork is well coated. Marinate in refrigerator 15 minutes.

Remove stems from shiitake mushrooms; reserve stems for another use. Slice caps, and set aside.

Bring broth to a boil in a saucepan; add vermicelli. Cook according to package directions, omitting salt and fat. Drain, reserving ½ cup broth. Set pasta aside; keep warm.

Remove pork from marinade, reserving marinade. Place marinade in a saucepan; bring to a boil. Remove from heat. Add reserved ½ cup broth and cornstarch to marinade, stirring until smooth. Set aside.

Coat a wok or large nonstick skillet with cooking spray; drizzle oil around top of wok, coating sides. Heat at medium-high (375°) until hot. Add shiitake and oyster mushrooms and green onions; stir-fry 2 minutes. Add pork; stir-fry 3 to 4 minutes or until browned. Add reserved marinade mixture and water chestnuts; stir-fry 2 minutes or until thickened. Serve over pasta. Yield: 4 servings.

Per Serving: Calories 431 (13% calories from fat)
Fat 6.4g (Sat 1.5g Mono 2.1g Poly 1.9g) Chol 74mg
Protein 32.7g Carbohydrate 56.3g Sodium 459mg
Exchanges: 3 Very Lean Meat, 3 Starch, 2 Vegetable

Szechuan Pork Fried Rice

1 (¾-pound) pork tenderloin
   Vegetable cooking spray
2 teaspoons peanut oil, divided
1 teaspoon peeled, minced gingerroot
½ teaspoon dried crushed red pepper
2 cloves garlic, minced
3 tablespoons low-sodium soy sauce
1½ cups snow pea pods
3½ cups cooked long-grain rice (cooked without salt or fat), chilled
½ cup coarsely shredded carrot
⅓ cup thinly sliced green onions

Trim fat from tenderloin; cut tenderloin into 1½-inch strips.

Coat a wok or large nonstick skillet with cooking spray; drizzle 1 teaspoon oil around top of wok, coating sides. Heat at medium-high (375°) until hot. Add pork, gingerroot, pepper, and garlic; stir-fry 3 to 4 minutes or until pork is browned. Transfer pork mixture to a shallow bowl; add soy sauce, and set aside.

Drizzle remaining 1 teaspoon oil around top of wok. Add snow peas; stir-fry 1 minute. Add rice and carrot; stir-fry 2 minutes. Add green onions and reserved pork mixture; stir-fry 3 to 4 minutes or until thoroughly heated. Yield: 4 servings.

Per Serving: Calories 340 (13% calories from fat)
Fat 4.8g (Sat 1.1g Mono 2.0g Poly 1.0g) Chol 55mg
Protein 23.1g Carbohydrate 47.9g Sodium 343mg
Exchanges: 2 Lean Meat, 3 Starch, 1 Vegetable

New Mexican Posole

1 (¾-pound) pork tenderloin
1 teaspoon chili powder
1 teaspoon ground cumin
1 teaspoon dried oregano
   Vegetable cooking spray
2 teaspoons vegetable oil
2 cloves garlic, minced
½ cup no-salt-added salsa
½ cup canned low-sodium chicken broth,
   undiluted
1 (15-ounce) can yellow hominy, rinsed and
   drained
1 (15-ounce) can no-salt-added black beans,
   rinsed and drained
⅓ cup thinly sliced green onions
⅓ cup chopped fresh cilantro
4 (8-inch) flour tortillas
   Lime wedges (optional)

Trim fat from tenderloin; cut tenderloin into 1-inch pieces.

Combine chili powder, cumin, and oregano in a large heavy-duty, zip-top plastic bag; add pork. Seal bag, and shake until pork is coated. Coat a large non-stick skillet with cooking spray; add oil. Place over medium-high heat until hot. Add pork and garlic; cook 3 minutes or until browned, stirring often. Add salsa and next 3 ingredients; bring to a boil. Reduce heat, and simmer, uncovered, 10 minutes, stirring occasionally. Stir in green onions and cilantro.

To serve, place 1 tortilla in each of 4 shallow bowls; spoon pork mixture evenly over tortillas. Garnish with lime wedges, if desired. Yield: 4 servings.

Per Serving: Calories 413 (19% calories from fat)
Fat 8.9g (Sat 1.8g Mono 3.0g Poly 2.8g) Chol 55mg
Protein 29.9g Carbohydrate 53.4g Sodium 480mg
Exchanges: 3 Lean Meat, 3 Starch, 1 Vegetable

TORTILLA FATS

We use both regular and fat-free flour tortillas in our recipes. What's the difference?

	Fat	Sodium
1 regular 8-inch tortilla	3 grams	203 mg
1 fat-free 8-inch tortilla	0 grams	340 mg

In recipes where there are several fat-containing ingredients, we opt for the fat-free version. If the other ingredients contribute very little fat, we use the regular. Fat-free tortillas dry out a little quicker than the regular tortillas. So we use the fat-free brands when there is plenty of sauce in the recipe, or when the dish doesn't bake long. However, your recipe will still work if you substitute one for the other.

posole (poh-SOH-leh): a thick soup-like Mexican dish of pork, hominy, and onion. It's traditionally served at Christmas, but we think you'll like it year 'round.

Ham- and
Cheese-
Stuffed
Potatoes

Ham- and Cheese-Stuffed Potatoes

4 (12-ounce) baking potatoes
2 tablespoons reduced-calorie margarine
2 cups fresh broccoli flowerets
½ cup chopped onion
½ cup canned low-sodium chicken broth,
    undiluted
1 cup diced reduced-fat, low-salt ham
¼ teaspoon freshly ground pepper
¼ cup plus 2 tablespoons nonfat sour cream,
    divided
    Vegetable cooking spray
½ cup (2 ounces) reduced-fat shredded
    Cheddar cheese

Scrub potatoes; prick each several times with a fork. Bake at 400° for 1 hour and 15 minutes or until done. Let cool slightly.

Melt margarine in a large nonstick skillet over medium-high heat. Add broccoli and onion; sauté 3 minutes. Add broth; bring to a boil. Cover, reduce heat, and simmer 5 minutes or until broccoli is tender. Remove from heat; stir in ham and pepper.

Cut a lengthwise strip from top of each potato; discard strips. Scoop out pulp, leaving ¼-inch-thick shells; set shells aside.

Place potato pulp in a bowl; add 2 tablespoons sour cream, and mash slightly. Stir in broccoli mixture. Spoon mixture evenly into potato shells.

Place potatoes in an 11- x 7- x 1½-inch baking dish coated with cooking spray. Bake at 400° for 15 to 20 minutes or until thoroughly heated. Top each potato with 2 tablespoons Cheddar cheese, and bake 3 additional minutes or until cheese melts. Top each with 1 tablespoon sour cream. Yield: 4 servings.

Per Serving: Calories 385 (21% calories from fat) Fat 8.9g (Sat 2.8g Mono 0.0g Poly 0.3g) Chol 26mg Protein 20.6g Carbohydrate 58.3g Sodium 491mg
Exchanges: 1 High-Fat Meat, 3 Starch, 2 Vegetable

1-POTATO, 2-POTATO, 3-POTATO, MORE!

There's more to topping a baked potato than sour cream and chives. Top it right, and a baked potato can be a whole meal.

Set toppings out on the counter, and let everybody top their own 'tater. Only your imagination limits the combinations.

Here are some ideas to get you started on a low-fat potato party for four:

Chili Potato

•**Chili Potato:** Top with Easy Sausage Chili (page 23) and nonfat sour cream.

•**Taco Potato:** Brown ½ pound ground round and ½ cup chopped onion in a nonstick skillet. Stir in ¼ cup salsa. Spoon mixture into a potato, and top with reduced-fat Cheddar and chopped green onions.

Taco Potato

•**Chef Salad Potato:** Top that spud with shredded lettuce, reduced-fat Cheddar and Swiss, minced carrot, celery, tomato, and fat-free Ranch dressing.

Chef Salad Potato

Pasta

Mediterranean
Spinach
Lasagna
(page 111)

pasta (PAHST-ah): noodles; often mixed with meats, vegetables, and sauces. Available in oodles of shapes that add interest to menus and texture to children's art projects.

Penne with Chunky Tomato Sauce
(page 112)

Old-Fashioned Spaghetti and Meatballs
(page 121)

Farfalle with Garbanzo Beans and Spinach

1 (10-ounce) package fresh spinach
14 ounces farfalle (bow tie pasta), uncooked
2 teaspoons olive oil, divided
3 cloves garlic, minced
½ cup canned low-sodium chicken broth, undiluted
½ teaspoon dried oregano
½ teaspoon salt
½ teaspoon freshly ground pepper
1 (15-ounce) can garbanzo beans (chick-peas), drained
1 (4-ounce) package crumbled feta cheese
Lemon wedges (optional)

Trim and chop spinach; set aside.

Cook pasta according to package directions, omitting salt and fat. Drain well.

Heat 1 teaspoon oil in a nonstick skillet over medium-high heat. Add garlic; sauté 3 minutes. Reduce heat; stir in broth and next 4 ingredients. Add spinach; cover and cook just until spinach wilts. Combine cooked pasta and spinach mixture in a large bowl. Add remaining 1 teaspoon oil and cheese; toss well. Garnish with lemon wedges, if desired. Serve immediately. Yield: 7 (1½-cup) servings.

Per Serving: Calories 336 (18% calories from fat) Fat 6.8g (Sat 2.7g Mono 1.9g Poly 0.7g) Chol 14mg Protein 13.8g Carbohydrate 53.5g Sodium 455mg
Exchanges: 3 Starch, 2 Vegetable, 1½ Fat

Vegetable Stroganoff

1 cup sliced carrot
1 cup broccoli flowerets
1 cup cauliflower flowerets
Vegetable cooking spray
1 teaspoon olive oil
1 (8-ounce) package presliced fresh mushrooms
3 cloves garlic, minced
½ teaspoon dried tarragon
¼ teaspoon low-sodium Worcestershire sauce
1 cup evaporated skimmed milk
1 cup nonfat sour cream
4 cups cooked fettuccine (cooked without salt or fat)
½ cup freshly grated Parmesan cheese
Freshly ground pepper
Fresh basil sprigs (optional)

Arrange carrot, broccoli, and cauliflower in a steamer basket over boiling water. Cover and steam 6 to 8 minutes or until vegetables are crisp-tender. Drain well.

Coat a large nonstick skillet with cooking spray; add oil. Place over medium-high heat until hot. Add mushrooms and garlic; sauté until tender. Add vegetables, tarragon, and Worcestershire sauce; stir well.

Combine milk and sour cream, stirring until smooth. Add to vegetable mixture, and cook until thoroughly heated. (Do not boil.) To serve, place 1 cup pasta on each serving plate; spoon 1 cup vegetable mixture over each serving. Sprinkle with Parmesan cheese and freshly ground pepper. Garnish with fresh basil sprigs, if desired. Yield: 4 servings.

Per Serving: Calories 401 (15% calories from fat) Fat 6.5g (Sat 2.8g Mono 2.1g Poly 0.8g) Chol 12mg Protein 23.5g Carbohydrate 61.1g Sodium 373mg
Exchanges: 1 Medium-Fat Meat, 3 Starch, 3 Vegetable

Creamy Fettuccine with Peas

8 ounces fettuccine, uncooked
1 clove garlic, peeled
¾ cup evaporated skimmed milk
1½ teaspoons all-purpose flour
½ cup freshly grated Parmesan cheese
¼ teaspoon salt
½ cup frozen English peas, thawed
¼ teaspoon freshly ground pepper

Cook pasta according to package directions, omitting salt and fat, and adding garlic. Drain; remove garlic. Mash garlic into a paste; set aside. Place pasta in a large bowl; set aside.

Combine milk and flour in a small, heavy saucepan, stirring with a wire whisk until smooth. Cook over medium heat, stirring constantly, until thickened and bubbly. Add garlic paste, cheese, and salt. Cook, stirring constantly, until cheese melts.

Add cheese sauce and peas to pasta; toss well. Sprinkle with freshly ground pepper, and serve immediately. Yield: 4 (1-cup) servings.

Per Serving: Calories 352 (10% calories from fat) Fat 4.0g (Sat 1.9g Mono 1.1g Poly 0.8g) Chol 8mg Protein 17.3g Carbohydrate 64.5g Sodium 373mg
Exchanges: ½ High-Fat Meat, 4 Starch, 1 Vegetable

NOODLE KNOWLEDGE

Since pasta is low-fat, low-sodium, and high-carbohydrate, you can enjoy it often in your heart-healthy diet. The chart on the right will help you identify some of the many types you'll see in the supermarket. If you can't find a specific type of pasta, substitute another of similar size or shape.

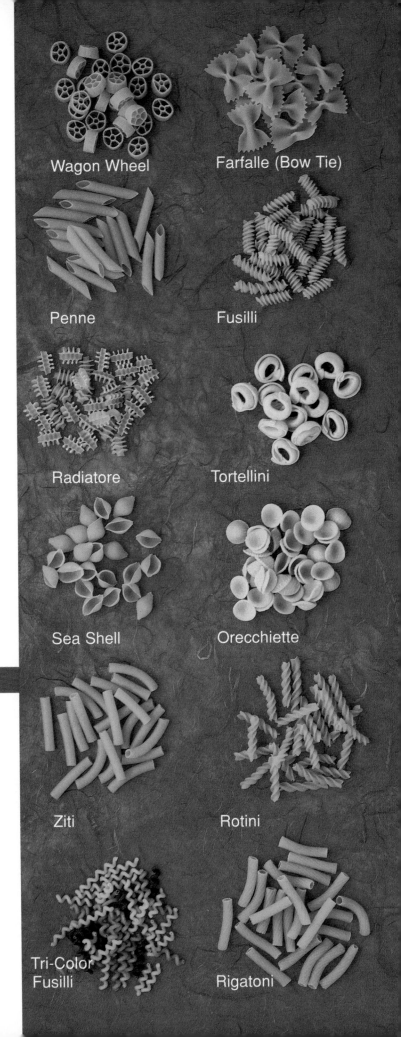

Wagon Wheel

Farfalle (Bow Tie)

Penne

Fusilli

Radiatore

Tortellini

Sea Shell

Orecchiette

Ziti

Rotini

Tri-Color Fusilli

Rigatoni

Fusilli with Roasted Peppers

3 sweet red peppers
3 yellow peppers
1 pound fusilli (corkscrew pasta), uncooked
½ cup sliced fresh basil
2 tablespoons balsamic vinegar
1 tablespoon olive oil
¾ teaspoon salt
½ teaspoon freshly ground pepper
4 ounces basil- and tomato-flavored feta cheese, crumbled

Place peppers in a 13- x 9- x 2-inch baking dish. Bake, uncovered, at 500° for 35 minutes or until charred, turning once. Remove from oven, and cover with foil. Let stand 20 minutes.

Cut a slit in each pepper. Let cool 10 to 15 minutes. Reserve roasted pepper liquid, and set aside. Remove and discard seeds, membranes, and skins from peppers; cut peppers into thin strips. Set aside.

Cook pasta according to package directions, omitting salt and fat; drain. Combine reserved pepper liquid, pepper strips, pasta, basil, and next 4 ingredients in a large serving bowl; toss well. Sprinkle with feta cheese. Yield: 6 (2-cup) servings.

Per Serving: Calories 384 (19% calories from fat)
Fat 8.2g (Sat 3.2g Mono 2.6g Poly 0.6g) Chol 17mg
Protein 13.2g Carbohydrate 62.6g Sodium 509mg
Exchanges: 4 Starch, 1 Vegetable, 1½ Fat

Fusilli with Fresh Tomato Sauce

4½ cups chopped tomato
½ cup sliced fresh basil
½ cup chopped onion
2 tablespoons olive oil
1½ tablespoons balsamic vinegar
¾ teaspoon salt
¾ teaspoon freshly ground pepper
1 pound fusilli (corkscrew pasta), uncooked
3 tablespoons freshly grated Romano cheese

Combine first 7 ingredients in a large bowl. Cover and chill at least 2 hours. (May chill overnight, if desired.)

Cook pasta according to package directions, omitting salt and fat; drain. Add cooked pasta to tomato mixture, tossing lightly. Sprinkle with cheese. Yield: 6 (2-cup) servings.

Per Serving: Calories 353 (18% calories from fat)
Fat 6.9g (Sat 1.4g Mono 3.8g Poly 1.0g) Chol 4mg
Protein 11.6g Carbohydrate 60.7g Sodium 347mg
Exchanges: 3½ Starch, 1 Vegetable, 1 Fat

Cheesy Macaroni and Veggies

8 cups water
8 ounces elbow macaroni, uncooked
2 cups sliced carrot
2 cups broccoli flowerets
1¾ cups (7 ounces) shredded reduced-fat sharp
    Cheddar cheese, divided
1 tablespoon reduced-calorie margarine
¼ teaspoon salt
¼ teaspoon freshly ground pepper
1 tablespoon all-purpose flour
1 cup evaporated skimmed milk, divided
    Vegetable cooking spray

Bring water to a boil in a Dutch oven. Add macaroni, carrot, and broccoli; cook 8 minutes or until macaroni is almost tender. Drain.

Return macaroni mixture to Dutch oven; add 1¼ cups cheese and next 3 ingredients; toss lightly.

Combine flour and 3 tablespoons milk in a small bowl; stir well with a wire whisk. Stir in remaining milk. Stir milk mixture into macaroni mixture. Spoon mixture into an 11- x 7- x 1½-inch baking dish coated with cooking spray. Cover and bake at 350° for 25 minutes. Uncover and sprinkle remaining ½ cup cheese over top of casserole. Bake 5 additional minutes or until cheese melts. Yield: 4 servings.

Per Serving: Calories 475 (24% calories from fat)
Fat 12.7g (Sat 6.0g Mono 3.5g Poly 1.6g) Chol 36mg
Protein 28.6g Carbohydrate 62.3g Sodium 645mg
Exchanges: 2 Medium-Fat Meat, 4 Starch, 1 Vegetable

Orecchiette with Kale and Sun-Dried Tomatoes

1 cup sun-dried tomatoes (packed without oil)
1 cup boiling water
1 teaspoon olive oil
¾ teaspoon dried crushed red pepper
4 large cloves garlic, minced
¼ teaspoon salt
1 pound orecchiette (bowl-shaped pasta),
    uncooked
7 cups chopped kale (about 1 bunch)
2 tablespoons freshly grated Romano cheese
6 kalamata olives, pitted and sliced

Combine tomatoes and water in a small bowl. Let stand 15 minutes; drain, reserving ½ cup water. Cut tomatoes into thin strips; set aside.

Heat oil in a small nonstick skillet over medium heat. Add pepper and garlic; sauté 1 minute. Remove from heat; stir in salt and tomato strips. Set aside.

Cook pasta according to package directions, omitting salt and fat; add kale during last 5 minutes of cooking time. Drain; place pasta mixture in a large serving bowl. Add tomato mixture and reserved ½ cup water to pasta, tossing lightly. Top with cheese and olives. Yield: 6 (2-cup) servings.

Per Serving: Calories 407 (10% calories from fat)
Fat 4.4g (Sat 0.8g Mono 1.2g Poly 0.7g) Chol 2mg
Protein 16.3g Carbohydrate 77.3g Sodium 692mg
Exchanges: 4 Starch, 3 Vegetable, 1 Fat

HAIL, KALE

Kale is a member of the cabbage family, but it grows in bunches of frilly leaves instead of in a compact head. It gets an A-plus in nutrition as a source of vitamins A and C, folic acid, calcium, and iron. And like most leafy greens, it's fat-free and cholesterol-free, low-calorie, and low-sodium. Use kale as you would spinach—cooked or tossed with other greens in a salad.

Mediterranean
Spinach
Lasagna

Mediterranean Spinach Lasagna

9 lasagna noodles, uncooked
  Vegetable cooking spray
2 cups sliced fresh mushrooms
1 cup shredded carrot
1 cup chopped onion
2 (8-ounce) cans no-salt-added tomato sauce
1 (6-ounce) can no-salt-added tomato paste
1 (2¼-ounce) can sliced ripe olives, drained
1½ teaspoons dried oregano
1 teaspoon dried basil
½ teaspoon pepper
1 (10-ounce) package frozen chopped spinach,
  thawed
1½ cups 1% low-fat cottage cheese
¼ cup plus 2 tablespoons nonfat cream cheese,
  softened
1 tablespoon lemon juice
1½ cups (6 ounces) shredded part-skim
  mozzarella cheese
¼ cup grated Parmesan cheese

Cook noodles according to package directions, omitting salt and fat. Drain and set aside.

Coat a large nonstick skillet with cooking spray; place over medium-high heat until hot. Add mushrooms, carrot, and onion; sauté 5 minutes.

Remove vegetable mixture from heat, and stir in tomato sauce, tomato paste, olives, oregano, basil, and pepper. Set mixture aside.

Drain spinach, and press between paper towels to remove excess moisture. Combine spinach, cottage cheese, nonfat cream cheese, and lemon juice. Set spinach mixture aside.

Place 3 lasagna noodles in bottom of an 11- x 7- x 1½-inch baking dish coated with vegetable cooking spray. Spoon one-third of spinach mixture over noodles. Spoon one-third of vegetable mixture over spinach mixture. Top with one-third of mozzarella cheese. Repeat layers twice with remaining noodles, spinach mixture, vegetable mixture, and mozzarella cheese. Top with Parmesan cheese. Bake, uncovered, at 325° for 30 to 35 minutes or until thoroughly heated. Let stand 10 minutes before serving. Yield: 6 servings.

Note: If desired, cover and chill overnight before baking. Bake, uncovered, at 325° for 45 minutes or until thoroughly heated.

Per Serving: Calories 379 (20% calories from fat)
Fat 8.3g (Sat 4.2g Mono 2.7g Poly 0.8g) Chol 25mg
Protein 27.0g Carbohydrate 50.0g Sodium 705mg
Exchanges: 2 Medium-Fat Meat, 3 Starch, 2 Vegetable

Pesto Penne with Green Beans and Potatoes

½ pound fresh green beans
12 cups water
3 cups cubed small round red potatoes
1 pound penne (short tubular pasta), uncooked
2 cups packed fresh basil leaves
¼ cup canned low-sodium chicken broth, undiluted
¼ cup 1% low-fat milk
¼ cup grated Romano cheese
1½ tablespoons olive oil
1 teaspoon salt
½ teaspoon freshly ground pepper
2 cloves garlic

Wash green beans; trim ends, and remove strings. Cut beans into 1-inch pieces. Set aside.

Bring water to a boil in a Dutch oven. Add potato, and cook, uncovered, 2 minutes. Stir in pasta; bring to a boil, and cook, uncovered, 5 minutes. Add beans, and cook 5 additional minutes or until potato and pasta are tender. Drain and set aside.

Position knife blade in food processor bowl. Add basil and remaining 7 ingredients; process 30 seconds or until smooth, stopping once to scrape down sides.

Place pasta mixture in a large bowl; add basil mixture, and toss well. Yield: 7 (1½-cup) servings.

Per Serving: Calories 349 (14% calories from fat)
Fat 5.3g (Sat 1.3g Mono 2.6g Poly 0.8g) Chol 5mg
Protein 12.3g Carbohydrate 62.9g Sodium 402mg
Exchanges: 3½ Starch, 1 Vegetable, 1 Fat

Penne with Chunky Tomato Sauce

Olive oil-flavored vegetable cooking spray
1 teaspoon olive oil
½ cup finely chopped onion
1 clove garlic, minced
2 (14½-ounce) cans no-salt-added whole tomatoes, undrained and chopped
½ cup no-salt-added tomato sauce
¼ teaspoon salt
¼ teaspoon freshly ground pepper
1 pound penne (short tubular pasta), uncooked
½ cup thinly sliced fresh basil
3 tablespoons freshly grated Parmesan cheese
Fresh basil sprigs (optional)

Coat a large nonstick skillet with cooking spray; add oil. Place over medium heat until hot. Add onion and garlic; sauté until tender. Add tomato and tomato sauce; bring to a boil. Reduce heat, and simmer, uncovered, 20 minutes or until thickened, stirring occasionally. Stir in salt and pepper.

Cook pasta according to package directions, omitting salt and fat; drain. Place pasta in a serving bowl; add tomato mixture; toss lightly. Sprinkle with sliced basil and cheese. Garnish with basil sprigs, if desired. Serve immediately. Yield: 6 (1½-cup) servings.

Per Serving: Calories 337 (7% calories from fat)
Fat 2.7g (Sat 0.7g Mono 0.9g Poly 0.6g) Chol 2mg
Protein 12.1g Carbohydrate 65.9g Sodium 164mg
Exchanges: 4 Starch, 1 Vegetable, ½ Fat

pesto (PEH-stoh): an uncooked Italian sauce traditionally made with fresh basil, garlic, pine nuts, Parmesan cheese, and olive oil. We omitted the pine nuts and decreased the amount of oil.

Penne with
Chunky
Tomato
Sauce

Vegetable Spaghettini

Olive oil-flavored vegetable cooking spray
2 teaspoons olive oil
3 cups julienne-sliced yellow squash
2 cups sliced fresh crimini mushrooms
½ teaspoon dried crushed red pepper
2 cloves garlic, minced
1½ cups coarsely chopped plum tomato
½ teaspoon salt
¼ pound fresh green beans
4 quarts water
8 ounces spaghettini, uncooked and broken in half
½ cup sliced carrot
1 tablespoon reduced-calorie margarine
1 tablespoon all-purpose flour
¾ cup evaporated skimmed milk
¼ cup canned no-salt-added chicken broth, undiluted
¼ cup grated Parmesan cheese

Coat a large nonstick skillet with cooking spray; add oil. Place over medium-high heat until hot. Add squash, mushrooms, crushed red pepper, and garlic; sauté 3 minutes. Add tomato and salt; sauté 5 additional minutes. Set aside, and keep warm.

Wash beans; trim ends, and remove strings. Cut beans into 1-inch pieces. Bring water to a boil in a Dutch oven; add beans, pasta, and carrot. Cook 8 to 10 minutes or until pasta is tender. Drain well; set aside, and keep warm.

Melt margarine in a small saucepan over low heat; add flour, stirring until smooth. Cook, stirring constantly, 1 minute. Gradually add milk and broth to mixture, stirring constantly. Cook over medium heat, stirring constantly, until thickened and bubbly.

Combine pasta mixture and vegetable mixture in a large bowl. Add sauce; toss well. Sprinkle with cheese. Serve warm. Yield: 4 (1½-cup) servings.

Per Serving: Calories 367 (18% calories from fat) Fat 7.3g (Sat 1.8g Mono 3.0g Poly 1.6g) Chol 6mg Protein 15.8g Carbohydrate 60.8g Sodium 489mg
Exchanges: 3 Starch, 3 Vegetable, 1½ Fat

THE PERFECT PASTA

Fettuccine Alfredo, spaghetti marinara—these well-known pasta and sauce combinations didn't come about by chance. Good Italian cooks know that you select the type of pasta based upon the sauce you plan to serve with it.

The rule of thumb is that the thinner the sauce, the longer the pasta. Long pasta types include spaghetti, linguine, and vermicelli. The twists and turns of short pastas such as penne, fusilli (corkscrew), and farfalle (bow tie) trap the chunky ingredients of a thicker sauce. So, fettuccine is the perfect pasta for creamy Alfredo sauce, while penne or ziti works well with a thick tomato sauce.

Stuffed Shells with Tomato Sauce

18 jumbo pasta shells, uncooked
1 (15-ounce) can garbanzo beans (chick-peas), drained
1¼ cups light ricotta cheese
¼ cup grated Romano cheese
¼ teaspoon salt
¼ teaspoon freshly ground pepper
1 egg white
1 clove garlic, minced
Olive oil-flavored vegetable cooking spray
¾ cup sliced fresh mushrooms
¼ cup minced onion
3½ cups peeled, seeded, and chopped plum tomato
¾ cup no-salt-added tomato juice
½ (6-ounce) can no-salt-added tomato paste
1 tablespoon chopped fresh basil
1 teaspoon chopped fresh oregano
⅛ teaspoon salt
1 bay leaf
½ cup (2 ounces) shredded part-skim mozzarella cheese

Cook shells according to package directions, omitting salt and fat. Drain and set aside.

Position knife blade in food processor bowl; add beans and next 6 ingredients. Process until smooth, stopping once to scrape down sides.

Coat a large nonstick skillet with cooking spray. Place over medium-high heat until hot. Add mushrooms and onion; sauté until tender. Add chopped tomato and next 6 ingredients; stir well. Bring to a boil; cover, reduce heat, and simmer 15 minutes, stirring occasionally. Uncover and cook 15 additional minutes. Remove and discard bay leaf. Set aside.

Spoon bean mixture evenly into shells. Spoon 1 cup tomato mixture into an 11- x 7- x 1½-inch baking dish coated with cooking spray. Arrange shells in prepared dish. Pour remaining tomato mixture over shells. Top with mozzarella cheese.

Cover and bake at 350° for 20 minutes. Uncover and bake 10 additional minutes. Yield: 6 servings.

Per Serving: Calories 328 (18% calories from fat)
Fat 6.6g (Sat 2.9g Mono 1.6g Poly 0.8g) Chol 17mg
Protein 19.6g Carbohydrate 50.2g Sodium 392mg
Exchanges: 1 Medium-Fat Meat, 3 Starch, 2 Vegetable

Shrimp and Cabbage on Capellini

16 unpeeled jumbo fresh shrimp
1 tablespoon dark sesame oil, divided
1½ tablespoons peeled, minced gingerroot
2 cloves garlic, minced
6 cups shredded Chinese cabbage
½ teaspoon salt
8 ounces capellini (angel hair pasta), uncooked

Peel and devein shrimp. Cut shrimp in half crosswise. Set aside.

Heat 1½ teaspoons oil in a large nonstick skillet over medium heat. Add gingerroot and garlic; sauté 1 minute. Add shrimp, and cook 3 to 5 minutes or until shrimp turn pink, stirring often. Remove shrimp from skillet, and keep warm.

Place cabbage and salt in skillet; cover and cook over medium heat 5 minutes, stirring once.

Cook pasta according to package directions, omitting salt and fat; drain. Place pasta in a serving bowl. Stir in remaining 1½ teaspoons oil. Top with cabbage and shrimp. Serve immediately. Yield: 6 (1½-cup) servings.

Per Serving: Calories 241 (16% calories from fat)
Fat 4.2g (Sat 0.6g Mono 1.2g Poly 1.7g) Chol 101mg
Protein 19.2g Carbohydrate 30.8g Sodium 333mg
Exchanges: 2 Lean Meat, 1½ Starch, 1 Vegetable

Farfalle with Smoked Salmon and Peas

Vegetable cooking spray
2 teaspoons reduced-calorie margarine
½ cup minced shallots
2 cups fresh Sugar Snap peas, trimmed
½ cup canned no-salt-added chicken broth, undiluted
2 tablespoons vodka
½ teaspoon freshly ground pepper
½ cup 1% low-fat milk
1 tablespoon all-purpose flour
8 ounces sliced smoked salmon, cut into thin strips
12 ounces farfalle (bow tie pasta), uncooked

Coat a large nonstick skillet with cooking spray; add margarine. Place over medium-high heat until margarine melts. Add shallots; sauté 1 to 2 minutes or until tender. Add peas; sauté 2 additional minutes. Stir in broth, vodka, and pepper; bring to a boil. Reduce heat, and simmer, uncovered, 3 minutes.

Combine milk and flour, stirring until smooth. Add to vegetable mixture in skillet, and cook, stirring constantly, until thickened and bubbly. Stir in smoked salmon. Remove from heat; set aside, and keep warm.

Cook pasta according to package directions, omitting salt and fat; drain well.

To serve, place pasta in a serving bowl; add salmon mixture, and toss lightly. Yield: 4 (2-cup) servings.

Per Serving: Calories 475 (11% calories from fat)
Fat 5.7g (Sat 1.1g Mono 1.9g Poly 1.7g) Chol 14mg
Protein 24.9g Carbohydrate 75.0g Sodium 489mg
Exchanges: 1 Medium-Fat Meat, 4 Starch, 3 Vegetable

Linguine with Mussels

2 pounds fresh mussels
12 ounces linguine, uncooked
Vegetable cooking spray
1 teaspoon olive oil
1½ cups chopped sweet red pepper
¼ cup chopped fresh basil, divided
½ teaspoon salt
¼ teaspoon dried crushed red pepper
4 large cloves garlic, minced
¾ cup dry white wine

Remove beards on mussels, and scrub shells with a brush. Discard opened, cracked, or heavy mussels (they're filled with sand). Set aside.

Cook pasta according to package directions, omitting salt and fat; drain well. Place in a serving bowl; keep warm.

Coat a nonstick skillet with cooking spray. Add olive oil; place over medium-high heat until hot. Add sweet red pepper, 2 tablespoons basil, salt, crushed red pepper, and garlic; cook, stirring constantly, 2 minutes.

Add mussels and wine. Cover and cook 5 minutes or until mussels open. (Discard any mussels that do not open.) Spoon mussels and wine mixture over pasta; sprinkle with remaining 2 tablespoons chopped basil. Yield: 4 servings.

Per Serving: Calories 434 (11% calories from fat)
Fat 5.2g (Sat 0.8g Mono 1.5g Poly 1.4g) Chol 29mg
Protein 23.9g Carbohydrate 71.3g Sodium 496mg
Exchanges: 1 Medium-Fat Meat, 4 Starch, 2 Vegetable

Angel Hair Pasta with Chicken and Snow Peas

2 teaspoons dark sesame oil
4 cups fresh snow pea pods, trimmed
1 cup julienne-sliced sweet yellow pepper
½ teaspoon dried crushed red pepper
8 ounces skinned, boned chicken breasts, cut
    into 1-inch pieces
1 (8-ounce) can sliced water chestnuts, drained
3 large cloves garlic, minced
½ teaspoon salt
⅛ teaspoon Chinese five-spice powder
8 ounces capellini (angel hair pasta), uncooked

Heat oil in a large nonstick skillet over medium-high heat. Add snow peas and next 5 ingredients; sauté 5 minutes or until chicken is done. Add salt and five-spice powder; cook 1 additional minute. Remove from heat, and set aside.

    Cook pasta according to package directions, omitting salt and fat; drain well. Combine snow pea mixture and pasta, tossing well. Yield: 4 (2-cup) servings.

Per Serving: Calories 370 (10% calories from fat)
Fat 4.2g (Sat 0.7g Mono 1.2g Poly 1.6g) Chol 33mg
Protein 23.1g Carbohydrate 58.2g Sodium 344mg
Exchanges: 1 Lean Meat, 3 Starch, 3 Vegetable

Penne with Grilled Chicken and Eggplant

1 (1-pound) eggplant
2 tablespoons balsamic vinegar
2 tablespoons canned low-sodium chicken broth
2 tablespoons chili powder
1 teaspoon garlic powder
8 ounces skinned, boned chicken breast tenders
    Vegetable cooking spray
1 pound penne (short tubular pasta), uncooked
1 cup seeded, diced tomato
¼ cup chopped fresh cilantro
1 tablespoon olive oil
1 tablespoon canned low-sodium chicken broth,
    undiluted
½ teaspoon salt
6 large pitted ripe olives, chopped

Cut eggplant lengthwise into 8 (¼-inch-thick) slices; place in an 11- x 7- x 1½-inch baking dish. Combine vinegar and 2 tablespoons broth; pour over eggplant. Cover and let stand 30 minutes, turning occasionally. Remove eggplant slices from marinade, discarding any remaining marinade.

    Combine chili and garlic powders in a large heavy-duty, zip-top plastic bag. Add chicken; seal bag, and shake until chicken is well coated.

    Coat grill rack with cooking spray; place on grill over medium-hot coals (350° to 400°). Place chicken on rack; grill, covered, 3 minutes on each side. Place eggplant on rack; grill, covered, 2 minutes on each side. Cut chicken and eggplant into 1-inch pieces.

    Cook pasta according to package directions, omitting salt and fat. Drain.

    Combine pasta, eggplant, chicken, tomato, and remaining ingredients; toss well. Yield: 6 (2-cup) servings.

Per Serving: Calories 380 (14% calories from fat)
Fat 5.7g (Sat 0.8g Mono 2.4g Poly 0.7g) Chol 23mg
Protein 19.2g Carbohydrate 61.0g Sodium 285mg
Exchanges: 1 Medium-Fat Meat, 3 Starch, 3 Vegetable

Turkey-Noodle Bake

8 ounces elbow macaroni, uncooked
¾ pound turkey sausage
½ cup sliced fresh mushrooms
½ cup chopped green pepper
½ cup chopped onion
1 tablespoon low-sodium Worcestershire sauce
2 cloves garlic, minced
2 (8-ounce) cans no-salt-added tomato sauce
½ teaspoon dried Italian seasoning
    Dash of salt
1 (12-ounce) carton 1% low-fat cottage cheese
1 (8-ounce) carton nonfat sour cream
1⅓ cups chopped green onions
2 tablespoons grated Romano cheese
    Vegetable cooking spray
½ cup (2 ounces) shredded reduced-fat sharp
    Cheddar cheese

Cook macaroni according to package directions, omitting salt and fat. Drain and set aside.

Cook turkey sausage and next 5 ingredients in a large nonstick skillet over medium-high heat until sausage is browned, stirring until it crumbles. Add cooked macaroni, tomato sauce, Italian seasoning, and salt; stir well.

Combine cottage cheese and next 3 ingredients. Spoon half of turkey mixture into a 13- x 9- x 2-inch baking dish coated with cooking spray. Spread cheese mixture over turkey mixture. Top with remaining turkey mixture. Cover and bake at 350° for 40 minutes; uncover and top with Cheddar cheese. Bake 5 additional minutes or until cheese melts. Yield: 8 servings.

Per Serving: Calories 327 (32% calories from fat)
Fat 11.7g (Sat 4.8g Mono 0.3g Poly 3.2g) Chol 32mg
Protein 21.1g Carbohydrate 32.9g Sodium 634mg
Exchanges: 2 Medium-Fat Meat, 2 Starch, 1 Vegetable

Rigatoni with Turkey Sausage

    Vegetable cooking spray
1 pound smoked turkey sausage, sliced
1 cup chopped onion
4 cloves garlic, minced
3 (14½-ounce) cans no-salt-added whole
    tomatoes, undrained and chopped
¼ cup dry white wine
⅛ teaspoon salt
3 bay leaves
12 ounces rigatoni (short tubular pasta),
    uncooked

Coat a Dutch oven with cooking spray; place over medium-high heat until hot. Add sausage, onion, and garlic; cook 3 minutes or until sausage is browned, stirring often.

Add tomato and next 3 ingredients; bring to a boil. Reduce heat, and simmer, uncovered, 25 minutes, stirring occasionally. Remove and discard bay leaves.

Cook pasta according to package directions, omitting salt and fat; drain. Place pasta in a large serving bowl; add sausage mixture, and toss well. Yield: 8 (1¼-cup) servings.

Per Serving: Calories 267 (8% calories from fat)
Fat 2.3g (Sat 0.2g Mono 0.1g Poly 0.8g) Chol 25mg
Protein 15.0g Carbohydrate 44.7g Sodium 650mg
Exchanges: 1 Lean Meat, 2½ Starch, 1 Vegetable

Spaghetti Carbonara

1 tablespoon all-purpose flour
1 cup evaporated skimmed milk
¼ cup frozen egg substitute, thawed
2 tablespoons chopped fresh parsley
1 teaspoon chopped fresh basil
1 clove garlic, minced
8 ounces spaghetti, uncooked
1 cup frozen English peas and carrots, thawed
¼ cup freshly grated Parmesan cheese
4 slices turkey bacon, cooked and crumbled
½ teaspoon freshly ground pepper

Place flour in a medium saucepan. Gradually add milk, stirring until smooth. Cook over medium heat, stirring constantly, until mixture is slightly thickened. Gradually stir about one-fourth of hot milk mixture into egg substitute. Add to remaining milk mixture, stirring constantly until thickened. Stir in parsley, basil, and garlic. Set aside, and keep warm.

Cook pasta according to package directions, omitting salt and fat. Drain well. Combine pasta and sauce in a large bowl; toss lightly. Add peas and carrots, cheese, and bacon; toss lightly. Sprinkle with pepper, and serve immediately. Yield: 4 (1½-cup) servings.

Per Serving: Calories 358 (13% calories from fat) Fat 5.1g (Sat 2.0g Mono 1.7g Poly 0.9g) Chol 17mg Protein 19.8g Carbohydrate 56.5g Sodium 437mg
Exchanges: 1 Medium-Fat Meat, 3 Starch, 2 Vegetable

BEYOND SPAGHETTI

A spaghetti noodle by any other name might be linguine or fettuccine. If one type of long pasta is not available, substitute another one of similar size. The chart on the right can help you identify the different sizes.

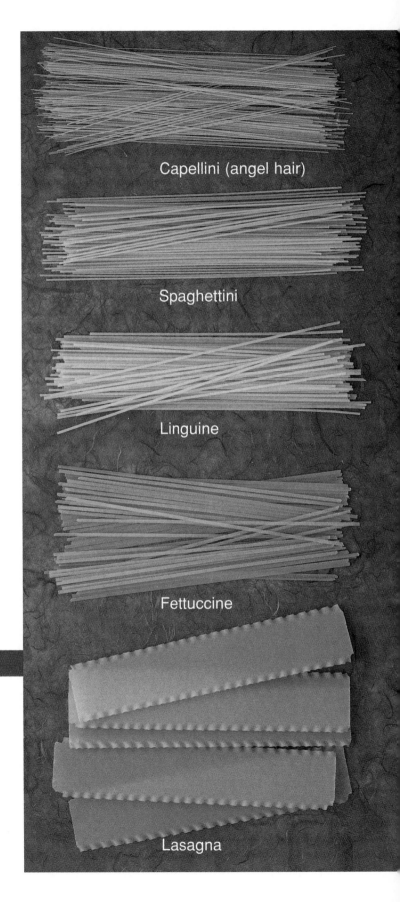

Capellini (angel hair)

Spaghettini

Linguine

Fettuccine

Lasagna

Old-Fashioned
Spaghetti and
Meatballs

Old-Fashioned Spaghetti and Meatballs

1 pound ground round
½ cup soft white breadcrumbs
¼ cup minced fresh parsley
3 tablespoons grated Parmesan cheese
2 teaspoons sugar
¼ teaspoon salt
¼ teaspoon freshly ground pepper
1 egg white
2 cloves garlic, minced
    Vegetable cooking spray
1 teaspoon olive oil
1 cup minced onion
4 (14½-ounce) cans no-salt-added whole
    tomatoes, undrained and chopped
1 (6-ounce) can no-salt-added tomato paste
½ teaspoon salt
⅛ teaspoon dried crushed red pepper
12 ounces spaghetti, uncooked

Combine first 9 ingredients, stirring well. Shape mixture into 18 (1½-inch) balls. Coat a large nonstick skillet with cooking spray. Place over medium-high heat until hot. Add meatballs; cook 10 minutes or until browned on all sides, turning occasionally. Remove meatballs from skillet. Drain and pat dry with paper towels.

Coat a Dutch oven with cooking spray; add oil. Place over medium heat until hot. Add onion; sauté 5 minutes or until onion is tender. Add tomato and next 3 ingredients; cover and cook 30 minutes, stirring often. Add meatballs, and cook 30 additional minutes.

Cook pasta according to package directions, omitting salt and fat; drain. Place in a large serving bowl. To serve, spoon meatball mixture over pasta. Yield: 6 servings.

Per Serving: Calories 445 (15% calories from fat) Fat 7.3g (Sat 2.4g Mono 2.9g Poly 0.7g) Chol 49mg Protein 29.0g Carbohydrate 66.3g Sodium 461mg **Exchanges:** 2 Lean Meat, 4 Starch, 1 Vegetable

FRUIT OF THE VINE

"Drink one glass of wine with dinner, and call me in the morning."

Current evidence suggests that drinking wine in moderation can reduce your risk of getting heart disease.

Moderate drinking is defined as 4 ounces of wine a day for women and 4 to 8 ounces a day for men.

But even though a little *vino* may not be bad for your heart, health experts caution against viewing wine as a medicine. The risks of drinking too much wine outweigh the heart benefits. As the American Heart Association states, "If you don't drink, don't start."

Pizza

Roasted
Pepper Pizza
(page 132)

pizza (peet-za): a flat, round yeast bread topped with sauce (traditionally tomato), vegetables, meat, cheese, and/or anything else edible.

Deep-Dish Italian Meatball Pizza (page 129)

Roasted Vegetable Pizza (page 135)

Build a Better Pizza

Everybody loves a pizza—why not make it a heart-healthy one? In this chapter we give you recipes for three tasty crusts, for a hearty (and freezable) tomato sauce, and for seven "Oh, Wow!" pizzas.

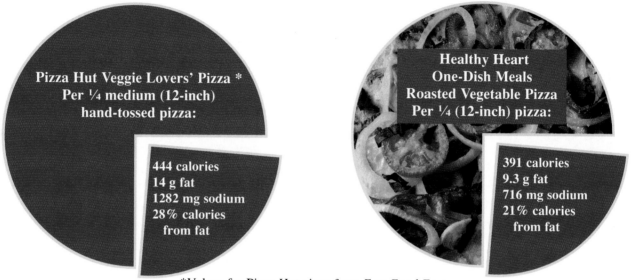

Pizza Hut Veggie Lovers' Pizza *
Per ¼ medium (12-inch)
hand-tossed pizza:

444 calories
14 g fat
1282 mg sodium
28% calories
from fat

Healthy Heart
One-Dish Meals
Roasted Vegetable Pizza
Per ¼ (12-inch) pizza:

391 calories
9.3 g fat
716 mg sodium
21% calories
from fat

*Values for Pizza Hut pizza from *Fast Food Facts,*
Marion J. Franz, 1994, page 65.

Why Not Just Order Out?

Sure, it's easier to pick up the phone and dial for pizza delivery. But the pizza that's delivered may not be as easy on your heart as a heart-smart homemade one. The local pizzaria usually piles on the meat and cheese, which piles on the fat and the sodium. Take a look at the difference in the pizzas above.

Make A Crust

For each pizza in this chapter, we suggest either a plain, whole wheat, or cornmeal crust recipe. All three crusts are similar in calories, fat, and sodium, so you can mix and match crusts and toppings to your heart's content. (The nutrient analysis is for the crust listed in the ingredient list.)

THE CRUST OF THE MATTER

Compare the nutrient values of our homemade crusts and a commercial crust:

	Calories per 1 crust	Calories per ¼ crust	Fat per ¼ crust	Sodium per ¼ crust	% Calories from fat
Plain Ol' Pizza Crust	758	190	3.7g	181mg	18%
Whole Wheat Pizza Crust	751	188	1.0g	148mg	5%
Cornmeal Pizza Crust	702	176	1.6g	151mg	8%
Commercial Pizza Crust	720	180	2.5g	390mg	13%

Plain Ol' Pizza Crust

2 tablespoons margarine
1 cup boiling water
1 package active dry yeast
1 teaspoon sugar
2½ cups bread flour, divided
½ teaspoon salt
⅛ teaspoon garlic powder
1 tablespoon bread flour
   Vegetable cooking spray

Place margarine in a large bowl; add boiling water, stirring until margarine melts. Cool to 115°.

Sprinkle yeast and sugar over water mixture, stirring until yeast and sugar dissolve. Let stand 10 minutes or until bubbly. Add 2 cups flour, salt, and garlic powder, stirring until blended. Gradually stir in enough of remaining ½ cup flour to make a medium-stiff dough.

Sprinkle 1 tablespoon flour evenly over work surface. Turn dough out onto floured surface, and knead until smooth and elastic (about 5 minutes). Place in a large bowl coated with cooking spray, turning to coat top. Cover and let rise in a warm place (85°), free from drafts, 35 to 40 minutes or until doubled in bulk.

Punch dough down, and let rest 5 minutes. Divide dough in half, and pat each portion into a 12-inch pizza pan coated with cooking spray. Bake according to pizza recipe directions. Yield: 2 (12-inch) crusts.

Per Crust: Calories 758 (18% calories from fat)
Fat 14.9g (Sat 2.7g Mono 5.4g Poly 4.9g) Chol 0mg
Protein 22.5g Carbohydrate 131.0g Sodium 723mg

Whole Wheat Pizza Crust

1 package active dry yeast
1 tablespoon sugar
1 cup warm water (105° to 115°)
2 cups bread flour, divided
1 cup whole wheat flour
½ teaspoon salt
1 tablespoon bread flour
   Vegetable cooking spray

Combine yeast, sugar, and warm water in a 2-cup liquid measuring cup; let stand 5 minutes.

Combine yeast mixture, 1 cup bread flour, whole wheat flour, and salt in a large bowl, stirring until well blended. Gradually stir in enough of remaining 1 cup bread flour to make a stiff dough.

Sprinkle 1 tablespoon flour evenly over work surface. Turn dough out onto floured surface, and knead until smooth and elastic (about 10 minutes). Place in a large bowl coated with cooking spray, turning to coat top. Cover and let rise in a warm place (85°), free from drafts, 1 hour or until doubled in bulk.

Punch dough down, and let rest 5 minutes. Divide dough in half, and pat each portion into a 12-inch pizza pan coated with cooking spray. Bake according to pizza recipe directions. Yield: 2 (12-inch) crusts.

Per Crust: Calories 751 (5% calories from fat)
Fat 4.0g (Sat 0.6g Mono 0.4g Poly 1.5g) Chol 0mg
Protein 26.5g Carbohydrate 153.6g Sodium 592mg

WHY MAKE YOUR OWN CRUST?

•**For the flavor:** There's nothing like sinking your teeth into a hearty, fresh-from-the-oven crust topped with tomato sauce and cheese.
•**For the fiber:** Try the Cornmeal Pizza Crust with 5.2 grams of fiber per crust, or the Whole Wheat Pizza Crust with 8.5 grams.
•**For the fun:** If you have flour, yeast, sugar, and salt in your pantry, you have a pizza crust. Ask a few friends to bring their favorite toppings, and you have a pizza party.
And if you're concerned about sodium, a homemade crust has about half as much sodium as a commercial crust.

Cornmeal Pizza Crust

1 package active dry yeast
2 teaspoons sugar
1 cup warm water (105° to 115°)
2 cups bread flour, divided
½ cup coarsely ground yellow cornmeal
1 teaspoon olive oil
½ teaspoon salt
2 cloves garlic, crushed
1 tablespoon bread flour
  Vegetable cooking spray
2 tablespoons coarsely ground yellow cornmeal

Combine yeast, sugar, and warm water in a 2-cup liquid measuring cup; let stand 5 minutes.

Combine yeast mixture, 1 cup flour, cornmeal, and next 3 ingredients in a large mixing bowl; beat at medium speed of an electric mixer until well blended. Gradually stir in enough of remaining 1 cup flour to make a stiff dough.

Sprinkle 1 tablespoon flour evenly over work surface. Turn dough out onto floured surface, and knead until smooth and elastic (about 5 minutes). Place in a large bowl coated with cooking spray, turning to coat top. Cover and let rise in a warm place (85°), free from drafts, 30 minutes or until doubled in bulk.

Punch dough down, and let rest 5 minutes. Coat 2 (12-inch) pizza pans with cooking spray, and sprinkle each with 1 tablespoon cornmeal. Divide dough in half, and pat each portion of dough into a prepared pan. Bake according to pizza recipe directions. Yield: 2 (12-inch) crusts.

Per Crust: Calories 702 (8% calories from fat)
Fat 6.5g (Sat 0.9g Mono 2.3g Poly 1.9g) Chol 0mg
Protein 21.6g Carbohydrate 138.3g Sodium 603mg

Classic Italian Tomato Sauce

  Vegetable cooking spray
2 teaspoons olive oil
1¼ cups minced onion
3 cloves garlic, minced
3 (14½-ounce) cans no-salt-added whole
    tomatoes, drained and finely chopped
¼ cup dry red wine
¼ cup sun-dried tomato paste
3 tablespoons chopped fresh basil
2 teaspoons sugar
½ teaspoon salt
½ teaspoon fennel seeds, crushed
¼ teaspoon pepper

Coat a large nonstick skillet with cooking spray; add oil, and place over medium-high heat until hot. Add onion and garlic; sauté until tender. Add tomato and remaining ingredients. Reduce heat; simmer, uncovered, 30 minutes or until thickened. Yield: 6 (½-cup) servings.

Note: This thick and chunky tomato sauce is great on pasta, too.

Per Serving: Calories 76 (35% calories from fat)
Fat 3.0g (Sat 0.4g Mono 1.9g Poly 0.3g) Chol 0mg
Protein 1.9g Carbohydrate 12.2g Sodium 239mg
Exchanges: 2 Vegetable, ½ Fat

FREEZE A CRUST

Each crust recipe makes two crusts. So if you're only making one pizza, just freeze the dough.
•After it rises, wrap the dough in plastic wrap, and place it in a heavy-duty, zip-top plastic bag to freeze.
•When you're ready to use it, thaw it in the refrigerator overnight.
•Then set it out, let it reach room temperature (it'll take about 30 minutes), and follow the rest of the recipe directions.

Classic
Italian
Tomato
Sauce

STIR UP A SAUCE

We use our Classic Italian Tomato Sauce recipe (page 126) in Deep-Dish Italian Meatball Pizza (page 129). You can spread this simple sauce on your choice of crusts and add a variety of low-fat, low-sodium toppings to create your own pizza recipe. For make-ahead ease, freeze 1-cup portions of the sauce in airtight containers for up to one month.

Artichoke and Bacon Pizza

½ recipe Plain Ol' Pizza Crust dough (page 125)
  Vegetable cooking spray
1 (6-ounce) jar marinated artichoke hearts
¾ cup part-skim ricotta cheese
1 teaspoon dried Italian seasoning
2 cloves garlic, minced
1 large tomato, sliced
2 ounces part-skim mozzarella cheese, thinly sliced
3 slices turkey bacon, cooked and crumbled
¼ teaspoon cracked pepper

Pat dough into a 12-inch pizza pan coated with cooking spray. Coat dough with cooking spray (to help crust brown). Bake at 425° on bottom rack of oven for 8 minutes.

Drain artichokes, reserving 1 tablespoon marinade. Finely chop artichokes. Combine chopped artichoke, reserved marinade, ricotta cheese, Italian seasoning, and garlic, stirring well. Spread cheese mixture over crust, leaving a ½-inch border. Arrange tomato slices over cheese mixture; arrange mozzarella over tomato. Sprinkle bacon and cracked pepper evenly over pizza.

Bake at 425° on bottom rack of oven for 15 to 17 minutes or until cheese melts and crust is lightly browned. Yield: 4 servings.

Per Serving: Calories 349 (31% calories from fat)
Fat 11.9g (Sat 4.9g Mono 3.9g Poly 2.0g) Chol 30mg
Protein 17.7g Carbohydrate 43.0g Sodium 561mg
Exchanges: 1 High-Fat Meat, 2 Starch, 2 Vegetable

Glazed Onion and Apple Pizza

½ recipe Whole Wheat Pizza Crust dough (page 125)
  Vegetable cooking spray
1 teaspoon olive oil
1 onion, thinly sliced and separated into rings
1½ teaspoons brown sugar
2 tablespoons dry red wine
1½ teaspoons balsamic vinegar
1 medium Granny Smith apple, cored and thinly sliced
¼ teaspoon salt
⅛ teaspoon ground red pepper
½ cup skim milk
1 tablespoon cornstarch
2 tablespoons light process cream cheese
2 ounces blue cheese, crumbled
2 tablespoons chopped walnuts, toasted

Pat dough into a 12-inch pizza pan coated with cooking spray. Bake at 425° on bottom rack of oven for 5 minutes.

Heat oil in a large nonstick skillet over medium-high heat. Add onion; sauté 2 minutes or until tender. Add brown sugar; cook 1 minute, stirring well. Add wine and vinegar; cover and cook 2 minutes. Uncover and cook 2 minutes or until liquid evaporates. Remove from heat; stir in apple, salt, and red pepper. Set aside.

Combine milk and cornstarch in a small saucepan; stir well. Bring to a boil; reduce heat to low. Simmer, stirring constantly, 2 minutes or until thickened. Remove from heat; add cream cheese, stirring until cheese melts. Let cool.

Spread cream cheese mixture over crust, leaving a ½-inch border. Spoon apple mixture over cream cheese mixture. Bake at 425° on bottom rack of oven for 12 minutes or until crust is lightly browned. Sprinkle with blue cheese and walnuts. Bake 5 additional minutes or until cheese melts. Let stand 10 minutes before serving. Yield: 4 servings.

Per Serving: Calories 344 (26% calories from fat)
Fat 9.8g (Sat 3.9g Mono 2.6g Poly 2.2g) Chol 15mg
Protein 12.9g Carbohydrate 52.5g Sodium 550mg
Exchanges: 3 Starch, 1 Vegetable, 2 Fat

Deep-Dish Italian Meatball Pizza

½ recipe Plain Ol' Pizza Crust dough (page 125)
  Vegetable cooking spray
½ (10-ounce) package frozen chopped spinach,
  thawed
¾ pound ground round
½ teaspoon fennel seeds, crushed
1 clove garlic, minced
½ cup soft breadcrumbs, toasted
2 tablespoons freshly grated Parmesan
  cheese
1 egg white
1 cup Classic Italian Tomato Sauce,
  divided (page 126)
1 cup nonfat cottage cheese
½ cup nonfat ricotta cheese
½ cup (2 ounces) shredded reduced-fat provolone
  cheese, divided
3 tablespoons chopped hot pickled
  pepper rings

Press pizza crust dough into bottom and up sides of a 9-inch round cakepan coated with cooking spray. Coat dough with cooking spray (to help crust brown). Bake at 425° on bottom rack of oven for 10 minutes.

Drain spinach, and press between paper towels to remove excess moisture. Combine spinach and next 3 ingredients; stir well. Add breadcrumbs, Parmesan cheese, and egg white, stirring well. Shape mixture into 12 meatballs. Coat a large nonstick skillet with cooking spray; place over medium-high heat until hot. Add meatballs, and cook 8 to 10 minutes or until browned. Drain and pat dry with paper towels.

Spread ½ cup Classic Italian Tomato Sauce over crust, leaving a ½-inch border. Combine cottage cheese, ricotta cheese, ¼ cup provolone cheese, and pepper rings. Spread half of cheese mixture over tomato sauce. Arrange meatballs over cheese mixture. Spoon remaining ½ cup tomato sauce and remaining cheese mixture around meatballs. Bake at 425° on bottom rack of oven for 15 minutes. Sprinkle with remaining ¼ cup provolone cheese, and bake 5 additional minutes or until cheese melts. Let stand 10 minutes before serving. Yield: 4 servings.

Per Serving: Calories 474 (29% calories from fat)
Fat 15.4g (Sat 5.3g Mono 5.1g Poly 1.8g) Chol 67mg
Protein 38.3g Carbohydrate 45.0g Sodium 793mg
Exchanges: 3½ Medium-Fat Meat, 2 Starch, 3 Vegetable

SODIUM SMARTS

The American Heart Association (AHA) says it's okay to have up to 3000 milligrams of sodium per day (unless your doctor has put you on a strict low-sodium diet). If you eat three meals a day, that works out to be about 1000 milligrams per meal. So you can have a serving of Deep-Dish Italian Meatball Pizza (793 milligrams sodium) for lunch and stay within the guidelines.

Grilled
Chicken
Pizza

Grilled Chicken Pizza

½ recipe Whole Wheat Pizza Crust dough
   (page 125)
   Vegetable cooking spray
2 ears fresh corn
3 (4-ounce) skinned, boned chicken breast halves
¼ cup plus 2 tablespoons fat-free barbecue sauce,
   divided
¾ cup diagonally sliced green onions
½ cup (2 ounces) shredded reduced-fat Cheddar
   cheese

Pat dough into a 12-inch pizza pan coated with cooking spray. Bake at 425° on bottom rack of oven for 5 minutes.

Remove and discard husks and silks from corn. Coat grill rack with cooking spray; place on grill over medium-hot coals (350° to 400°). Place corn on rack; grill, covered, 20 minutes or until tender and slightly charred, turning often. Remove from grill, and cut corn from cob. Place chicken on rack; grill, covered, 5 minutes on each side or until done, basting with 3 tablespoons barbecue sauce. Let chicken cool, and tear into bite-size pieces.

Spread remaining 3 tablespoons barbecue sauce over crust, leaving a ½-inch border. Top with corn, chicken, and green onions. Bake at 425° on bottom rack of oven for 10 minutes or until crust is lightly browned. Sprinkle with cheese, and bake 2 additional minutes or until cheese melts. Yield: 4 servings.

Per Serving: Calories 427 (14% calories from fat)
Fat 6.8g (Sat 2.5g Mono 1.8g Poly 1.3g) Chol 62mg
Protein 32.0g Carbohydrate 61.0g Sodium 586mg
Exchanges: 3 Lean Meat, 4 Starch

Mushroom Lovers' Pizza

½ recipe Whole Wheat Pizza Crust dough
   (page 125)
   Vegetable cooking spray
8 (¼-inch-thick) slices portobello mushrooms
¾ cup dry Marsala, divided
1 teaspoon olive oil
2 cloves garlic, minced
4 ounces sliced fresh mushrooms
4 ounces shiitake mushrooms, coarsely chopped
2 tablespoons freshly grated Parmesan cheese
1 tablespoon lemon juice
1 (2¼-ounce) can sliced ripe olives, drained
½ cup (2 ounces) shredded reduced-fat Swiss
   cheese
¼ cup shredded fresh basil

Pat dough into a 12-inch pizza pan coated with cooking spray. Bake at 425° on bottom rack of oven for 5 minutes.

Place portobello mushrooms in a large nonstick skillet; add ¼ cup wine. Bring to a boil; cover, reduce heat, and simmer 10 minutes or until mushrooms are tender. Remove from skillet; set aside. Wipe skillet dry with a paper towel.

Coat skillet with cooking spray; add oil. Place over medium-high heat until hot. Add garlic, 4 ounces sliced fresh mushrooms, and shiitake mushrooms; sauté until tender. Add remaining ½ cup wine. Bring to a boil; reduce heat, and simmer, uncovered, until liquid evaporates.

Position knife blade in food processor bowl; add shiitake mushroom mixture, Parmesan cheese, lemon juice, and olives. Process 10 seconds or until almost smooth.

Spread shiitake mushroom mixture over crust, leaving a ½-inch border. Arrange portobello mushrooms over mushroom mixture; sprinkle with Swiss cheese. Bake at 425° on bottom rack of oven for 12 minutes or until crust is lightly browned and cheese melts. Remove from oven, and sprinkle with basil. Let stand 10 minutes before serving. Yield: 4 servings.

Per Serving: Calories 313 (23% calories from fat)
Fat 7.9g (Sat 2.6g Mono 2.5g Poly 1.1g) Chol 11mg
Protein 15.3g Carbohydrate 47.5g Sodium 375mg
Exchanges: 1 High-Fat Meat, 3 Starch, 1 Vegetable

ROAST A PEPPER

It's easy to add roasted pepper flavor to recipes. Just follow these steps: First, cut each pepper in half lengthwise. Take out the stem, seeds, and white membranes.

Flatten each half

•**Flatten** each pepper half with the palm of your hand. Place the peppers, skin sides up, on a baking sheet.

Broil halves

•**Broil** the peppers for 15 to 20 minutes or until they look charred and blistered. Then, using tongs or a fork, transfer the peppers to a bowl of ice water; let them soak until they're cool enough to handle.

Peel skins

•**Peel** off the blistered skins with a knife.

Roasted Pepper Pizza

3 medium-size sweet red peppers
3 medium-size sweet yellow peppers
½ recipe Whole Wheat Pizza Crust dough
   (page 125)
   Vegetable cooking spray
3 tablespoons pesto sauce
1 (4-ounce) package crumbled basil- and tomato-
   flavored feta cheese

Cut peppers in half lengthwise; remove and discard seeds, stems, and membranes. Flatten pepper halves with palm of hand; place, skin sides up, on a baking sheet. Broil 5½ inches from heat (with electric oven door partially opened) 15 to 20 minutes or until skins are charred. Place in ice water until cool; peel and discard skins.

Place red peppers in container of an electric blender; cover and process until smooth, stopping once to scrape down sides. Place puree in a small saucepan; bring to a boil. Reduce heat, and simmer 8 to 10 minutes or until thickened and the consistency of tomato paste. Repeat procedure with yellow peppers.

Pat dough into a 12-inch pizza pan coated with cooking spray. Bake at 425° on bottom rack of oven for 8 minutes.

Spread pesto sauce over crust, leaving a ½-inch border. Spoon red pepper paste over half of crust; spoon yellow pepper paste over other half of crust. Sprinkle with cheese. Bake at 425° on bottom rack of oven for 12 to 14 minutes or until crust is lightly browned. Let stand 10 minutes before serving. Yield: 4 servings.

Note: If you want to vary the recipe, use either all red or all yellow peppers, or change the design as we did in the photo.

Per Serving: Calories 344 (28% calories from fat) Fat 10.8g (Sat 5.1g Mono 3.4g Poly 1.4g) Chol 26mg Protein 13.1g Carbohydrate 50.9g Sodium 538mg
Exchanges: 3 Starch, 1 Vegetable, 2 Fat

Roasted
Pepper
Pizza

Roasted
Vegetable
Pizza

Roasted Vegetable Pizza

1 medium-size eggplant, peeled and cut into
  ¼-inch-thick slices
1 medium onion, cut into ¼-inch-thick slices
1 medium-size green pepper, seeded and cut
  into ¼-inch-thick slices
2 small yellow squash, cut into ¼-inch-thick
  slices
  Vegetable cooking spray
½ recipe Cornmeal Pizza Crust dough (page 126)
¾ cup evaporated skimmed milk
1 tablespoon plus 1 teaspoon cornstarch
¾ cup grated Asiago cheese
2 tablespoons dry white wine
¼ teaspoon pepper
⅛ teaspoon salt
  Dash of garlic powder
3 plum tomatoes, cut into ¼-inch-thick slices
3 tablespoons freshly grated Parmesan cheese
¼ cup shredded fresh basil

Arrange first 4 ingredients on a baking sheet coated
with cooking spray; coat vegetables with cooking
spray. Broil 5½ inches from heat (with electric oven
door partially opened) 3 minutes. Turn vegetables;
coat with cooking spray. Broil 3 additional minutes
or until vegetables are tender. Set aside.

Pat dough into a 12-inch pizza pan coated with
cooking spray. Bake at 425° on bottom rack of oven
for 5 minutes.

Combine milk and cornstarch in a small saucepan,
stirring until smooth. Bring to a boil over medium
heat, stirring constantly, and boil 1 minute. Remove
from heat; stir in Asiago cheese and next 4 ingredients. Spread cheese mixture over crust, leaving a
½-inch border; arrange roasted vegetables and tomato
over cheese mixture. Sprinkle with Parmesan cheese
and basil. Bake at 425° on bottom rack of oven for
15 to 18 minutes or until crust is lightly browned. Let
stand 10 minutes before serving. Yield: 4 servings.

Per Serving: Calories 391 (21% calories from fat)
Fat 9.3g (Sat 4.7g Mono 2.7g Poly 0.9g) Chol 20mg
Protein 21.1g Carbohydrate 57.4g Sodium 716mg
Exchanges: 1 High-Fat Meat, 3 Starch, 2 Vegetable

Asiago (ah-SYAH-go) **cheese:** an Italian hard cheese with a rich, nutty flavor; can be used
instead of fresh Parmesan cheese.

Poultry

Island
Chicken
(page 150)

poultry (POLE-tree): chicken, turkey, or any other domestic bird eaten three to five nights a week by people trying to eat healthfully. Because poultry is low in fat and high in nutrients, a chicken in every pot is not such a bad idea.

Baked Chicken Stew (page 146)   Grilled Chicken and Vegetables (page 153)

MAKE AN ARTICHOKE CUP

Slice off top

•**Slice** ½ inch off the top of each artichoke. Cut off the stem end, and remove any loose leaves from the bottom.

Trim top

•**Trim** the top quarter off each leaf with scissors, removing the spiny tips. Cook the artichokes until they're tender.

Spread leaves

•**Spread** the leaves apart, and use a spoon to scrape out the fuzzy center. Now you have a cup to fill.

Chicken-Stuffed Artichokes

    4 large artichokes (about ¾ pound each)
    4 lemon wedges
1⅓ cups chopped cooked chicken breast (skinned
        before cooking and cooked without salt)
    1 cup chopped celery
    ¾ cup fat-free mayonnaise
    ½ cup chopped green onions
    ¼ cup chopped fresh parsley
    2 tablespoons chopped almonds, toasted
    1 teaspoon chopped garlic
    1 (8-ounce) can sliced water chestnuts, drained
    1 cup canned no-salt-added chicken broth,
        undiluted
    ¼ cup grated Romano cheese
    ¼ cup chopped fresh parsley
        Lemon slices (optional)

Wash artichokes by plunging them up and down in cold water. Cut off stem ends, and trim ½ inch from top of each artichoke. Remove any loose bottom leaves. With scissors, trim away one-fourth of each outer leaf. Rub tops and edges of leaves with lemon wedges to prevent discoloration.

Place artichokes in a Dutch oven; add water to depth of 2 inches. Bring to a boil; cover, reduce heat, and simmer 30 minutes or until artichokes are tender. Drain; let cool. Spread leaves apart; scrape out fuzzy thistle centers (chokes) with a spoon, and discard. Set artichokes aside.

Combine chicken and next 7 ingredients in a large bowl; stir well. Spoon chicken mixture evenly into artichoke cavities. Arrange artichokes in a 13- x 9- x 2-inch baking dish. Pour broth into dish around artichokes. Cover and bake at 350° for 30 minutes. Uncover and sprinkle with cheese; bake 10 additional minutes or until cheese melts. Sprinkle with ¼ cup parsley, and serve with lemon slices, if desired. Yield: 4 servings.

Per Serving: Calories 224 (19% calories from fat)
Fat 4.8g (Sat 1.6g Mono 2.1g Poly 0.7g) Chol 23mg
Protein 14.2g Carbohydrate 34.2g Sodium 819mg
Exchanges: 1 Medium-Fat Meat, 2 Starch, 1 Vegetable

Creamy Chicken with Skillet Cornbread

2½ cups small broccoli flowerets
1½ cups thinly sliced carrot
 ½ cup all-purpose flour
1½ cups 1% low-fat milk, divided
1½ cups canned no-salt-added beef broth,
    undiluted
 ¼ cup dry white wine
 1 tablespoon reduced-calorie margarine, melted
 ½ cup low-fat sour cream
 1 tablespoon lemon juice
 1 teaspoon freshly ground pepper
 ½ teaspoon salt
 4 cups cubed cooked chicken breast (skinned
    before cooking and cooked without salt)
1½ cups sliced fresh mushrooms
    Vegetable cooking spray
 ¼ cup (1 ounce) shredded reduced-fat sharp
    Cheddar cheese
    Skillet Cornbread

Arrange broccoli and carrot in a steamer basket over boiling water. Cover and steam 3 minutes or until crisp-tender.

Combine flour and ¼ cup milk; stir until smooth. Combine flour mixture, remaining 1¼ cups milk, broth, wine, and margarine in a medium saucepan. Cook over medium heat, stirring constantly with a wire whisk, until mixture is thickened and bubbly. Remove from heat; stir in sour cream, lemon juice, ground pepper, and salt. Add steamed vegetables, chicken, and mushrooms; stir well. Spoon mixture into an 11- x 7- x 1½-inch baking dish coated with cooking spray. Cover and bake at 325° for 35 minutes.

Uncover, sprinkle with Cheddar cheese, and bake 5 additional minutes or until cheese melts.

To serve, place 1 wedge of Skillet Cornbread on each plate. Spoon chicken mixture evenly over cornbread wedges. Yield: 8 servings.

Skillet Cornbread

1½ cups yellow cornmeal
 ¾ cup all-purpose flour
 2 teaspoons baking powder
 1 teaspoon baking soda
 ½ teaspoon salt
 2 cups nonfat buttermilk
1½ tablespoons vegetable oil
 1 egg yolk, lightly beaten
 3 egg whites, lightly beaten
    Vegetable cooking spray

Combine first 5 ingredients in a large bowl; make a well in center of mixture. Combine buttermilk and next 3 ingredients; add to cornmeal mixture, stirring just until dry ingredients are moistened.

Spoon batter into a preheated 10-inch cast-iron skillet coated with cooking spray. Bake at 450° for 20 to 25 minutes or until cornbread is lightly browned. Cut into wedges, and remove from skillet immediately. Yield: 8 wedges.

Per Serving: Calories 377 (23% calories from fat) Fat 9.7g (Sat 3.3g Mono 2.8g Poly 2.4g) Chol 76mg Protein 25.5g Carbohydrate 45.8g Sodium 651mg
Exchanges: 2 Medium-Fat Meat, 3 Starch, 1 Vegetable

Chicken
Enchilada
Casserole

Chicken Enchilada Casserole

½ cup no-salt-added salsa
½ cup canned low-sodium chicken broth, undiluted
1 teaspoon ground cumin
3 (8-ounce) cans no-salt-added tomato sauce
3 cups cubed cooked chicken breast (skinned before cooking and cooked without salt)
3 tablespoons chopped pickled jalapeño peppers
1 (15-ounce) can no-salt-added black beans, rinsed and drained
12 (6-inch) corn tortillas
1½ cups (6 ounces) shredded reduced-fat sharp Cheddar cheese
½ cup (2 ounces) shredded reduced-fat Monterey Jack cheese
¾ cup low-fat sour cream
½ cup chopped green onions

Combine first 4 ingredients; stir well. Spread ¾ cup mixture in bottom of a 13- x 9- x 2-inch baking dish.

Combine chicken, pepper, black beans, and ½ cup tomato sauce mixture in a medium bowl. Stir well. Spoon chicken mixture evenly down centers of tortillas. Roll up tortillas; place, seam side down, on sauce mixture in baking dish. Top with remaining sauce mixture and cheeses. Cover and bake at 350° for 25 minutes. Top with sour cream, and sprinkle with green onions. Yield: 6 servings.

Per Serving: Calories 458 (28% calories from fat)
Fat 14.4g (Sat 7.1g Mono 3.5g Poly 1.4g) Chol 73mg
Protein 33.9g Carbohydrate 50.1g Sodium 724mg
Exchanges: 3 Medium-Fat Meat, 3 Starch, 1 Vegetable

Chicken Shepherd's Pies

5 cups peeled, cubed baking potato
⅓ cup 1% low-fat milk
⅓ cup low-fat sour cream
¼ cup grated Romano cheese
¼ teaspoon salt
¼ teaspoon pepper
1 (10-ounce) package frozen cut green beans
1½ cups canned no-salt-added chicken broth, undiluted and divided
1½ tablespoons cornstarch
    Vegetable cooking spray
½ teaspoon vegetable oil
½ cup chopped onion
2 teaspoons minced garlic
¼ teaspoon salt
¼ teaspoon pepper
1 (8-ounce) package presliced fresh mushrooms
2 cups chopped cooked chicken breast (skinned before cooking and cooked without salt)

Place potato in a large saucepan; add water to cover. Bring to a boil; cover, reduce heat, and simmer 10 minutes or until tender. Drain potato, and place in a large bowl. Add milk and next 4 ingredients. Beat at medium speed of an electric mixer 2 minutes or until smooth. Set aside, and keep warm.

Cook green beans according to package directions, omitting salt; drain. Set aside, and keep warm.

Combine 2 tablespoons broth and cornstarch in a small bowl, stirring well. Set aside.

Coat a large nonstick skillet with cooking spray; add oil. Place over medium-high heat until hot. Add onion and next 4 ingredients; sauté 5 minutes. Add cornstarch mixture and remaining broth to skillet, stirring constantly. Bring to a boil; reduce heat, and simmer, uncovered, 5 minutes or until thickened, stirring often. Add green beans and chicken; cook until heated.

Spoon chicken mixture evenly into 4 (2-cup) baking dishes. Top with mashed potato mixture, and place on a large baking sheet. Bake at 450° for 25 minutes or until bubbly and golden. Yield: 4 servings.

Per Serving: Calories 383 (17% calories from fat)
Fat 7.4g (Sat 3.5g Mono 2.0g Poly 0.9g) Chol 52mg
Protein 24.2g Carbohydrate 55.8g Sodium 456mg
Exchanges: 2 Lean Meat, 3 Starch, 2 Vegetable

Chicken Strata

8 (1-ounce) slices white bread
   Butter-flavored vegetable cooking spray
2 cups cubed cooked chicken breast (skinned
   before cooking and cooked without salt)
1 cup sliced fresh mushrooms
½ cup chopped green pepper
½ cup chopped onion
½ cup 1% low-fat cottage cheese
½ teaspoon pepper
⅛ teaspoon salt
1½ cups 1% low-fat milk
½ cup frozen egg substitute, thawed
½ cup (2 ounces) shredded reduced-fat sharp
   Cheddar cheese

Trim crusts from bread; reserve crusts for another use. Cut bread into ½-inch cubes.

Arrange half of bread cubes in an 8-inch square baking dish coated with vegetable cooking spray. Combine chicken and next 6 ingredients, and stir well. Spoon chicken mixture over bread cubes in baking dish. Top with remaining bread cubes.

Combine milk and egg substitute; stir well. Pour mixture over bread cubes. Cover and chill 8 hours.

Bake, uncovered, at 350° for 55 minutes; sprinkle with Cheddar cheese. Bake 5 additional minutes or until cheese melts. Let stand 10 minutes before serving. Yield: 4 servings.

Per Serving: Calories 319 (20% calories from fat)
Fat 7.2g (Sat 3.1g Mono 2.2g Poly 1.0g) Chol 52mg
Protein 31.2g Carbohydrate 31.1g Sodium 630mg
Exchanges: 3 Lean Meat, 2 Starch

Leek and Chicken Tart

1 cup all-purpose flour
¼ teaspoon salt
3 tablespoons vegetable oil
2 tablespoons cold water
½ pound fresh asparagus spears
   Vegetable cooking spray
1½ cups chopped leeks
½ cup chopped onion
1 clove garlic, minced
1 cup shredded cooked chicken breast (skinned
   before cooking and cooked without salt)
¾ cup 1% low-fat milk
¾ cup frozen egg substitute, thawed
½ teaspoon salt
¼ teaspoon pepper
¼ teaspoon dried thyme

Combine flour and ¼ teaspoon salt; stir well. Combine oil and water; add to flour mixture, stirring just until dry ingredients are moistened. Shape dough into a ball; cover with plastic wrap. Chill 30 minutes.

Place dough between 2 sheets of heavy-duty plastic wrap. Roll to ⅛-inch thickness; remove top sheet of plastic wrap. Invert and fit pastry into a 9-inch quiche dish or pieplate; seal to edge of dish. Remove remaining sheet of plastic wrap. Prick bottom and sides of pastry with a fork. Bake at 400° for 10 minutes or until lightly browned. Cool on a wire rack.

Snap off tough ends of asparagus. Remove scales from stalks with a knife or vegetable peeler, if desired. Cut asparagus into 1-inch pieces.

Coat a large nonstick skillet with cooking spray; place over medium-high heat until hot. Add leeks, onion, and garlic; sauté 3 minutes. Add asparagus; sauté until asparagus is crisp-tender. Add chicken; cook until thoroughly heated, stirring often. Spoon mixture into prepared crust.

Combine milk and remaining 4 ingredients. Pour over vegetable mixture. Bake at 350° for 25 to 30 minutes or until set. Let stand 10 minutes before slicing. Yield: 4 servings.

Per Serving: Calories 347 (33% calories from fat)
Fat 12.7g (Sat 2.6g Mono 3.7g Poly 5.5g) Chol 33mg
Protein 22.2g Carbohydrate 35.6g Sodium 566mg
Exchanges: 2 Medium-Fat Meat, 2 Starch, 1 Vegetable

Cashew Chicken

½ cup dry white wine
¼ cup low-sodium soy sauce
1 tablespoon peeled, grated gingerroot
1 clove garlic, crushed
1½ pounds skinned, boned chicken breasts,
   cut into strips
½ pound fresh green beans
   Vegetable cooking spray
1 tablespoon dark sesame oil, divided
½ cup diagonally-sliced celery
½ cup diagonally-sliced carrot
½ cup sliced green onions
1 (10½-ounce) can low-sodium chicken broth
3 tablespoons low-sodium soy sauce
1 tablespoon plus 2 teaspoons cornstarch
1 tablespoon brown sugar
⅓ cup chopped unsalted roasted cashews
6 cups cooked long-grain rice (cooked without
   salt or fat)

Combine first 4 ingredients in a heavy-duty, zip-top plastic bag; add chicken. Seal bag, and shake until chicken is well coated. Marinate in refrigerator 1 hour, turning bag occasionally. Remove chicken from marinade; discard marinade.

Wash green beans; trim ends, and remove strings. Cut beans diagonally into 1½-inch pieces.

Coat a wok or large nonstick skillet with cooking spray; drizzle 2 teaspoons oil around top of wok, coating sides. Heat at medium-high (375°) until hot. Add green beans, celery, carrot, and onions; stir-fry 5 minutes or until vegetables are crisp-tender. Remove vegetables from wok, and set aside.

Add remaining 1 teaspoon oil to wok. Add chicken; stir-fry 3 to 4 minutes or until chicken is lightly browned.

Combine broth and next 3 ingredients, stirring well. Add broth mixture to wok; stir-fry 1 to 2 minutes or until mixture is thickened and bubbly. Add vegetables and cashews; stir-fry 1 minute or until thoroughly heated. Serve over rice. Yield: 6 servings.

Per Serving: Calories 462 (17% calories from fat) Fat 8.8g (Sat 1.6g Mono 3.8g Poly 2.1g) Chol 66mg Protein 33.1g Carbohydrate 60.0g Sodium 369mg
Exchanges: 3 Lean Meat, 3 Starch, 3 Vegetable

Ginger Chicken Stir-Fry

¾ cup canned no-salt-added chicken broth, undiluted
1 tablespoon cornstarch
3 tablespoons dry sherry
2 tablespoons low-sodium soy sauce
1 tablespoon peeled, minced gingerroot
1 teaspoon sugar
2 teaspoons minced garlic
¼ teaspoon salt
 Vegetable cooking spray
1½ teaspoons dark sesame oil, divided
2 cups broccoli flowerets
1 cup thinly sliced carrot
1½ cups cubed zucchini
1 cup thinly sliced onion
1 green onion, cut diagonally into 1-inch slices
1 pound skinned, boned chicken breasts, cut into 1-inch pieces
4 cups cooked long-grain rice (cooked without salt or fat)

Combine first 8 ingredients in a small bowl; stir well, and set aside.

Coat a wok or large nonstick skillet with cooking spray; drizzle ½ teaspoon oil around top of wok. Heat at medium-high (375°) until hot. Add broccoli and carrot; stir-fry 2 minutes. Add zucchini, onion, and green onions; stir-fry 2 minutes. Remove vegetables from wok; set aside.

Add remaining 1 teaspoon oil to wok. Add chicken; stir-fry 3 to 4 minutes or until chicken is lightly browned. Return vegetables to wok. Stir cornstarch mixture; add to wok. Stir-fry 1 minute or until thoroughly heated. Serve over rice. Yield: 4 servings.

Per Serving: Calories 439 (8% calories from fat)
Fat 3.9g (Sat 0.8g Mono 1.1g Poly 1.1g) Chol 66mg
Protein 33.9g Carbohydrate 64.8g Sodium 452mg
Exchanges: 3 Very Lean Meat, 4 Starch, 1 Vegetable

Chicken and Potato Dumplings

 Vegetable cooking spray
1 cup chopped onion
1 cup sliced celery
2 cloves garlic, minced
1¼ pounds skinned, boned chicken breasts, cut into 1-inch pieces
4 cups canned no-salt-added chicken broth, undiluted
2 cups sliced carrot
½ teaspoon pepper
½ teaspoon salt
1 bay leaf
2¼ cups instant mashed potato flakes, divided
⅔ cup water
½ cup skim milk
1 tablespoon reduced-calorie margarine
½ teaspoon salt
¼ teaspoon pepper
½ cup frozen egg substitute, thawed
½ cup all-purpose flour

Coat a Dutch oven with cooking spray; place over medium-high heat until hot. Add onion, celery, and garlic; sauté until tender. Add chicken and next 5 ingredients. Bring to a boil; cover, reduce heat, and simmer 15 minutes. Gradually add 1 cup potato flakes, stirring constantly. Bring to a boil.

Combine water and next 4 ingredients in a medium saucepan; bring to a boil. Add remaining 1¼ cups potato flakes, egg substitute, and flour, stirring well. Remove from heat. Drop dough by rounded tablespoonfuls into boiling chicken mixture. Cook, uncovered, over medium heat 10 minutes or until potato dumplings are firm. Remove and discard bay leaf. Yield: 6 servings.

Per Serving: Calories 282 (9% calories from fat)
Fat 2.9g (Sat 0.6g Mono 0.8g Poly 0.9g) Chol 55mg
Protein 28.3g Carbohydrate 33.2g Sodium 577mg
Exchanges: 3 Very Lean Meat, 2 Starch, 1 Vegetable

Baked Chicken Fajitas

½ cup fresh lime juice
1 tablespoon balsamic vinegar
1 tablespoon minced garlic
2 teaspoons ground cumin
1 teaspoon chili powder
1 teaspoon vegetable oil
1 pound skinned, boned chicken breasts, cut into thin strips
¼ cup canned low-sodium chicken broth, undiluted
1 medium-size green pepper, seeded and cut into ¼-inch-wide strips
1 medium-size sweet yellow pepper, seeded and cut into ¼-inch-wide strips
1 large onion, cut in half lengthwise and sliced into strips
Vegetable cooking spray
8 (8½-inch) fat-free flour tortillas
2 cups chopped tomato
½ cup low-fat sour cream

Combine first 6 ingredients in a heavy-duty, zip-top plastic bag; add chicken. Seal bag, and shake until chicken is well coated. Marinate in refrigerator 1 hour, turning occasionally.

Remove chicken from marinade, reserving marinade. Place marinade in a small saucepan; add broth, and bring to a boil. Remove from heat, and set aside.

Place peppers and onion in a 13- x 9- x 2-inch baking dish coated with cooking spray. Bake, uncovered, at 400° for 10 minutes. Stir in chicken. Pour marinade mixture over chicken and vegetables. Bake 15 to 18 minutes or until chicken is done.

Wrap tortillas in aluminum foil. Bake at 325° for 15 minutes.

Spoon chicken and vegetables evenly down centers of tortillas, using a slotted spoon; roll up tortillas. Top each with ¼ cup chopped tomato and 1 tablespoon sour cream. Yield: 4 servings (serving size: 2 fajitas).

Per Serving: Calories 483 (17% calories from fat)
Fat 9.1g (Sat 3.4g Mono 2.6g Poly 1.8g) Chol 82mg
Protein 35.1g Carbohydrate 65.8g Sodium 778mg
Exchanges: 3 Lean Meat, 4 Starch, 1 Vegetable

Thai Chicken Kabobs

⅔ cup canned no-salt-added chicken broth, undiluted
¼ cup firmly packed brown sugar
2 tablespoons low-sodium soy sauce
2 tablespoons lemon juice
2 teaspoons dried crushed red pepper
2 teaspoons curry powder
1 pound skinned, boned chicken breasts, cut into 1½-inch pieces
2 medium zucchini, cut into 1¼-inch pieces
2 medium-size yellow squash, cut into 1¼-inch pieces
2 medium-size sweet red peppers, seeded and cut into 1¼-inch pieces
Vegetable cooking spray
4 cups cooked long-grain rice (cooked without salt or fat)

Combine first 6 ingredients in a large heavy-duty, zip-top plastic bag. Add chicken; seal bag, and shake until chicken is well coated. Marinate chicken in refrigerator 8 hours, turning bag occasionally.

Remove chicken from marinade, reserving marinade. Place marinade in a small saucepan; bring to a boil. Remove from heat, and set aside. Thread chicken evenly onto 4 (12-inch) skewers. Thread zucchini, squash, and sweet red pepper alternately onto 4 additional 12-inch skewers.

Coat grill rack with cooking spray; place on grill over medium-hot coals (350° to 400°). Place vegetable skewers on rack; grill, covered, 5 minutes, turning and basting with reserved marinade. Place chicken skewers on rack; grill chicken and vegetables, covered, 5 additional minutes or until vegetables are tender and chicken is done, turning and basting often with marinade. Remove vegetables and chicken from skewers.

To serve, place 1 cup rice on each plate; top evenly with vegetables and chicken. Yield: 4 servings.

Per Serving: Calories 470 (8% calories from fat)
Fat 4.1g (Sat 1.0g Mono 1.1g Poly 0.9g) Chol 70mg
Protein 33.0g Carbohydrate 74.1g Sodium 274mg
Exchanges: 2 Lean Meat, 4 Starch, 3 Vegetable

Peachy Chicken Kabobs

½ cup lime juice
2 tablespoons low-sodium soy sauce
2 teaspoons brown sugar
2 teaspoons dark sesame oil
1 teaspoon hot sauce
1½ pounds skinned, boned chicken breast halves, cut into 1-inch-wide strips
3 green peppers, seeded and cut lengthwise into 6 pieces
6 medium-size firm, ripe peaches, peeled, halved, and pitted
3 medium-size purple onions, cut into 6 wedges
  Vegetable cooking spray
3 cups cooked long-grain rice (cooked without salt or fat)

Combine first 5 ingredients; stir well, and set aside.

Thread chicken evenly onto 3 (12-inch) skewers. Thread pepper, peach halves, and onion alternately onto 6 (12-inch) skewers.

Coat grill rack with cooking spray; place on grill over medium-hot coals (350° to 400°). Place chicken and vegetable-peach skewers on rack; grill, covered, 10 to 12 minutes or until vegetables and peaches are tender and chicken is done, turning and basting often with lime juice mixture. Remove chicken, vegetables, and peaches from skewers.

To serve, place ½ cup rice on each plate; top evenly with chicken, vegetables, and peaches. Yield: 6 servings.

Per Serving: Calories 354 (13% calories from fat) Fat 5.2g (Sat 1.1g Mono 1.7g Poly 1.5g) Chol 70mg Protein 29.9g Carbohydrate 46.5g Sodium 202mg
Exchanges: 3 Very Lean Meat, 2 Starch, 1 Fruit

Baked Chicken Stew

1¼ pounds skinned, boned chicken breasts, cut into 1-inch pieces
⅓ cup all-purpose flour
1 teaspoon garlic powder
½ teaspoon pepper
3 cups peeled, cubed potato
3 cups sliced onion
2 cups sliced carrot
1 cup canned no-salt-added chicken broth, undiluted
2 tablespoons low-sodium Worcestershire sauce
1 (15¼-ounce) can no-salt-added whole-kernel corn, drained
1 (14½-ounce) can no-salt-added whole tomatoes, undrained and chopped
1 (8-ounce) can no-salt-added tomato sauce
1 teaspoon chili powder
1 bay leaf
  Vegetable cooking spray
1 (12-ounce) can refrigerated buttermilk biscuits

Combine first 4 ingredients in a heavy-duty, zip-top plastic bag; shake well. Combine chicken mixture, potato, and next 9 ingredients in a large bowl, stirring well. Place in a 4-quart baking dish coated with cooking spray. Cover and bake at 325° for 2 hours or until potato is tender, stirring occasionally.

Separate biscuits, and cut each biscuit into fourths. Remove baking dish from oven. Remove and discard bay leaf. Place biscuit pieces over top of chicken mixture. Bake, uncovered, at 375° for 10 to 12 minutes or until biscuits are lightly browned. Yield: 6 servings.

Note: Although this hearty chicken stew bakes for 2 hours, it doesn't require much prep time from the cook. It takes just a few minutes to put the ingredients together; then it's ready to serve when it comes out of the oven.

Per Serving: Calories 459 (12% calories from fat) Fat 6.2g (Sat 1.2g Mono 2.5g Poly 1.0g) Chol 55mg Protein 30.8g Carbohydrate 71.6g Sodium 545mg
Exchanges: 2 Lean Meat, 4 Starch, 2 Vegetable

Baked
Chicken
Stew

South-of-the-Border Chicken and Pasta

Vegetable cooking spray
1½ teaspoons olive oil
1 pound skinned, boned chicken breasts, cut into strips
1 cup diced green pepper
1 cup sliced green onions
2 tablespoons seeded, minced jalapeño pepper
1 tablespoon minced garlic
1 (8-ounce) package presliced fresh mushrooms
¾ cup canned no-salt-added chicken broth, undiluted
¼ cup dry red wine
2 tablespoons dark brown sugar
1½ tablespoons chili powder
1 tablespoon low-sodium Worcestershire sauce
1 teaspoon dry mustard
2 (8-ounce) cans no-salt-added tomato sauce
1½ cups diagonally sliced fresh green beans
4 ounces mostaccioli (tubular pasta), uncooked
1 cup (4 ounces) shredded manchego cheese

Coat a large nonstick skillet with cooking spray; add olive oil. Place over medium-high heat until hot. Add chicken, and cook 8 to 10 minutes or until chicken is tender, stirring often. Remove from skillet; set aside, and keep warm. Add green pepper and next 3 ingredients to skillet; sauté 2 minutes. Add mushrooms; sauté 2 minutes. Add broth and next 6 ingredients; cook, stirring constantly, 2 to 3 minutes or until thoroughly heated. Remove from heat, and set aside.

Arrange green beans in a steamer basket over boiling water. Cover and steam 5 minutes or until crisp-tender. Drain well.

Cook pasta according to package directions, omitting salt and fat; drain well. Combine pasta, chicken, tomato sauce mixture, and beans; toss well. Spoon mixture into an 11- x 7- x 1½-inch baking dish coated with vegetable cooking spray. Cover and bake at 350° for 15 minutes. Uncover, sprinkle with shredded cheese, and bake 5 minutes or until cheese melts. Yield: 4 (2-cup) servings.

Per Serving: Calories 473 (26% calories from fat)
Fat 13.5g (Sat 6.3g Mono 2.4g Poly 1.4g) Chol 90mg
Protein 40.9g Carbohydrate 48.6g Sodium 285mg
Exchanges: 4 Lean Meat, 3 Starch, 1 Vegetable

manchego (man-CHAY-go) **cheese:** a mild-flavored, part-skim milk cheese similar to reduced-fat Monterey Jack. The two can be used interchangeably in most recipes.

Bourbon Chicken and Vegetables

Vegetable cooking spray
2 teaspoons olive oil
4 (4-ounce) skinned, boned chicken breast halves
½ teaspoon salt
½ teaspoon pepper
8 ounces fresh mushrooms, quartered
8 ounces zucchini, cut into ¼-inch-thick slices
½ cup canned no-salt-added chicken broth,
    undiluted
3 tablespoons bourbon
2 teaspoons reduced-calorie margarine
1 tablespoon chopped fresh parsley
4 cups cooked long-grain rice (cooked without
    salt or fat)

Coat a large nonstick skillet with cooking spray; add oil. Place over medium-high heat until hot. Add chicken; cook 3 minutes on each side. Sprinkle with salt and pepper. Place mushrooms and zucchini over chicken. Pour broth and bourbon over chicken and vegetables. Cover, reduce heat, and simmer 15 minutes. Uncover and cook 5 additional minutes. Transfer chicken and vegetables to a serving platter, using a slotted spoon; keep warm.

Bring chicken broth mixture in skillet to a boil; cook 2 minutes. Add margarine and parsley, stirring until margarine melts.

To serve, place 1 cup rice on each plate, and top evenly with chicken mixture. Spoon chicken broth mixture evenly over chicken and vegetables. Yield: 4 servings.

Per Serving: Calories 398 (13% calories from fat)
Fat 5.6g (Sat 0.9g Mono 2.5g Poly 1.1g) Chol 66mg
Protein 32.1g Carbohydrate 52.8g Sodium 390mg
Exchanges: 3 Very Lean Meat, 3 Starch, 1 Vegetable

ALCOHOL AWAY

A little dash of spirits—wine, liqueur, or liquor—adds a splash of flavor to your recipes, but no fat, cholesterol, or sodium. And the amount of alcohol that remains in the food depends on the type of liquor and the cooking time.

For example, if you add 3 to 4 tablespoons of liquor to a dish just before serving it, 85 percent of the alcohol stays in the food. When you cook that same amount of alcohol for 20 to 30 minutes, only about 35 percent of the alcohol remains. If you use a cup of wine in a slow-cooked stew, only about 5 percent of the alcohol stays, but all of the flavor is still there.

Of course, if you choose not to use alcohol, you can always substitute an equal amount of another liquid like fruit juice or broth.

Country Captain Chicken

3 tablespoons all-purpose flour
½ teaspoon paprika
¼ teaspoon ground red pepper
6 (4-ounce) skinned, boned chicken breast halves
  Vegetable cooking spray
2 tablespoons reduced-calorie margarine
2 cups chopped green pepper
1½ cups chopped onion
½ cup chopped fresh parsley
1½ tablespoons curry powder
1 teaspoon pepper
½ teaspoon ground nutmeg
½ teaspoon salt
2 cloves garlic, minced
½ cup raisins
2 (14½-ounce) cans no-salt-added whole tomatoes, undrained and chopped
4 cups water
2 cups long-grain rice, uncooked
¾ teaspoon ground turmeric

Combine first 3 ingredients in a heavy-duty, zip-top plastic bag; add chicken. Seal bag, and shake until chicken is well coated.

Coat a Dutch oven with cooking spray; add margarine. Place over medium heat until margarine melts. Add chicken; cook until browned. Drain and pat dry. Wipe drippings from Dutch oven.

Coat Dutch oven with cooking spray; place over medium-high heat until hot. Add green pepper and next 7 ingredients; sauté 5 minutes. Add raisins, tomato, and chicken; bring to a boil. Cover, reduce heat; simmer 20 minutes or until chicken is tender.

Bring water to a boil in a medium saucepan; stir in rice and turmeric. Cover, reduce heat, and simmer 20 minutes or until rice is tender and water is absorbed.

To serve, place 1 cup rice on each plate. Spoon chicken mixture evenly over rice. Yield: 6 servings.

Per Serving: Calories 470 (10% calories from fat) Fat 5.0g (Sat 1.0g Mono 1.5g Poly 1.7g) Chol 66mg Protein 33.5g Carbohydrate 72.3g Sodium 332mg
Exchanges: 2 Lean Meat, 4 Starch, 2 Vegetable

Island Chicken

Olive oil-flavored vegetable cooking spray
1½ teaspoons olive oil
6 (4-ounce) skinned, boned chicken breast halves
1½ tablespoons all-purpose flour
1½ cups unsweetened orange juice
½ cup canned no-salt-added chicken broth, undiluted
1 cup fresh pineapple chunks
⅓ cup raisins
½ teaspoon salt
½ teaspoon pepper
¼ teaspoon dried crushed red pepper
⅛ teaspoon ground cloves
1 large green pepper, seeded and cut into 1-inch pieces
6 cups cooked long-grain rice (cooked without salt or fat)
  Orange wedges (optional)

Coat a large nonstick skillet with cooking spray; add oil. Place over medium-high heat until hot. Add chicken; cook 2 minutes on each side or until lightly browned. Remove chicken from skillet, and set aside.

Add flour to skillet; cook, stirring constantly, 20 seconds. Add orange juice and broth, deglazing skillet by scraping particles that cling to bottom. Add pineapple and next 6 ingredients, stirring well. Add chicken. Bring to a boil; cover, reduce heat, and simmer 30 to 35 minutes or until chicken is done.

To serve, place 1 cup rice on each plate. Top each serving with chicken; spoon pineapple mixture evenly over chicken. Garnish with orange wedges, if desired. Yield: 6 servings.

Per Serving: Calories 436 (7% calories from fat) Fat 3.4g (Sat 0.6g Mono 1.2g Poly 0.6g) Chol 66mg Protein 31.6g Carbohydrate 67.9g Sodium 284mg
Exchanges: 3 Very Lean Meat, 4 Starch, 1 Fruit

Island
Chicken

Grilled
Chicken
and
Vegetables

Grilled Chicken and Vegetables

8 small round red potatoes, halved
2 small eggplants
1 cup canned no-salt-added chicken broth, undiluted
¼ cup reduced-calorie ketchup
3 tablespoons lemon juice
3 tablespoons dry sherry
3 tablespoons low-sodium soy sauce
2 tablespoons minced garlic
2 teaspoons coarsely ground pepper
2 teaspoons chopped fresh cilantro
1½ teaspoons chopped fresh dill
1 teaspoon vegetable oil
4 (4-ounce) skinned, boned chicken breast halves
1 large sweet red pepper, quartered lengthwise
1 large zucchini, quartered lengthwise
   Vegetable cooking spray
   Fresh dill sprigs (optional)

Place potato in a medium saucepan; add water to cover. Bring to a boil; cover, reduce heat, and simmer 12 minutes. Drain and set aside.

Slice each eggplant in half lengthwise; slice halves lengthwise into ½-inch-thick strips. Set aside.

Combine broth and next 9 ingredients in a medium bowl; stir well. Pour ⅓ cup broth mixture into a large heavy-duty, zip-top plastic bag. Set aside remaining broth mixture. Add potato, eggplant, chicken, red pepper, and zucchini to bag; seal bag, and shake until chicken and vegetables are well coated. Marinate in refrigerator 3 hours, turning bag occasionally. Remove chicken and vegetables from marinade; discard marinade.

Coat grill rack with cooking spray; place on grill over medium-hot coals (350° to 400°). Place potato on rack; grill, covered, 10 minutes, basting occasionally with reserved broth mixture. Turn potato; place chicken and remaining vegetables on rack. Grill potatoes, chicken, and vegetables, covered, 5 minutes on each side or until chicken is done and vegetables are tender, basting occasionally with reserved broth mixture. Garnish with fresh dill sprigs, if desired. Yield: 4 servings.

Per Serving: Calories 397 (12% calories from fat)
Fat 5.3g (Sat 1.2g Mono 1.4g Poly 1.5g) Chol 70mg
Protein 33.9g Carbohydrate 51.8g Sodium 381mg
Exchanges: 3 Very Lean Meat, 3 Starch, 1 Vegetable

Citrus-Grilled Chicken, Squash, and Potatoes

½ cup unsweetened orange juice
⅓ cup balsamic vinegar
1 tablespoon minced garlic
1 teaspoon coarsely ground pepper
2 teaspoons sesame oil
½ teaspoon salt
   Vegetable cooking spray
4 (4-ounce) skinned, boned chicken breast halves
8 small round red potatoes
2 medium zucchini, cut in half lengthwise
2 medium-size yellow squash, cut in half lengthwise
2 medium-size purple onions, each cut into 4 slices

Combine first 6 ingredients; set aside.

Coat grill rack with cooking spray; place on grill over medium-hot coals (350° to 400°). Place chicken and remaining 4 ingredients on rack; grill, covered, 8 minutes on each side, basting often with juice mixture. Remove onion from grill, and keep warm. Grill chicken and remaining vegetables 2 to 3 additional minutes or until chicken is done and vegetables are tender. Transfer chicken and vegetables to a serving platter. Yield: 4 servings.

Per Serving: Calories 337 (16% calories from fat) Fat 5.9g (Sat 1.3g Mono 2.0g Poly 1.8g) Chol 70mg Protein 31.9g Carbohydrate 40.4g Sodium 372mg
Exchanges: 3 Lean Meat, 2 Starch, 2 Vegetable

Roasted Chicken and Vegetables

1 (3-pound) broiler-fryer, skinned
1 teaspoon olive oil
   Vegetable cooking spray
12 small round red potatoes
2 cups thinly sliced leeks
1 cup Sugar Snap peas, trimmed
6 small squash, cut into 1-inch-thick slices
6 small zucchini cut into 1-inch-thick slices
3 heads Belgian endive, sliced lengthwise
1 cup canned low-sodium chicken broth, undiluted
¼ cup dry white wine
½ teaspoon salt
½ teaspoon pepper
½ teaspoon minced fresh thyme
3 tablespoons all-purpose flour
¼ cup water
   Fresh thyme (optional)

Trim fat from chicken. Remove giblets and neck from chicken; reserve for another use. Rinse chicken under cold water; pat dry. Brush chicken with olive oil. Place chicken, breast side up, on a rack in a large roasting pan coated with cooking spray. Insert meat thermometer in meaty part of thigh, making sure it does not touch the bone.

Add potatoes to roasting pan. Bake, uncovered, at 350° for 1 hour. Add leeks and next 4 ingredients to roasting pan. Combine broth and next 4 ingredients; pour over chicken and vegetables. Bake 45 additional minutes or until meat thermometer registers 185°, basting occasionally with pan juices.

Transfer chicken and vegetables to a serving platter; keep warm. Pour pan juices through a wire-mesh strainer into a small saucepan, discarding solids. Combine flour and water, stirring until smooth; stir into pan juices. Cook over medium-high heat, stirring constantly, until thickened. Serve sauce with chicken and vegetables. Garnish with fresh thyme, if desired. Yield: 6 servings.

Per Serving: Calories 251 (14% calories from fat) Fat 3.9g (Sat 1.0g Mono 0.9g Poly 1.0g) Chol 76mg Protein 27.9g Carbohydrate 25.6g Sodium 296mg
Exchanges: 3 Very Lean Meat, 1 Starch, 2 Vegetable

Roasted
Chicken and
Vegetables

Romano Chicken, Eggplant, and Potatoes

¼ cup grated Romano cheese
1½ teaspoons freshly ground pepper
1½ teaspoons dried oregano
½ teaspoon garlic powder
¼ teaspoon salt
1 teaspoon paprika
3 medium baking potatoes
3 small eggplants (about 2¼ pounds)
  Olive oil-flavored vegetable cooking spray
6 (6-ounce) skinned chicken breast halves
2 teaspoons olive oil

Combine first 6 ingredients in a small bowl; stir well. Set aside. Cut each potato into 6 wedges. Cut eggplants lengthwise into quarters.

Place chicken and potato in a large shallow roasting pan coated with cooking spray. Coat chicken and potato with cooking spray. Bake, uncovered, at 375° for 25 minutes; turn potatoes, and add eggplant. Brush chicken and vegetables with oil; sprinkle with cheese mixture. Bake, uncovered, 20 minutes or until chicken and vegetables are done. Yield: 6 servings.

Per Serving: Calories 282 (15% calories from fat)
Fat 4.7g (Sat 1.5g Mono 1.9g Poly 0.6g) Chol 71mg
Protein 31.9g Carbohydrate 29.0g Sodium 242mg
Exchanges: 3½ Very Lean Meat, 1 Starch, 2 Vegetable

Turkey à la King

1 tablespoon reduced-calorie margarine
1 pound turkey breast cutlets, cut into 1-inch
  pieces
¼ cup chopped onion
¼ cup sliced fresh mushrooms
¼ cup plus 2 tablespoons all-purpose flour
1 (12-ounce) can evaporated skimmed milk
1 cup frozen peas and carrots, thawed
½ teaspoon pepper
  Dash of salt
1 (2-ounce) jar diced pimiento, drained
4 whole wheat English muffins, split and toasted
¼ teaspoon paprika

Melt margarine in a large nonstick skillet over medium heat. Add turkey and onion; sauté 3 to 5 minutes or until turkey is browned. Add mushrooms; sauté 1 minute.

Add flour to skillet; cook, stirring constantly, 1 minute. Gradually add milk, stirring constantly. Add peas and carrots and next 3 ingredients. Cook, stirring constantly, until mixture is thickened and bubbly.

To serve, spoon turkey mixture evenly over muffin halves; sprinkle with paprika. Serve immediately. Yield: 4 servings.

Per Serving: Calories 454 (11% calories from fat)
Fat 5.3g (Sat 1.1g Mono 1.2g Poly 1.9g) Chol 71mg
Protein 40.9g Carbohydrate 58.2g Sodium 595mg
Exchanges: 4 Very Lean Meat, 3 Starch, 2 Vegetable

Turkey and Dressing Casserole

1 cup yellow cornmeal
1¼ teaspoons baking powder
¼ teaspoon baking soda
¼ teaspoon salt
¾ cup nonfat buttermilk
¼ cup frozen egg substitute, thawed
1 (4½- ounce) can green chiles, undrained
   Vegetable cooking spray
4 cups chopped cooked turkey breast
3 cups canned no-salt-added chicken broth,
   undiluted
1 cup chopped onion
1 cup chopped celery
½ cup frozen egg substitute, thawed
2 tablespoons chopped fresh parsley
½ teaspoon rubbed sage
¼ teaspoon salt
¼ teaspoon pepper
⅛ teaspoon hot sauce
1½ tablespoons reduced-calorie margarine
3 tablespoons all-purpose flour
1 cup evaporated skimmed milk
½ cup canned no-salt-added chicken broth,
   undiluted
¼ teaspoon salt
⅛ teaspoon pepper

Combine first 4 ingredients in a medium bowl; make a well in center of mixture. Combine buttermilk, ¼ cup egg substitute, and green chiles; add buttermilk mixture to dry ingredients, stirring just until dry ingredients are moistened. Spoon batter into a preheated 8-inch cast-iron skillet coated with vegetable cooking spray. Bake at 425° for 15 minutes or until golden. Remove cornbread from skillet, and cool slightly on a wire rack.

Crumble cornbread into a large bowl. Add turkey and next 9 ingredients, stirring well. Spoon mixture into a 13- x 9- x 2-inch baking dish coated with cooking spray. Bake, uncovered, at 350° for 1 hour. Cover and bake 30 additional minutes.

Melt margarine in a medium saucepan over medium heat; add flour, and stir until smooth. Cook, stirring constantly, 1 minute. Gradually add milk and chicken broth; cook, stirring constantly, until mixture is thickened. Remove from heat; stir in ¼ teaspoon salt and ⅛ teaspoon pepper. Serve gravy with casserole. Yield: 6 servings.

Per Serving: Calories 343 (14% calories from fat)
Fat 5.5g (Sat 1.4g Mono 1.3g Poly 1.8g) Chol 63mg
Protein 36.6g Carbohydrate 33.3g Sodium 606mg
Exchanges: 4 Very Lean Meat, 2 Starch, 1 Vegetable

LET'S TALK TURKEY

 Don't wait until the holidays to enjoy these nutrition benefits of turkey—

•**Low-Calorie:** A 3-ounce cooked portion of skinless turkey breast has only 134 calories.

•**Low-Fat:** Cooked turkey breast has less than 1 gram of fat per ounce.

•**Low-Saturated Fat:** You get only 0.2 grams saturated fat in a 3-ounce serving.

•**Low-Sodium:** When roasted without salt, a 3-ounce portion of turkey breast only has 44 milligrams of sodium.

•**High-Protein:** 81 percent of the calories in turkey breast meat are from protein (compared to 77 percent for chicken breast meat).

Savory Turkey-Stuffed Peppers

6 medium-size green peppers
1 cup orzo (rice-shaped pasta), uncooked
  Vegetable cooking spray
1½ pounds freshly ground raw turkey
¾ cup diced onion
¾ cup diced celery
½ cup golden raisins
¼ cup pine nuts, toasted
¼ cup frozen egg substitute, thawed
1 tablespoon lemon juice
1 tablespoon low-sodium Worcestershire sauce
1½ teaspoons brown sugar
1½ teaspoons pepper
1 teaspoon salt
½ teaspoon dried oregano
2 (8-ounce) cans no-salt-added tomato sauce
¾ cup canned no-salt-added chicken broth,
  undiluted

Cut peppers in half lengthwise; remove and discard seeds and membranes. Cook peppers in boiling water to cover 5 minutes. Drain.

Cook orzo according to package directions, omitting salt and fat. Drain well.

Coat a large nonstick skillet with cooking spray; place over medium heat until hot. Add turkey, onion, and celery; cook until turkey is browned, stirring until it crumbles.

Place turkey mixture in a large bowl. Add orzo, raisins, and next 9 ingredients; stir well. Spoon turkey mixture evenly into pepper halves.

Place pepper halves in a 15- x 10- x 2-inch baking dish. Pour chicken broth into dish around peppers. Bake, uncovered, at 350° for 30 minutes or until thoroughly heated. Yield: 6 servings.

Per Serving: Calories 398 (16% calories from fat) Fat 7.0g (Sat 1.6g Mono 1.7g Poly 2.5g) Chol 74mg Protein 33.6g Carbohydrate 51.4g Sodium 533mg
Exchanges: 3 Lean Meat, 3 Starch, 1 Vegetable

TRANSLATING TURKEY LABELS

Not all ground turkey is created equal. Some forms of ground turkey are higher in fat than others, so check the label to make sure you know what you're buying.
- **Ground white meat:** white meat only (lowest fat variety)
- **Ground turkey meat:** meat minus skin and fat (may contain dark meat)
- **Ground turkey:** meat plus skin and fat (no fat is added, but the skin and fat naturally on the bird goes into the grind)

Spaghetti Squash Italiano

1 (4-pound) spaghetti squash
  Olive oil-flavored vegetable cooking spray
1 cup finely chopped onion
1 tablespoon minced garlic
1 cup chopped zucchini
1 cup finely chopped mushrooms
¾ pound freshly ground raw turkey
2 ounces reduced-fat, low-salt ham, chopped
1 (25-ounce) jar fat-free tomato-basil
    spaghetti sauce
1 tablespoon chopped fresh oregano
1 tablespoon chopped fresh basil
1 teaspoon freshly ground pepper
½ teaspoon dried crushed red pepper
3 tablespoons freshly grated Parmesan cheese

Wash squash; cut in half lengthwise. Remove and discard seeds. Place squash halves, cut sides down, in a 13- x 9- x 2-inch baking dish coated with cooking spray. Add water to dish to depth of ½ inch. Bake at 375° for 40 minutes or until squash is tender; let cool slightly. Using a fork, remove spaghetti-like strands; discard shells. Set strands aside, and keep warm.

Coat a large nonstick skillet with cooking spray; place over medium-high heat until hot. Add onion and garlic; sauté 2 minutes. Add zucchini, and sauté 2 minutes. Add mushrooms; sauté 2 additional minutes. Remove vegetables from skillet, and set aside.

Coat skillet with cooking spray; add turkey. Cook over medium-high heat until turkey is browned, stirring until it crumbles. Add vegetable mixture, ham, and next 5 ingredients. Cook over medium heat until thoroughly heated.

To serve, spoon turkey mixture over spaghetti squash; sprinkle with cheese. Yield: 4 servings.

Per Serving: Calories 320 (17% calories from fat)
Fat 5.9g (Sat 2.2g Mono 1.4g Poly 1.3g) Chol 66mg
Protein 29.3g Carbohydrate 41.2g Sodium 606mg
Exchanges: 3 Lean Meat, 2 Starch, 2 Vegetable

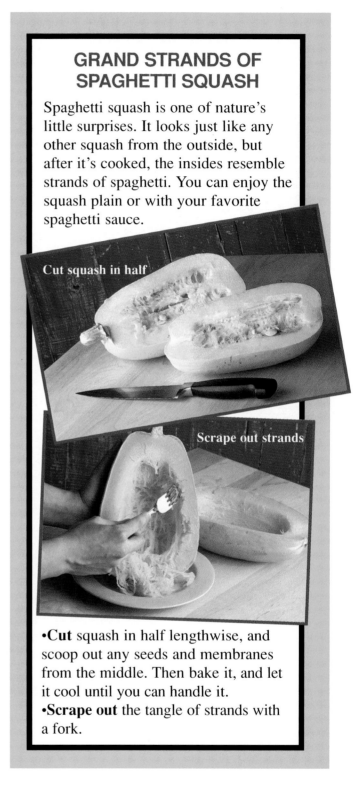

GRAND STRANDS OF SPAGHETTI SQUASH

Spaghetti squash is one of nature's little surprises. It looks just like any other squash from the outside, but after it's cooked, the insides resemble strands of spaghetti. You can enjoy the squash plain or with your favorite spaghetti sauce.

Cut squash in half

Scrape out strands

•**Cut** squash in half lengthwise, and scoop out any seeds and membranes from the middle. Then bake it, and let it cool until you can handle it.
•**Scrape out** the tangle of strands with a fork.

Italian Sausage with Peppers and Onions

Italian Sausage with Peppers and Onions

Olive oil-flavored vegetable cooking spray
¾ pound smoked Italian turkey sausage, cut into ¾-inch-thick slices
2 cups sliced onion
1 cup sliced green pepper
1 cup sliced sweet yellow pepper
1 cup fat-free, no-salt-added spaghetti sauce
1 (8-ounce) can no-salt-added tomato sauce
½ cup water
1 tablespoon minced garlic
1 teaspoon dried Italian seasoning
6 (1-inch-thick) slices French bread, toasted
Hot sauce (optional)

Coat a large nonstick skillet with cooking spray; place over medium heat until hot. Add sausage, onion, green pepper, and yellow pepper; cook 10 minutes, stirring occasionally. Add spaghetti sauce and next 4 ingredients; bring to a boil. Reduce heat; simmer, uncovered, 10 minutes. Spoon turkey mixture evenly over bread slices. Sprinkle with hot sauce, if desired. Yield: 6 servings.

Per Serving: Calories 269 (22% calories from fat)
Fat 6.7g (Sat 2.8g Mono 2.8g Poly 2.2g) Chol 32mg
Protein 13.5g Carbohydrate 38.2g Sodium 841mg
Exchanges: 1 High-Fat Meat, 2 Starch, 1 Vegetable

Creole Red Beans and Rice

Vegetable cooking spray
¾ pound smoked turkey sausage, thinly sliced
2 cups chopped onion
1½ cups chopped green pepper
1 cup chopped celery
4 cloves garlic, minced
2 (16-ounce) cans no-salt-added kidney beans, drained
2 (14½-ounce) cans no-salt-added stewed tomatoes, undrained
1 teaspoon dried oregano
1 teaspoon pepper
2 teaspoons hot sauce
3 cups cooked long-grain rice (cooked without salt or fat)
⅓ cup chopped fresh parsley

Coat a Dutch oven with cooking spray; place over medium heat until hot. Add sausage; cook 3 minutes or until browned, stirring often. Add onion, green pepper, celery, and garlic; sauté 10 minutes or until vegetables are tender. Stir in beans and next 4 ingredients; bring to a boil. Reduce heat, and simmer, uncovered, 15 minutes, stirring occasionally.

Combine rice and parsley in a bowl. To serve, spoon ½ cup rice mixture into each bowl. Spoon sausage mixture evenly over rice. Yield: 6 servings.

Per Serving: Calories 437 (26% calories from fat)
Fat 12.7g (Sat 4.6g Mono 0.1g Poly 4.2g) Chol 60mg
Protein 21.1g Carbohydrate 61.3g Sodium 496mg
Exchanges: 1 High-Fat Meat, 3 Starch, 3 Vegetable

Salads

Scallop
Salad
(page 179)

salad (SAL-ed): a combination of vegetables (often lettuce and tomatoes), fruit, meat, fish, grains, or pasta limited only by the imagination. Usually served with dressing and a cracker or two.

Roasted Chicken Salad with Goat Cheese Crostini (page 185)

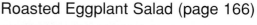

Roasted Eggplant Salad (page 166)

Antipasto Platter

1 (10-ounce) package frozen artichoke hearts
¾ cup canned no-salt-added chicken broth, undiluted
¼ cup white balsamic vinegar
1 teaspoon dried oregano
2 teaspoons minced garlic
2 teaspoons olive oil
⅛ teaspoon pepper
1½ cups small fresh mushrooms, halved
⅔ cup chopped purple onion
1 (15-ounce) can garbanzo beans (chick-peas), drained
1 (15-ounce) can no-salt-added kidney beans, drained
6 cups torn romaine lettuce
4 ounces thinly sliced fat-free turkey ham, cut into thin strips
4 ounces part-skim mozzarella cheese, thinly sliced
2 medium-size sweet red peppers, seeded and thinly sliced
2 medium cucumbers, sliced

Cook artichoke hearts according to package directions, omitting salt and fat. Drain well.

Combine broth and next 5 ingredients in a jar; cover tightly, and shake vigorously.

Combine artichoke hearts, mushrooms, and next 3 ingredients in a large bowl; add ½ cup broth mixture, and toss well. Cover and chill 2 hours, stirring occasionally.

Place romaine lettuce on a large serving platter; spoon bean mixture onto lettuce in center of platter. Arrange ham strips, cheese, sweet red pepper, and cucumber around bean mixture. Drizzle remaining broth mixture over salad. Yield: 4 servings.

Per Serving: Calories 412 (25% calories from fat)
Fat 11.3g (Sat 4.1g Mono 3.8g Poly 2.3g) Chol 32mg
Protein 29.6g Carbohydrate 52.4g Sodium 522mg
Exchanges: 3 Lean Meat, 3 Starch, 1 Vegetable

Tuscan Bread and Bean Salad

8 (1-ounce) slices Italian bread (¾ inch thick)
1½ cups seeded, diced tomato
1 cup peeled, diced cucumber
½ cup grated Parmesan cheese
½ cup diced celery
½ cup chopped purple onion
¼ cup chopped fresh parsley
¼ cup fat-free Italian dressing
2 tablespoons minced fresh basil
3 tablespoons sliced ripe olives
2 tablespoons white wine vinegar
1 (15-ounce) can cannellini beans, rinsed and drained

Cut bread into cubes. Arrange bread cubes in a single layer in a 15- x 10- x 1-inch jellyroll pan. Bake at 375° for 20 minutes or until golden. Remove from oven, and let cool completely.

Combine tomato and remaining 10 ingredients in a large bowl; toss well. Add toasted bread cubes to bean mixture just before serving; toss lightly. Serve immediately. Yield: 5 (2-cup) servings.

Per Serving: Calories 285 (15% calories from fat)
Fat 4.9g (Sat 2.5g Mono 1.7g Poly 0.7g) Chol 9mg
Protein 14.8g Carbohydrate 45.6g Sodium 775mg
Exchanges: ½ High-Fat Meat, 2 Starch, 2 Vegetable

Barley and Roasted Vegetable Salad

3 ears fresh corn
2 medium zucchini, cut in half lengthwise
Vegetable cooking spray
2 medium-size sweet red peppers
1 cup pearl barley, uncooked
8 cups water
1 (15-ounce) can no-salt-added kidney beans, drained
¾ cup sliced green onions
¼ cup minced fresh cilantro
¼ cup white wine vinegar
1 tablespoon olive oil
1 tablespoon low-sodium soy sauce
¾ teaspoon ground cumin
¼ teaspoon salt

Remove and discard husks and silks from corn. Place corn and zucchini, cut sides up, on a baking sheet coated with cooking spray. Cut peppers in half lengthwise; remove and discard seeds and membranes. Place peppers, skin sides up, on baking sheet; flatten with palm of hand.

Broil vegetables 5½ inches from heat (with electric oven door partially opened) 15 to 20 minutes or until peppers are charred. Remove peppers from baking sheet, and place in ice water until cool. Broil corn and zucchini 5 additional minutes or until lightly browned, turning often. Let cool. Remove peppers from water; peel and discard skins. Coarsely chop peppers. Cut corn from cob. Slice zucchini into ½-inch slices.

Combine barley and water in a large saucepan. Bring to a boil; cover, reduce heat, and simmer 30 minutes or until barley is tender. Drain well.

Combine roasted vegetables, barley, beans, green onions, and cilantro; toss lightly. Combine vinegar and remaining 4 ingredients in a jar; cover tightly, and shake vigorously. Pour vinegar mixture over barley mixture; toss lightly. Let stand 15 minutes before serving. Yield: 4 (2¼-cup) servings.

Per Serving: Calories 360 (14% calories from fat)
Fat 5.5g (Sat 0.8g Mono 2.8g Poly 1.2g) Chol 0mg
Protein 13.5g Carbohydrate 68.0g Sodium 266mg
Exchanges: 4 Starch, 1 Vegetable, 1 Fat

VINEGAR—NOT JUST SOUR GRAPES

Vinegars used to come in only two types: white and cider. Today they're flavored with everything from tarragon to raspberries, and are used in a variety of recipes from salad dressings to desserts. Thanks to these great vinegar flavors, you can add new life to vinaigrettes for green salads. Just mix a little bit of oil and a high-flavored vinegar for a vinaigrette that goes a long way toward making your low-fat salad a taste sensation.

Discover some new vinegar-food pairings: tarragon vinegar and chicken; balsamic vinegar with beef; red wine vinegar on grilled vegetables; raspberry vinegar on fresh strawberries. Any way you try them, vinegars add flavor without fat.

White Bean and Radicchio Salad

2½ cups shredded radicchio (about 2 small heads)
⅓ cup finely chopped shallots
¼ cup chopped fresh oregano
3 tablespoons red wine vinegar
3 tablespoons canned no-salt-added chicken broth, undiluted
2 tablespoons finely chopped ripe olives
1 tablespoon olive oil
½ teaspoon freshly ground pepper
3 ounces feta cheese, crumbled
2 (15-ounce) cans cannellini beans, rinsed and drained
4 large yellow or red tomatoes, cut into ½-inch-thick slices

Combine first 10 ingredients in a large bowl; toss well. Cover and chill at least 2 hours, stirring occasionally.

To serve, arrange tomato slices evenly on 4 plates; top evenly with bean mixture. Yield: 4 servings.

Per Serving: Calories 320 (28% calories from fat)
Fat 10.1g (Sat 4.0g Mono 4.2g Poly 1.2g) Chol 19mg
Protein 17.3g Carbohydrate 43.3g Sodium 574mg
Exchanges: 1 High-Fat Meat, 2 Starch, 2 Vegetable

Roasted Eggplant Salad

8 ounces fresh shiitake mushrooms
1½ pounds eggplant, peeled and cut into 1-inch cubes
1¼ cups frozen whole-kernel corn, thawed
Olive oil-flavored vegetable cooking spray
4 ounces reduced-fat Havarti cheese, diced
1 cup finely chopped sweet red pepper
½ cup chopped green onions
1 tablespoon sesame seeds, toasted
3 tablespoons white wine vinegar
3 tablespoons low-sodium soy sauce
1 tablespoon lemon juice
2 teaspoons olive oil
5 (8-inch) pita bread rounds
5 green leaf lettuce leaves

Remove and discard mushroom stems. Place mushrooms, eggplant, and corn in a large roasting pan coated with cooking spray. Coat eggplant mixture with cooking spray; toss, and coat again with cooking spray. Bake at 450° for 20 minutes or until lightly browned, stirring occasionally. Let cool.

Combine eggplant mixture, cheese, and next 3 ingredients in a large bowl; toss lightly.

Combine vinegar and next 3 ingredients in a jar; cover tightly, and shake vigorously. Pour vinegar mixture over vegetable mixture; toss lightly.

Cut each pita round into 8 wedges; place on a baking sheet coated with cooking spray. Bake at 400° for 5 minutes or until crisp.

To serve, place lettuce on 5 plates. Top each with 1½ cups vegetable mixture. Serve with toasted pita wedges. Yield: 5 servings (1 serving: 1½ cups vegetable mixture plus 8 pita wedges).

Per Serving: Calories 318 (25% calories from fat)
Fat 8.9g (Sat 3.0g Mono 1.8g Poly 1.0g) Chol 15mg
Protein 13.1g Carbohydrate 45.1g Sodium 604mg
Exchanges: 2 Starch, 3 Vegetable, 2 Fat

Roasted
Eggplant
Salad

Vegetable Pasta Salad

¼ cup red wine vinegar
1 tablespoon olive oil
¾ teaspoon freshly ground pepper
½ teaspoon salt
3 cloves garlic, minced
5 cups chopped ripe tomato (about 5 medium)
½ cup finely chopped purple onion
4 cups whole wheat rotini (corkscrew pasta),
    uncooked
1 pound medium zucchini, cut lengthwise into
    ½-inch-thick slices
1 pound large yellow squash, cut lengthwise into
    ½-inch-thick slices
  Olive-oil flavored vegetable cooking spray
10 ounces part-skim mozzarella cheese, cubed
¾ cup coarsely chopped fresh basil
3 tablespoons sliced ripe olives

Combine first 5 ingredients in a large bowl; stir well.
Add tomato and onion. Set aside.

Cook pasta according to package directions; drain
and add to tomato mixture. Toss well; cover and set
aside.

Arrange zucchini and squash slices on a baking
sheet coated with cooking spray. Coat vegetables with
cooking spray. Broil 3 inches from heat (with electric
oven door partially opened) 10 minutes on each side
or until golden.

Cut zucchini and squash into 1-inch pieces. Add
zucchini, squash, cheese, basil, and olives to pasta
mixture; toss well. Cover and chill thoroughly. Yield:
9 (2-cup) servings.

Per Serving: Calories 249 (29% calories from fat)
Fat 8.0g (Sat 3.5g Mono 2.8g Poly 0.5g) Chol 18mg
Protein 13.6g Carbohydrate 32.3g Sodium 314mg
Exchanges: 1 High-Fat Meat, 1½ Starch, 2 Vegetable

Bistro Beef Salad

1 pound small round red potatoes, quartered
⅔ cup no-salt-added salsa
¼ cup red wine vinegar
2 teaspoons olive oil
6 cups torn red leaf lettuce
2 cups torn curly endive
¾ pound cooked lean roast beef, thinly sliced
1½ cups cherry tomato halves
1 cup thinly sliced cucumber
1 cup thinly sliced purple onion, separated
    into rings

Cook potato in a medium saucepan in boiling water to
cover 10 to 15 minutes or until tender. Drain well, and
let cool.

Combine salsa, red wine vinegar, and oil, stirring
mixture well.

To serve, place 1½ cups lettuce and ½ cup endive
on each of 4 plates. Arrange potato, beef, tomato,
cucumber, and onion evenly over lettuce and endive.
Spoon salsa mixture evenly over salads. Yield: 4
servings.

Per Serving: Calories 322 (23% calories from fat)
Fat 8.4g (Sat 2.5g Mono 4.1g Poly 0.7g) Chol 61mg
Protein 30.4g Carbohydrate 32.1g Sodium 144mg
Exchanges: 3 Lean Meat, 2 Starch, 1 Vegetable

Sesame Beef-Quinoa Salad

1 cup quinoa, uncooked
  Vegetable cooking spray
2 cups water
2 tablespoons sesame seeds
1 teaspoon curry powder
½ cup unsweetened orange juice
3 tablespoons lime juice
1 tablespoon peeled, grated gingerroot
1 tablespoon canned no-salt-added beef broth,
  undiluted
1 teaspoon sesame oil
½ teaspoon salt
¼ teaspoon pepper
2 cups cubed cooked lean roast beef
1½ cups finely chopped carrot
1½ cups finely chopped cabbage
½ cup minced green onions
8 green leaf lettuce leaves

Place quinoa in a small bowl; cover with warm water, and rub quinoa between hands (water will be cloudy). Drain and repeat procedure until water is clear; drain quinoa well.

Place quinoa in a large nonstick skillet coated with cooking spray; cook over medium heat, stirring constantly, until quinoa is lightly browned.

Bring 2 cups water to a boil in a medium saucepan; add quinoa. Cover, reduce heat, and simmer 12 minutes or until tender; transfer to a large bowl, and set aside.

Place sesame seeds in skillet coated with cooking spray; cook over medium heat, stirring constantly, until lightly browned. Add to quinoa.

Cook curry powder in skillet over medium heat, stirring constantly, 2 minutes or until fragrant. Stir in orange juice, lime juice, and gingerroot; bring to a boil. Remove from heat. Stir in broth and next 3 ingredients; add to quinoa mixture. Stir in beef and next 3 ingredients. Cover and chill, stirring mixture occasionally.

To serve, place lettuce on 4 plates. Top each with 2 cups quinoa mixture. Yield: 4 (2-cup) servings.

Per Serving: Calories 389 (26% calories from fat)
Fat 11.2g (Sat 2.6g Mono 4.1g Poly 2.8g) Chol 51mg
Protein 30.0g Carbohydrate 43.3g Sodium 394mg
Exchanges: 3 Lean Meat, 2½ Starch, 1 Vegetable

KEEN ON QUINOA

Tired of rice? Then substitute quinoa (pronounced KEEN-wah) in any recipe that calls for rice.
You'll get three benefits—
1. A unique texture variation (and delicate flavor) similar to couscous
2. A grain that cooks in half the time of rice
3. A great nutrition boost because quinoa contains more protein than any other grain
No wonder the ancient Incas dubbed quinoa "the mother grain."

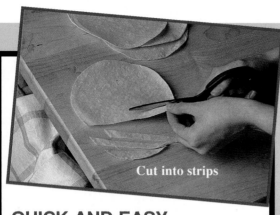

Cut into strips

QUICK AND EASY TORTILLA TIPS

Turn corn tortillas into tasty strips, chips, or even bowls to serve with Mexican meals.

•**Cut** corn tortillas into strips with kitchen scissors. Toast and serve them with the taco salad, or cut the tortillas into wedges to make low-fat chips.

•**Make** little bowls for serving salsa or low-fat salad dressing. Microwave a 6-inch tortilla at HIGH

Make bowls for serving

10 seconds to soften it. Then line a custard cup or small bowl with the tortilla, and prick it with a fork. Microwave at HIGH 1½ to 2 minutes or until it's crisp. Let it cool; then spoon in salsa.

Taco Salad Supreme

3 (6-inch) corn tortillas
   Vegetable cooking spray
½ pound freshly ground raw turkey
1 cup chopped onion
1 cup frozen whole-kernel corn, thawed
2 tablespoons minced jalapeño pepper
2 teaspoons chili powder
1 teaspoon ground cumin
1 (15-ounce) can no-salt-added black beans, rinsed and drained
2 tablespoons white wine vinegar
1 tablespoon lime juice
1 teaspoon chili powder
1 teaspoon vegetable oil
¼ teaspoon salt
¼ teaspoon ground red pepper
8 cups thinly sliced romaine lettuce leaves
1 cup (4 ounces) shredded reduced-fat Cheddar cheese
1 cup seeded, diced tomato
¼ cup minced fresh cilantro
2 tablespoons sliced ripe olives
½ cup nonfat sour cream

Coat tortillas on both sides with cooking spray; cut into ¼-inch-wide strips. Place in a single layer on an ungreased baking sheet; bake at 400° for 15 minutes.

Coat a nonstick skillet with cooking spray; place over medium heat until hot. Add turkey and next 3 ingredients; cook over medium heat until turkey is done, stirring until it crumbles. Stir in chili powder, cumin, and beans; cook until thoroughly heated. Set aside.

Combine vinegar and next 5 ingredients; cover and shake vigorously.

Combine lettuce and vinaigrette. Place 2 cups lettuce mixture on each plate. Spoon turkey mixture over lettuce. Top with cheese and remaining 4 ingredients; serve with tortilla strips. Yield: 4 servings.

Per Serving: Calories 377 (25% calories from fat) Fat 10.6g (Sat 4.3g Mono 3.0g Poly 2.1g) Chol 56mg Protein 32.7g Carbohydrate 39.7g Sodium 512mg
Exchanges: 3 Lean Meat, 2 Starch, 2 Vegetable

Taco Salad
Supreme

Lamb Tabbouleh Salad

1 cup bulgur, uncooked
1½ cups boiling water
1 cup seeded, diced tomato
½ cup chopped fresh parsley
½ cup minced green onions
2 tablespoons minced fresh mint
1 (15-ounce) can garbanzo beans (chick-peas), drained
¼ cup lemon juice
¼ cup canned low-sodium chicken broth, undiluted
2 teaspoons olive oil
½ teaspoon freshly ground pepper
¼ teaspoon salt
¾ pound lean boneless leg of lamb, cut into ½-inch-thick slices
   Vegetable cooking spray
5 cups torn romaine lettuce

Combine bulgur and water in a large bowl; let stand 1 hour or until bulgur is tender and liquid is absorbed. Add tomato and next 4 ingredients; stir well.

Combine lemon juice and next 4 ingredients, stirring well. Place lamb slices on rack of a broiler pan coated with cooking spray. Brush lamb with 2 tablespoons lemon juice mixture. Broil 5½ inches from heat (with electric oven door partially opened) 3 to 4 minutes on each side or to desired degree of doneness. Cut lamb into ½-inch pieces.

Add remaining lemon juice mixture and lamb to bulgur mixture; toss well. To serve, place lettuce evenly on 4 salad plates. Top evenly with bulgur mixture. Yield: 4 (1½-cup) servings.

Per Serving: Calories 409 (21% calories from fat)
Fat 9.5g (Sat 2.2g Mono 4.1g Poly 1.6g) Chol 51mg
Protein 29.0g Carbohydrate 55.5g Sodium 345mg
Exchanges: 2 Medium-Fat Meat, 3 Starch, 2 Vegetable

Succotash Rice Salad

2½ cups cooked white basmati rice (cooked without salt or fat)
1¾ cups cooked baby lima beans (cooked without salt or fat)
1¾ cups frozen whole-kernel corn, thawed
¾ cup diced reduced-fat, low-salt ham
¾ cup thinly sliced celery
¾ cup finely chopped onion
¼ cup finely chopped fresh cilantro
½ cup fat-free Ranch-style dressing
2 tablespoons lime juice
1 tablespoon white wine vinegar
½ teaspoon ground oregano
½ teaspoon freshly ground pepper
3 medium tomatoes, sliced

Combine first 7 ingredients in a large bowl; toss lightly, and set aside.

Combine Ranch-style dressing and next 4 ingredients; add to rice mixture, and toss lightly. Cover and chill thoroughly, stirring occasionally.

To serve, place tomato slices on a serving platter; spoon rice mixture over tomato. Yield: 5 servings.

Per Serving: Calories 320 (4% calories from fat)
Fat 1.5g (Sat 0.3g Mono 0.1g Poly 0.2g) Chol 9mg
Protein 13.5g Carbohydrate 65.5g Sodium 506mg
Exchanges: 4 Starch, 1 Vegetable

succotash (SUHK-uh-tash): a traditional favorite in the American South; made of lima beans, corn, and whatever other vegetables happen to be left over.

Greens with Ham and Pears

½ cup plain nonfat yogurt
2 tablespoons brown sugar
2 tablespoons sherry vinegar
¼ teaspoon apple pie spice
   Dash of salt
4 cups torn Bibb lettuce
1 cup torn curly endive
1 cup loosely packed fresh watercress
6 (1-ounce) slices lean turkey ham, cut into
   thin strips
2 medium-size ripe pears (about ¾ pound),
   cored and thinly sliced
3 tablespoons finely chopped walnuts,
   toasted
   Swiss Cheese Toast

Combine first 5 ingredients in a small bowl, stirring well. Cover and chill 1 hour.

Arrange lettuce, endive, and watercress evenly on 4 plates. Arrange turkey ham and pear slices over greens. Drizzle 3 tablespoons yogurt mixture over each, and sprinkle with walnuts. Serve with Swiss Cheese Toast. Yield: 4 servings (1 serving: one-fourth of salad mixture plus 3 slices cheese toast).

Swiss Cheese Toast

 1 tablespoon Dijon mustard
12 (¾-inch-thick) slices French baguette,
   toasted
½ cup (2 ounces) shredded reduced-fat Swiss
   cheese
 1 tablespoon minced fresh chives

Spread mustard evenly over one side of bread slices. Combine cheese and chives; sprinkle over mustard.

Place on a baking sheet, and broil 3 inches from heat (with electric oven door partially opened) 1 to 2 minutes or until cheese melts. Yield: 12 slices.

Per Serving: Calories 280 (27% calories from fat)
Fat 8.4g (Sat 2.3g Mono 1.3g Poly 2.9g) Chol 26mg
Protein 16.5g Carbohydrate 34.7g Sodium 583mg
Exchanges: 1 High-Fat Meat, 2 Starch, 1 Vegetable

ELEVATING THE GRAINS

The U.S. Dietary Guidelines recommend a diet that includes plenty of grain products. And the Food Guide Pyramid shows that six to eleven servings of bread, cereal, rice, or pasta are the basis of a healthy diet.

So when you top a salad with croutons or serve it with toasted bread or crackers, you're on your way to healthy eating.

Start with some of these ideas for salad sidekicks:

- •breadsticks
- •reduced-fat wheat crackers
- •low-fat croutons
- •French bread

- •Melba toast
- •rice cakes
- •hard rolls
- •baked tortilla chips

Wilted
Greens and
Black-Eyed
Pea Salad

Wilted Greens and Black-Eyed Pea Salad

1 (10-ounce) package frozen black-eyed peas, thawed
4 cups torn fresh spinach
4 cups torn escarole
1 medium-size sweet red pepper, seeded and cut into ¼-inch-thick strips
  Vegetable cooking spray
6 ounces reduced-fat, low-salt ham, cut into ¾-inch strips
2 teaspoons olive oil
1½ cups finely chopped onion
¼ cup balsamic vinegar
2 tablespoons honey
2 tablespoons water
  Toasted Cornbread

Cook peas according to package directions, omitting salt. Set aside.

Combine spinach, escarole, and red pepper strips in a large bowl; set aside.

Coat a large nonstick skillet with cooking spray; add ham, and sauté over medium heat until browned. Add ham to spinach mixture.

Add oil to skillet; place over medium heat until hot. Add onion, and sauté until tender. Stir in vinegar, honey, and water; bring to a boil. Remove from heat, and pour over spinach mixture. Add black-eyed peas to spinach mixture; toss lightly.

To serve, place one cornbread rectangle on each of 4 plates. Spoon one-half of spinach mixture evenly over cornbread rectangles. Top each serving with a second rectangle, and spoon remaining spinach mixture evenly over cornbread. Yield: 4 servings.

Toasted Cornbread

½ cup all-purpose flour
½ cup yellow cornmeal
2 tablespoons sugar
½ teaspoon baking powder
¼ teaspoon salt
¾ cup nonfat buttermilk
¼ cup frozen egg substitute, thawed
  Vegetable cooking spray
1 tablespoon reduced-calorie margarine, melted

Combine first 5 ingredients in a medium bowl. Combine buttermilk and egg substitute; add to dry ingredients, stirring just until dry ingredients are moistened. Pour batter into a 9-inch square pan coated with cooking spray. Bake at 350° for 30 minutes. Remove from oven, and let cornbread cool completely on a wire rack.

Cut cornbread into 8 rectangles. Place rectangles on a baking sheet; brush with one-half of melted margarine. Broil 3 inches from heat (with electric oven door partially opened) 1 to 2 minutes or until lightly browned. Turn cornbread; brush with remaining melted margarine. Broil 3 inches from heat (with electric oven door partially opened) 1 to 2 additional minutes or until lightly browned. Yield: 8 rectangles.

Per Serving: Calories 430 (17% calories from fat)
Fat 7.9g (Sat 2.1g Mono 2.5g Poly 1.3g) Chol 22mg
Protein 22.3g Carbohydrate 70.4g Sodium 610mg
Exchanges: 1 High-Fat Meat, 4 Starch, 2 Vegetable

Oriental Pork Salad

1 pound boneless center-cut pork loin chops
    (½ inch thick)
¼ cup lemon juice
3 tablespoons low-sodium soy sauce
1 tablespoon peeled, grated gingerroot
¼ teaspoon dried crushed red pepper
2 cloves garlic, minced
1 tablespoon tahini (sesame seed paste)
2 teaspoons sugar
4 cups thinly sliced romaine lettuce
3 cups thinly sliced Napa cabbage
1 cup julienne-sliced jicama
24 miniature teriyaki-flavored rice cakes

Trim fat from pork; cut pork into ½-inch strips, and place in a shallow dish. Combine lemon juice and next 4 ingredients, stirring well. Drizzle 3 tablespoons lemon juice mixture over pork. Cover and marinate in refrigerator 2 hours. Set remaining lemon juice mixture aside.

Add tahini and sugar to remaining lemon juice mixture; stir well, and set aside. Combine romaine lettuce, cabbage, and jicama in a bowl; toss, and set aside.

Remove pork from marinade, discarding marinade. Place pork in a large nonstick skillet, and cook over medium heat 5 to 7 minutes or until done.

To serve, place 2 cups lettuce mixture on each of 4 plates. Top evenly with pork strips. Drizzle lemon juice mixture evenly over salads. Serve with rice cakes. Yield: 4 (2-cup) servings.

Per Serving: Calories 335 (35% calories from fat) Fat 13.0g (Sat 4.0g Mono 5.4g Poly 2.2g) Chol 74mg Protein 27.5g Carbohydrate 25.7g Sodium 510mg **Exchanges:** 3 Medium-Fat Meat, 1 Starch, 2 Vegetable

Grilled Salmon on Greens

1¼ pounds medium-size round red potatoes,
    halved
¾ pound fresh green beans, trimmed
1 tablespoon lemon juice
2 teaspoons low-sodium Worcestershire sauce
1 teaspoon olive oil
1 pound salmon fillets
    Vegetable cooking spray
1 cup seeded, diced tomato
¼ cup balsamic vinegar
2 tablespoons Dijon mustard
1 teaspoon sugar
1 teaspoon olive oil
½ teaspoon low-sodium Worcestershire sauce
1 clove garlic
¼ cup sliced ripe olives
8 cups mixed baby salad greens

Cook potatoes in a saucepan in boiling water to cover 12 minutes or just until tender. Drain and let cool.

Cook green beans in saucepan in boiling water 3 to 5 minutes or until crisp-tender; drain and cool slightly. Cut beans in half crosswise.

Combine lemon juice, Worcestershire sauce, and 1 teaspoon olive oil; brush mixture on salmon. Coat grill rack with cooking spray; place on grill over medium-hot coals (350° to 400°). Place salmon and potato on rack; grill, covered, 6 minutes on each side or until fish flakes easily when tested with a fork. Remove salmon and potato from grill. Flake salmon into large chunks with a fork; cut potato into quarters.

Combine diced tomato and next 6 ingredients in container of an electric blender or food processor; cover and process until smooth, stopping once to scrape down sides.

Combine salmon, potato, beans, ½ cup tomato mixture, and olives; toss lightly.

To serve, place 2 cups salad greens on each of 4 plates. Spoon salmon mixture evenly over greens. Drizzle remaining tomato mixture evenly over salads. Yield: 4 servings.

Per Serving: Calories 391 (32% calories from fat) Fat 14.1g (Sat 2.3g Mono 7.1g Poly 2.7g) Chol 77mg Protein 30.2g Carbohydrate 36.9g Sodium 395mg **Exchanges:** 3 Medium-Fat Meat, 2 Starch, 1 Vegetable

Tuna Niçoise Salad

1¼ pounds small round red potatoes
8 ounces fresh green beans, trimmed
2 tablespoons dry white wine
½ cup plus 2 tablespoons white wine vinegar, divided
¼ cup canned low-sodium chicken broth, undiluted
1 tablespoon capers, drained
1 tablespoon Dijon mustard
1 teaspoon dried thyme
2 teaspoons olive oil
½ teaspoon sugar
8 cups mixed baby salad greens
½ (12-ounce) jar roasted red peppers, drained and cut into thin strips
2 (6-ounce) cans low-sodium chunk light tuna in water, drained
4 large pitted ripe olives, sliced
2 hard-cooked egg whites, chopped

Cook potatoes in a saucepan in boiling water to cover 15 minutes. Drain and let cool; cut into thin slices.

Cook beans in a medium saucepan in boiling water 3 to 5 minutes or until beans are crisp-tender; drain and chill.

Place potato in a shallow dish. Combine wine and 2 tablespoons vinegar. Drizzle over potato, turning to coat; set aside.

Combine remaining ½ cup vinegar, chicken broth, capers, Dijon mustard, dried thyme, olive oil, and sugar; stir well with a wire whisk.

Combine salad greens and ½ cup vinegar mixture, tossing lightly. To serve, place 2 cups salad greens on each of 4 plates. Arrange potato, beans, red pepper, tuna, and olives on salad greens. Drizzle remaining vinegar mixture evenly over salads. Sprinkle evenly with chopped egg whites. Yield: 4 servings.

Per Serving: Calories 267 (14% calories from fat) Fat 4.1g (Sat 0.6g Mono 2.1g Poly 0.6g) Chol 19mg Protein 23.5g Carbohydrate 32.6g Sodium 460mg
Exchanges: 2 Lean Meat, 2 Starch, 1 Vegetable

niçoise (nee-SWAHZ): a term describing foods from Nice, a city on the French Riviera. A traditional salad niçoise contains tomatoes, black olives, anchovies, green beans, tuna, and hard-cooked eggs.

Scallop
Salad

Scallop Salad

¾ cup plus 2 tablespoons unsweetened
    orange juice
1 tablespoon peeled, minced gingerroot
1 tablespoon plus 1 teaspoon Dijon mustard
2 teaspoons olive oil
2 cloves garlic, crushed
1 pound sea scallops
½ pound fresh asparagus spears
    Vegetable cooking spray
1 teaspoon olive oil
6 cups mixed baby salad greens
2 medium oranges, peeled and sectioned
    Orange zest (optional)
    Freshly ground pepper (optional)

Combine first 5 ingredients in a jar. Cover tightly, and shake vigorously.

Pour ½ cup orange juice mixture into a heavy-duty, zip-top plastic bag. Set remaining juice mixture aside. Add scallops to bag; seal bag, and shake until scallops are well coated. Marinate in refrigerator 30 minutes, turning bag occasionally.

Snap off tough ends of asparagus. Remove scales from stalks with a knife or vegetable peeler, if desired. Cut asparagus into 2-inch pieces. Set aside.

Remove scallops from marinade, discarding marinade. Coat a 10-inch cast-iron skillet with cooking spray; add 1 teaspoon oil. Place over medium-high heat until hot. Add scallops, and cook 5 minutes or until browned, turning once. Remove scallops from skillet; keep warm. Add asparagus to skillet; sauté until crisp-tender.

To serve, place 1½ cups greens on each of 4 plates. Arrange scallops, asparagus, and orange sections evenly over greens.

Pour remaining orange juice mixture through a wire-mesh strainer. Discard garlic and gingerroot remaining in strainer. Drizzle 2 tablespoons orange juice mixture over each salad. If desired, sprinkle with orange zest and pepper. Yield: 4 servings.

Per Serving: Calories 220 (21% calories from fat)
Fat 5.2g (Sat 0.6g Mono 2.6g Poly 0.8g) Chol 37mg
Protein 23.5g Carbohydrate 21.1g Sodium 344mg
Exchanges: 3 Very Lean Meat, 1 Vegetable, 1 Fruit

Tropical Seafood Salad

1 pound unpeeled medium-size fresh shrimp
2 small ripe mangoes, peeled and seeded
¼ cup fresh lime juice
1½ tablespoons finely chopped jalapeño pepper
1½ tablespoons dark rum
1½ teaspoons olive oil
¾ teaspoon freshly ground pepper
¼ teaspoon salt
    Vegetable cooking spray
1 teaspoon olive oil
1 (6-ounce) tuna steak (1 inch thick)
6 cups torn fresh spinach leaves
½ cup diced purple onion
8 plain breadsticks

Peel and devein shrimp; set aside.

Coarsely chop 1 mango. Slice remaining mango into ¼-inch-thick slices; set aside. Combine chopped mango, lime juice, and next 5 ingredients in container of an electric blender or food processor. Cover and process until smooth, stopping once to scrape down sides; set aside.

Coat a large nonstick skillet with cooking spray; add 1 teaspoon olive oil, and place over medium-high heat until hot. Add shrimp, and sauté 3 minutes. Remove from skillet, and set aside. Add tuna to skillet, and cook 4 minutes on each side or until fish flakes easily when tested with a fork. Remove from heat, and let cool completely. Flake tuna into large pieces with a fork.

To serve, place 1½ cups spinach on each of 4 plates. Arrange sliced mango, shrimp, and tuna evenly over spinach; sprinkle with onion. Drizzle mango mixture evenly over salads. Serve with breadsticks. Yield: 4 servings.

Per Serving: Calories 280 (23% calories from fat)
Fat 7.2g (Sat 1.5g Mono 3.2g Poly 1.7g) Chol 127mg
Protein 25.1g Carbohydrate 26.6g Sodium 379mg
Exchanges: 3 Lean Meat, 1 Starch, 1 Fruit

Seafood Couscous Salad

1 pound unpeeled medium-size
   fresh shrimp
5¼ cups water, divided
1½ cups couscous, uncooked
½ pound fresh lump crabmeat, drained
1½ cups seeded, chopped plum tomato
1 cup diced celery
½ cup chopped green onions
⅓ cup chopped fresh mint
2 tablespoons capers
¼ cup plus 2 tablespoons fresh lemon juice
¼ cup plus 2 tablespoons canned low-sodium
   chicken broth, undiluted
1 tablespoon olive oil
1½ teaspoons Dijon mustard
1 clove garlic, minced
1 head Boston lettuce, torn

Peel and devein shrimp. Bring 3 cups water to a boil in a saucepan; add shrimp, and cook 3 to 5 minutes or until shrimp turn pink. Drain well; rinse with cold water. Chill.

Bring remaining 2¼ cups water to a boil in a saucepan. Remove from heat. Add couscous; cover and let stand 10 minutes or until couscous is tender and liquid is absorbed. Fluff couscous with a fork, and transfer to a serving bowl. Add shrimp, crabmeat, and next 5 ingredients; toss well.

Combine lemon juice and next 4 ingredients; stir well with a wire whisk. Pour over couscous mixture; toss well. Cover and chill. To serve, place lettuce evenly on 6 plates. Spoon couscous mixture evenly over lettuce. Yield: 6 (1½-cup) servings.

Note: To make this recipe and Shrimp and Black Bean Salad super-quick, buy peeled and deveined shrimp.

Per Serving: Calories 285 (13% calories from fat) Fat 4.2g (Sat 0.5g Mono 1.9g Poly 0.7g) Chol 112mg Protein 22.9g Carbohydrate 39.8g Sodium 556mg
Exchanges: 2 Lean Meat, 2½ Starch, 1 Vegetable

Shrimp and Black Bean Salad

¼ cup canned low-sodium chicken broth,
   undiluted
¼ cup sherry vinegar
1½ teaspoons Dijon mustard
1 teaspoon olive oil
1 teaspoon ground cumin
½ teaspoon dried oregano
1½ pounds unpeeled large fresh shrimp
   Vegetable cooking spray
1 teaspoon olive oil
1 cup frozen whole-kernel corn
1 tablespoon minced garlic
1 cup diced sweet red pepper
½ cup sliced green onions
1 jalapeño pepper, seeded and minced
1 (15-ounce) can no-salt-added black beans,
   drained
⅓ cup chopped fresh cilantro
2 cups mixed salad greens
1 cup quartered cherry tomatoes

Combine first 6 ingredients; stir well with a wire whisk. Set aside.

Peel and devein shrimp. Coat a large nonstick skillet with cooking spray; add 1 teaspoon oil. Place over medium-high heat until hot. Add shrimp. Sauté 3 minutes or until shrimp turn pink. Remove shrimp from skillet; set aside, and keep warm.

Add corn and garlic to skillet; sauté 2 minutes. Reduce heat to medium; add shrimp, red pepper, and next 3 ingredients. Cook 2 minutes or until thoroughly heated. Remove from heat; stir in cilantro and broth mixture. Cover and chill.

To serve, arrange ½ cup salad greens and ¼ cup tomato quarters on each of 4 plates. Top evenly with shrimp mixture. Yield: 4 (1½-cup) servings.

Per Serving: Calories 313 (16% calories from fat) Fat 5.6g (Sat 0.9g Mono 2.1g Poly 1.4g) Chol 194mg Protein 34.1g Carbohydrate 29.5g Sodium 296mg
Exchanges: 4 Very Lean Meat, 1½ Starch, 1 Vegetable

Shrimp and Black Bean Salad

Jamaican Shrimp and Rice Salad

⅓ cup lime juice
3 tablespoons low-sodium Worcestershire sauce
1 tablespoon reduced-calorie ketchup
2 teaspoons hot sauce
2 teaspoons vegetable oil
2 teaspoons molasses
¼ teaspoon freshly ground pepper
1 large clove garlic, crushed
3 cups cooked long-grain rice (cooked without salt or fat)
½ cup chopped fresh cilantro
½ cup chopped green onions
1 (15-ounce) can no-salt-added black beans, rinsed and drained
1 (7-ounce) jar roasted red peppers in water, drained and chopped
1½ pounds unpeeled medium-size fresh shrimp
Vegetable cooking spray

Combine first 8 ingredients in a large bowl; set 1 table-spoon of mixture aside. Add rice and next 4 ingredients to remaining juice mixture. Stir well; set aside.

Peel and devein shrimp. Place shrimp on rack of a broiler pan coated with cooking spray, and brush with reserved 1 tablespoon lime juice mixture. Broil 5½ inches from heat (with electric oven door partially opened) 2 minutes on each side or until shrimp turn pink. Add shrimp to rice mixture, and stir. Serve salad immediately, or cover and chill. Yield: 4 (2-cup) servings.

Per Serving: Calories 391 (9% calories from fat)
Fat 3.9g (Sat 0.8g Mono 0.9g Poly 1.6g) Chol 166mg
Protein 27.1g Carbohydrate 61.3g Sodium 288mg
Exchanges: 2 Lean Meat, 3 Starch, 2 Vegetable

Greek Shrimp Salad

2 pounds unpeeled medium-size fresh shrimp
6 cups water
2¾ cups cooked orzo (cooked without salt or fat)
¾ cup chopped green onions
3 ounces crumbled feta cheese with peppercorns
3 tablespoons minced fresh dill
3 tablespoons lemon juice
1 tablespoon olive oil
¼ teaspoon salt
¾ cup peeled, chopped cucumber
1 cup cherry tomatoes, halved
15 Bibb lettuce leaves
Cucumber slices (optional)

Peel and devein shrimp. Bring water to a boil in a saucepan; add shrimp, and cook 3 to 5 minutes or until shrimp turn pink. Drain well, and rinse with cold water.

Combine shrimp, orzo, and next 3 ingredients in a large bowl. Combine lemon juice, oil, and salt; add to shrimp mixture, and toss lightly. Cover and chill at least 8 hours.

To serve, add chopped cucumber and tomato to shrimp mixture; toss well. Place 3 lettuce leaves on each of 5 salad plates. Spoon shrimp mixture evenly over lettuce. Garnish with cucumber slices, if desired. Yield: 5 (1½-cup) servings.

Per Serving: Calories 311 (24% calories from fat)
Fat 8.2g (Sat 3.3g Mono 3.1g Poly 1.0g) Chol 192mg
Protein 27.2g Carbohydrate 32.2g Sodium 526mg
Exchanges: 3 Lean Meat, 1½ Starch, 1 Vegetable

Asian Chicken Salad

⅓ cup canned low-sodium chicken broth, undiluted
3 tablespoons rice wine vinegar
2 tablespoons low-sodium soy sauce
1½ tablespoons lemon juice
2 teaspoons dark sesame oil
1½ teaspoons Chinese five-spice powder
¼ teaspoon salt
3 small cloves garlic, minced
1 pound skinned, boned chicken breasts
1 (10-ounce) package fresh spinach, washed and trimmed
1 (8-ounce) package Chinese-style noodles
⅔ cup chopped fresh cilantro
½ cup sliced green onions
1 tablespoon peeled, grated gingerroot
1 medium-size sweet red pepper, seeded and thinly sliced
2 tablespoons chopped unsalted dry roasted peanuts

Combine first 8 ingredients in a jar; cover tightly, and shake. Slice chicken diagonally into ½-inch slices.

Set aside 2 cups spinach leaves. Stack remaining spinach leaves, and cut into thin slices; set aside.

Cook noodles according to package directions, omitting salt and fat; drain. Transfer noodles to a large bowl; add ⅓ cup broth mixture, sliced spinach, cilantro, green onions, and gingerroot; toss lightly.

Pour remaining broth mixture into a large nonstick skillet; place over medium-high heat until hot. Add chicken; sauté 2 minutes. Add red pepper; sauté 3 to 4 minutes or until pepper is tender.

To serve, place ½ cup spinach leaves on each of 4 plates. Arrange noodle and chicken mixtures over spinach; sprinkle with peanuts. Yield: 4 servings.

Per Serving: Calories 407 (14% calories from fat) Fat 6.2g (Sat 1.1g Mono 2.3g Poly 3.5g) Chol 66mg Protein 29.6g Carbohydrate 56.6g Sodium 470mg
Exchanges: 2½ Lean Meat, 3 Starch, 2 Vegetable

CLOVE CLAIMS

Although the results are *not* conclusive, research shows that garlic may help protect you from heart disease by—
•Decreasing blood cholesterol
•Decreasing blood fats
•Thinning the blood
•Decreasing high blood pressure
•Increasing circulation in the limbs
Go ahead and enjoy the distinctive flavor garlic adds to food. Your heart may thank you for it.

Roasted Chicken
Salad with
Goat Cheese
Crostini

Roasted Chicken Salad with Goat Cheese Crostini

2 large carrots, scraped
8 cups torn fresh spinach leaves
1 cup thinly sliced purple onion
¾ cup sliced yellow squash
3 tablespoons chopped dried tomatoes
2 tablespoons chopped fresh tarragon
3 tablespoons rice wine vinegar
1 tablespoon balsamic vinegar
1 teaspoon sugar
1 teaspoon olive oil
¼ teaspoon dry mustard
⅛ teaspoon salt
1 clove garlic, minced
12 ounces skinned, boned roasted chicken,
    cut into ¾-inch pieces
    Goat Cheese Crostini

Cut carrots into long, thin strips using a vegetable peeler. Combine carrot, spinach, and next 3 ingredients in a large bowl. Set aside.

    Combine tarragon and next 7 ingredients in a small jar; cover tightly, and shake vigorously.

    Add vinegar mixture to spinach mixture, and toss well. Place spinach mixture evenly on 4 plates. Top evenly with chicken. Serve with Goat Cheese Crostini. Yield: 4 servings.

Goat Cheese Crostini

2 ounces goat cheese
1 tablespoon minced fresh tarragon
½ teaspoon freshly ground pepper
4 (¾-inch-thick) baguette slices, toasted

Combine first 3 ingredients in a small bowl; mash well with a fork. Spread mixture evenly on slices of bread, and broil 3 inches from heat (with electric oven door partially opened) 1 minute or until thoroughly heated. Yield: 4 slices.

Per Serving: Calories 356 (29% calories from fat)
Fat 11.3g (Sat 4.0g Mono 3.9g Poly 1.8g) Chol 83mg
Protein 33.6g Carbohydrate 30.2g Sodium 569mg
Exchanges: 3½ Lean Meat, 1 Starch, 3 Vegetable

QUICK CHICK

When a recipe calls for cooked chicken, you can use roasted chicken from the fresh poultry section or from the deli of your grocery store. It usually comes packaged as a whole chicken with the skin, which sometimes has seasonings rubbed on it. To reduce the fat and sodium, be sure to remove the skin before using the chicken.

Chicken Salad in Cantaloupe

3 cups shredded cooked chicken breast
1½ cups peeled, seeded, and cubed papaya
1 cup finely chopped sweet red pepper
¼ cup minced fresh cilantro
3 tablespoons white balsamic vinegar
1½ tablespoons lime juice
1½ tablespoons Dijon mustard
1 tablespoon plus 1 teaspoon honey
2 teaspoons olive oil
¼ teaspoon ground red pepper
2 small cantaloupes
    Lime wedges (optional)

Combine first 4 ingredients; toss well. Combine balsamic vinegar and next 5 ingredients; stir well. Pour vinegar mixture over chicken mixture; toss lightly. Cover and chill.

Cut each cantaloupe in half; remove and discard seeds. If necessary, cut a thin slice from bottom of each melon half so that it will sit flat. Spoon chicken mixture evenly into melon halves. Garnish with lime wedges, if desired. Yield: 4 servings.

Per Serving: Calories 366 (19% calories from fat)
Fat 7.7g (Sat 1.9g Mono 3.2g Poly 1.2g) Chol 96mg
Protein 38.4g Carbohydrate 37.5g Sodium 281mg
Exchanges: 5 Very Lean Meat, 1 Starch, 1½ Fruit

Mediterranean Potato-Chicken Salad

1 clove garlic
½ cup chopped fresh parsley
1 tablespoon capers, drained
6 pimiento-stuffed olives
⅓ cup plain nonfat yogurt
¼ cup reduced-calorie mayonnaise
1 tablespoon balsamic vinegar
2 teaspoons Dijon mustard
1 pound small round red potatoes
1 pound skinned, boned chicken breasts
1½ cups halved cherry tomatoes
8 romaine lettuce leaves

Position knife blade in food processor bowl. Drop garlic through food chute with processor running; process 3 seconds or until garlic is minced. Add parsley, capers, and olives. Process 10 seconds or until finely minced. Transfer mixture to a small bowl. Stir in yogurt and next 3 ingredients. Cover and chill.

Place potatoes in a large saucepan; add water to cover. Bring to a boil; cover, reduce heat, and simmer 10 minutes. Add chicken; cover and cook 10 to 15 minutes or until potato is tender and chicken is done. Drain well, and let cool.

Cut potatoes into ½-inch-thick slices. Cut chicken into ½-inch cubes. Place potato and chicken in a large bowl. Add tomato; toss lightly. Pour yogurt mixture over potato mixture, and toss lightly. Serve immediately, or cover and chill up to 8 hours.

To serve, place 2 lettuce leaves on each of 4 plates. Spoon potato mixture evenly over lettuce. Yield: 4 (1¼-cup) servings.

Per Serving: Calories 296 (24% calories from fat)
Fat 7.8g (Sat 1.5g Mono 1.1g Poly 3.4g) Chol 76mg
Protein 30.6g Carbohydrate 25.4g Sodium 707mg
Exchanges: 3 Lean Meat, 1 Starch, 2 Vegetable

Mexican Chicken and Pasta Salad

12 ounces tri-color fusilli (corkscrew pasta),
    uncooked
2 large carrots, scraped
½ cup fat-free Ranch-style dressing
2 tablespoons lime juice
1 teaspoon chili powder
1 teaspoon ground cumin
½ teaspoon hot sauce
3½ cups coarsely shredded roasted chicken breast
2½ cups seeded, diced tomato
¾ cup chopped fresh cilantro
½ cup chopped purple onion
1 (15½-ounce) can golden hominy, drained

Cook pasta according to package directions, omitting salt and fat. Drain and set aside.

Slice carrots diagonally; cut slices into thin strips. Add to pasta.

Combine dressing and next 4 ingredients. Add to pasta mixture; toss well. Add chicken and remaining ingredients; toss well. Cover and chill at least 3 hours. Yield: 6 servings.

Per Serving: Calories 448 (14% calories from fat)
Fat 7.1g (Sat 1.7g Mono 2.2g Poly 1.8g) Chol 67mg
Protein 31.4g Carbohydrate 62.9g Sodium 396mg
Exchanges: 2 Lean Meat, 3 Starch, 3 Vegetable

Pesto Chicken and Rice Salad

¼ teaspoon pepper
⅛ teaspoon salt
1½ pounds skinned chicken breasts
    Vegetable cooking spray
3 cups cooked long-grain rice (cooked without
    salt or fat)
1 cup chopped celery
½ cup 1% low-fat cottage cheese
⅓ cup reduced-calorie mayonnaise
⅓ cup nonfat buttermilk
2 cloves garlic
1 cup chopped fresh basil
¼ cup grated Parmesan cheese
2 tablespoons slivered almonds, toasted
4 medium tomatoes, cut into wedges
    Fresh basil sprigs (optional)

Sprinkle pepper and salt over chicken; place chicken in a 13- x 9- x 2-inch baking dish coated with cooking spray. Bake at 375° for 35 minutes or until chicken is tender. Let cool. Bone chicken, and cut into bite-size pieces.

Combine chicken, rice, and celery in a large bowl; toss lightly.

Position knife blade in food processor bowl; add cottage cheese and next 3 ingredients. Process until smooth. Add chopped basil; process until blended. Pour basil mixture over rice mixture; toss lightly. Stir in Parmesan cheese and almonds.

To serve, spoon 1½ cups rice mixture onto each of 4 plates. Arrange tomato wedges evenly around rice mixture. Garnish with basil sprigs, if desired. Yield: 4 (1½-cup) servings.

Per Serving: Calories 472 (24% calories from fat)
Fat 12.8g (Sat 2.3g Mono 2.7g Poly 1.3g) Chol 90mg
Protein 40.1g Carbohydrate 47.7g Sodium 559mg
Exchanges: 4 Lean Meat, 3 Starch, 1 Vegetable

Blue Cheese, Turkey, and Rice Salad

3 cups water
1 (6-ounce) package wild rice
1 medium-size sweet red pepper
3 cups trimmed, chopped fresh spinach leaves
1¾ cups chopped cooked turkey breast
½ cup thinly sliced celery
2 tablespoons chopped pecans, toasted
3 ounces blue cheese, crumbled
¼ cup white wine vinegar
3 tablespoons canned low-sodium chicken
    broth, undiluted
2 tablespoons honey
1 tablespoon Dijon mustard
2 teaspoons hot sauce
1 teaspoon vegetable oil
12 large spinach leaves

Combine water and rice in a medium saucepan; bring to a boil. Cover, reduce heat, and simmer 50 to 60 minutes or until rice is tender. Drain well; let cool.

Cut pepper in half lengthwise; remove and discard seeds and membrane. Place pepper, skin side up, on a baking sheet, and flatten with palm of hand. Broil 5½ inches from heat (with electric oven door partially opened) 15 to 20 minutes or until charred. Place in ice water until cool; peel and discard skin. Dice pepper.

Combine rice, red pepper, chopped spinach, and next 4 ingredients in a large bowl; toss lightly.

Combine vinegar and next 5 ingredients in a jar; cover tightly, and shake vigorously. Pour vinegar mixture over rice mixture, and toss well. Cover and chill thoroughly.

To serve, place 3 spinach leaves on each of 4 plates. Top evenly with rice mixture. Yield: 4 (1½-cup) servings.

Per Serving: Calories 416 (28% calories from fat)
Fat 12.8g (Sat 5.1g Mono 4.0g Poly 2.3g) Chol 55mg
Protein 30.2g Carbohydrate 46.7g Sodium 526mg
Exchanges: 3 Medium-Fat Meat, 3 Starch, 1 Vegetable

GO WILD WITH RICE

Did you know that wild rice is not really rice? It's a long-grain marsh grass native to the Great Lakes region of the United States.

If you enjoy the nutty flavor and chewy texture of wild rice, but don't have an hour to wait for it to cook, look for the quick-cooking varieties that are now available.

Indonesian Turkey-Rice Salad

1½ pounds skinned, boned turkey breast, cut into
    1-inch cubes
1 teaspoon chili powder
½ teaspoon ground cinnamon
    Vegetable cooking spray
1 teaspoon vegetable oil
3½ cups snow pea pods, trimmed and thinly sliced
3 cups cooked brown rice (cooked without salt
    or fat)
½ cup sliced green onions
½ cup raisins
1 (8-ounce) can sliced water chestnuts, drained
½ cup reduced-calorie mayonnaise
⅓ cup rice wine vinegar
2 tablespoons lime juice
2 tablespoons reduced-sodium teriyaki sauce
1 teaspoon sugar
¼ teaspoon salt
¼ teaspoon ground ginger
¼ teaspoon garlic powder

Combine turkey, chili powder, and cinnamon in a
medium bowl; stir well.

Coat a large nonstick skillet with cooking spray;
add oil. Place over medium-high heat until hot. Add
turkey mixture, and sauté 5 minutes or until turkey is
no longer pink. Combine turkey mixture, snow peas,
and next 4 ingredients in a large bowl; toss well.

Combine mayonnaise and remaining 7 ingredients;
stir well with a wire whisk. Add mayonnaise mixture
to rice mixture; toss lightly. Cover and chill 1 hour.
Yield: 6 (1½-cup) servings.

Per Serving: Calories 374 (22% calories from fat)
Fat 9.0g (Sat 1.7g Mono 0.9g Poly 4.7g) Chol 75mg
Protein 31.5g Carbohydrate 39.8g Sodium 435mg
Exchanges: 3 Lean Meat, 2½ Starch, 1 Vegetable

Turkey and Grain Salad

6 cups water
¾ cup wild rice, uncooked
½ cup pearl barley, uncooked
½ pound smoked turkey breast, diced
2 cups diced Red Delicious apple
¾ cup sliced green onions
¾ cup diced celery
¼ cup plus 1 tablespoon cider vinegar
¼ cup frozen apple juice concentrate, thawed
    and undiluted
1 tablespoon olive oil
1 tablespoon Dijon mustard
1 teaspoon dried thyme
½ teaspoon freshly ground pepper
12 red leaf lettuce leaves

Combine water, wild rice, and barley in a large
saucepan; bring to a boil. Cover, reduce heat, and
simmer 45 minutes or until rice and barley are tender.
Drain. Add turkey and next 3 ingredients; toss well.

Combine vinegar and next 5 ingredients. Pour over
rice mixture; toss well. Cover and chill 3 hours, stirring occasionally.

To serve, place 2 lettuce leaves on each of 6 plates.
Spoon rice mixture over lettuce. Yield: 6 (1½-cup)
servings.

Per Serving: Calories 295 (14% calories from fat)
Fat 4.7g (Sat 0.8g Mono 1.9g Poly 1.2g) Chol 22mg
Protein 17.4g Carbohydrate 50.6g Sodium 412mg
Exchanges: 1 Lean Meat, 3 Starch, 1 Vegetable

Soups and

Black-Eyed Pea
Gumbo
(page 203)

Stews

soups and stews (soops-'n'-stooz): liquid foods that are full of pasta, rice, vegetables, meat, poultry, or seafood. Especially good to eat on cold days or when you have the flu.

Cioppino (page 215)   Wagon Wheel Beef Soup (page 199)

Beer-Cheese Soup

Vegetable cooking spray
1 tablespoon reduced-calorie margarine
1 cup peeled, chopped baking potato
½ cup diced carrot
½ cup diced zucchini
½ cup chopped onion
½ cup chopped green pepper
1 cup flat light beer
¼ cup water
¼ teaspoon ground red pepper
1 (14¼-ounce) can no-salt-added chicken broth
2 cups evaporated skimmed milk
½ cup all-purpose flour
1 (8-ounce) loaf light process cheese spread, cubed
1 tablespoon minced fresh parsley
Peppered Toast Triangles

Coat a Dutch oven with cooking spray; add margarine. Place over medium-high heat until margarine melts. Add potato and next 4 ingredients; sauté until crisp-tender.

Add beer and next 3 ingredients, stirring well. Bring to a boil; cover, reduce heat, and simmer 30 minutes.

Combine milk and flour, stirring until smooth. Add flour mixture to vegetable mixture. Cook over medium heat, stirring constantly, until mixture is thickened and bubbly. Add cheese and parsley, stirring until cheese melts. To serve, ladle soup into individual bowls, and serve with Peppered Toast Triangles. Yield: 5 servings (serving size: 1½ cups soup and 3 toast triangles).

Peppered Toast Triangles

1 tablespoon reduced-calorie margarine, melted
2 teaspoons minced fresh parsley
⅛ teaspoon dried crushed red pepper
Dash of coarsely ground pepper
2 (1-ounce) slices sourdough bread, trimmed

Combine first 4 ingredients; brush mixture evenly over one side of bread slices. Cut each slice into 4 squares; cut each square into 2 triangles. Place triangles on a baking sheet. Bake at 350° for 10 minutes or until crisp and lightly browned. Yield: 16 triangles.

Per Serving: Calories 333 (23% calories from fat) Fat 8.4g (Sat 3.8g Mono 1.1g Poly 1.3g) Chol 20mg Protein 21.1g Carbohydrate 41.9g Sodium 896mg
Exchanges: 1 High-Fat Meat, 2 Starch, 2 Vegetable

Black and White Bean Soup

1 pound dried black beans
1 pound dried Great Northern beans
1 tablespoon olive oil
1 cup chopped onion
2 teaspoons garlic powder
2 teaspoons ground cumin
2 teaspoons ground oregano
2 teaspoons ground coriander
½ teaspoon salt
½ teaspoon ground red pepper
1 (4-ounce) can chopped green chiles
3 (14¼-ounce) cans no-salt-added chicken broth
½ cup chopped fresh parsley
   Nonfat sour cream (optional)
   Fresh parsley sprigs (optional)

Sort and wash beans; place beans in a large Dutch oven. Cover with water to a depth of 2 inches above beans. Bring to a boil; cover, remove from heat, and let stand for 1 hour. Drain beans, and set aside.

   Place oil in Dutch oven; place over medium-high heat until hot. Add onion and next 7 ingredients; sauté until onion is tender. Add broth and beans. Bring to a boil; cover, reduce heat, and simmer 1½ hours or until beans are tender. Stir in chopped parsley. To serve, ladle soup into individual bowls. Garnish with nonfat sour cream and parsley sprigs, if desired. Yield: 8 (1½-cup) servings.

Per Serving: Calories 430 (7% calories from fat)
Fat 3.4g (Sat 0.6g Mono 1.5g Poly 0.8g) Chol 0mg
Protein 25.3g Carbohydrate 76.2g Sodium 163mg
Exchanges: 1 Lean Meat, 4 Starch, 3 Vegetable

Black-Eyed Pea and Barley Soup

1 cup medium barley, uncooked
1 cup chopped onion
1 cup chopped sweet red pepper
1 tablespoon dried parsley flakes
1 teaspoon garlic powder
1 teaspoon ground cumin
½ teaspoon salt
⅛ teaspoon ground cloves
5 (14¼-ounce) cans no-salt-added beef broth
1 (1-pound) package frozen black-eyed peas

Combine all ingredients in a Dutch oven; bring to a boil. Cover, reduce heat, and simmer 1 hour. Yield: 6 (2-cup) servings.

Per Serving: Calories 273 (4% calories from fat)
Fat 1.1g (Sat 0.3g Mono 0.2g Poly 0.3g) Chol 0mg
Protein 11.5g Carbohydrate 51.7g Sodium 217mg
Exchanges: 3 Starch, 1 Vegetable

ALL SOAKED UP

Get a step ahead for soup making. When you soak dried beans overnight, soak more than you need and freeze the extra. The next time you need dried beans, just thaw the presoaked ones.

   Or go ahead and cook the beans right after you've soaked them, and freeze the cooked beans for up to one month. Then all you'll have to do when you're ready to use them is heat them with the other ingredients.

Lentil Soup with Cheese Biscuits

1 pound dried lentils
7½ cups water
2 cups chopped onion
1 cup chopped carrot
½ teaspoon freshly ground pepper
8 cloves garlic, minced
½ teaspoon salt
Cheese Biscuits

Combine first 6 ingredients in a Dutch oven. Bring to a boil; cover, reduce heat, and simmer 35 to 40 minutes or until lentils are tender. Stir in salt. Transfer 2 cups lentil mixture to container of an electric blender; cover and process until pureed. Stir pureed mixture into remaining lentil mixture.

To serve, ladle soup into individual bowls and top each serving with a Cheese Biscuit. Yield: 6 servings (serving size: 1½ cups soup and 1 biscuit).

Cheese Biscuits

1½ cups all-purpose flour
2 teaspoons baking powder
½ teaspoon baking soda
¼ teaspoon salt
¼ cup (1 ounce) shredded reduced-fat
   Cheddar cheese
¼ cup frozen egg substitute, thawed
1 tablespoon vegetable oil
1 (8-ounce) carton plain low-fat yogurt
Vegetable cooking spray

Combine first 4 ingredients in a bowl; make a well in center of mixture. Combine cheese and next 3 ingredients; add to flour mixture, stirring just until dry ingredients are moistened.

Drop dough by ⅓ cupfuls, 2 inches apart, onto a baking sheet coated with cooking spray. Bake at 400° for 13 to 15 minutes or until golden. Yield: 6 biscuits.

Per Serving: Calories 465 (10% calories from fat) Fat 5.0g (Sat 1.5g Mono 1.0g Poly 1.7g) Chol 5mg Protein 29.8g Carbohydrate 77.5g Sodium 493mg
Exchanges: 2 Lean Meat, 5 Starch, 1 Vegetable

Jambalaya Stew

4 cups water
2½ cups chopped tomato
1½ cups chopped green pepper
1 cup chopped onion
1 teaspoon dried Italian seasoning
1 teaspoon chili powder
1 teaspoon hot sauce
¾ teaspoon salt
3 cloves garlic, minced
1 bay leaf
2 cups instant rice, uncooked
3 (8-ounce) cans no-salt-added tomato sauce
2 (15-ounce) cans no-salt-added red kidney
   beans, undrained
1 (16-ounce) package frozen sliced okra, thawed

Combine first 10 ingredients in a large Dutch oven. Bring to a boil; reduce heat, and cook, uncovered, 5 minutes. Add rice and remaining ingredients. Bring to a boil; reduce heat, and cook, uncovered, 5 minutes or until okra is tender. Remove and discard bay leaf. Yield: 8 (2-cup) servings.

Per Serving: Calories 302 (4% calories from fat) Fat 1.2g (Sat 0.2g Mono 0.1g Poly 0.6g) Chol 0mg Protein 14.0g Carbohydrate 61.3g Sodium 257mg
Exchanges: 3 Starch, 3 Vegetable

Jambalaya
Stew

Potato-Onion Soup

Vegetable cooking spray
4 cups sliced onion
1 tablespoon water
2 tablespoons all-purpose flour
3 (14¼-ounce) cans no-salt-added beef broth, divided
3 cups frozen southern-style hash brown potatoes
1 tablespoon Dijon mustard
2 teaspoons low-sodium Worcestershire sauce
½ teaspoon pepper
¼ teaspoon salt
6 cloves garlic, minced
6 (1-ounce) slices French bread
1¼ cups (5 ounces) shredded reduced-fat Swiss cheese

Coat a Dutch oven with cooking spray; place over medium-high heat until hot. Add onion; sauté 5 minutes or until tender. Add water; reduce heat to medium-low. Cook, uncovered, 25 to 30 minutes or until onion is golden, stirring occasionally.

Sprinkle flour over onion; gradually stir in 1 can broth. Bring to a boil, stirring constantly. Add remaining 2 cans broth, potato, and next 5 ingredients. Bring to a boil; cover, reduce heat, and simmer 15 minutes.

Place 6 ovenproof bowls on a baking sheet. Place 1 bread slice in each bowl; ladle 1½ cups soup into each bowl. Sprinkle evenly with cheese. Broil 5½ inches from heat (with electric oven door partially opened) 4 minutes or until cheese is golden. Yield: 6 servings.

Per Serving: Calories 268 (17% calories from fat) Fat 5.2g (Sat 2.5g Mono 0.3g Poly 0.5g) Chol 15mg Protein 13.7g Carbohydrate 39.5g Sodium 442mg
Exchanges: 1 Medium-Fat Meat, 2 Starch, 2 Vegetable

SMILE AND SAY CHEESE

 Swiss, Cheddar, Colby, and Monterey Jack cheeses all come in reduced-fat versions that have about 35 to 40 percent less fat than their regular counterparts.

But these reduced-fat cheeses contain slightly more sodium than the regular cheeses. For example, regular Cheddar has 176 milligrams of sodium per ounce; reduced-fat Cheddar has 205 milligrams.

So, any way you slice it, you need to pay attention to the amount of fat *and* sodium in cheese.

White Bean and Pepper Soup

Vegetable cooking spray
1 cup chopped onion
1 cup chopped sweet red pepper
½ teaspoon black pepper
½ teaspoon dried dillweed
3 cloves garlic, minced
4 cups canned no-salt-added chicken broth, undiluted
2 (15-ounce) cans Great Northern beans, undrained
½ cup peeled, chopped cucumber
½ cup chopped green onions

Coat a large Dutch oven with cooking spray; place over medium-high heat until hot. Add 1 cup chopped onion, sweet red pepper, black pepper, dillweed, and garlic; sauté until vegetables are tender. Add broth and beans. Bring to a boil; reduce heat, and simmer, uncovered, 20 minutes. Stir in cucumber and green onions. Yield: 6 (1½-cup) servings.

Per Serving: Calories 203 (4% calories from fat)
Fat 0.8g (Sat 0.2g Mono 0.1g Poly 0.3g) Chol 0mg
Protein 13.1g Carbohydrate 36.3g Sodium 392mg
Exchanges: 1 Very Lean Meat, 2 Starch, 1 Vegetable

Gingered Beef Stew

1 pound lean boneless beef round steak, cut into 2-inch strips
¼ cup all-purpose flour
Vegetable cooking spray
1 cup chopped onion
3 (14¼-ounce) cans no-salt-added beef broth
2 tablespoons low-sodium soy sauce
1 teaspoon garlic powder
1 teaspoon ground ginger
½ teaspoon pepper
4 cups peeled, cubed baking potato
2 cups sliced carrot

Combine meat and flour in a heavy-duty, zip-top plastic bag; seal bag, and shake well to coat meat.

Coat a Dutch oven with cooking spray. Place over medium-high heat until hot; add meat mixture, and cook until meat is browned, stirring often. Stir in onion; cook until tender, stirring often. Add broth and next 4 ingredients; cover, reduce heat, and simmer 30 minutes, stirring occasionally. Add potato and carrot; cover and cook 15 to 17 minutes or until vegetables are tender. Yield: 5 (2-cup) servings.

Per Serving: Calories 307 (12% calories from fat)
Fat 4.1g (Sat 1.4g Mono 1.5g Poly 0.3g) Chol 52mg
Protein 25.4g Carbohydrate 38.0g Sodium 237mg
Exchanges: 2 Lean Meat, 2 Starch, 2 Vegetable

Wagon
Wheel
Beef Soup

Wagon Wheel Beef Soup

Vegetable cooking spray
¾ pound ground round
1 cup chopped onion
3 cups cooked wagon wheel pasta (cooked
    without salt or fat)
3 cups commercial low-fat spaghetti sauce
½ teaspoon ground oregano
2 (14¼-ounce) cans no-salt-added beef broth
1 (15-ounce) can no-salt-added red kidney beans

Coat a Dutch oven with cooking spray; place over
medium-high heat until hot. Add meat and onion, and
cook over medium heat until browned, stirring until
meat crumbles. Drain and pat dry with paper towels.
Wipe drippings from Dutch oven with a paper towel.
Return meat mixture to Dutch oven; add cooked pasta
and remaining ingredients. Cook until thoroughly
heated. Yield: 5 (2-cup) servings.

Per Serving: Calories 445 (17% calories from fat)
Fat 8.4g (Sat 2.2g Mono 2.5g Poly 0.7g) Chol 57mg
Protein 34.2g Carbohydrate 58.5g Sodium 521mg
Exchanges: 3 Lean Meat, 3 Starch, 3 Vegetable

Sauerbraten Stew

¼ cup all-purpose flour
½ teaspoon salt
½ teaspoon dry mustard
½ teaspoon pepper
1 pound lean boneless beef round steak,
    cut into ½-inch pieces
    Vegetable cooking spray
1 cup thinly sliced onion
1 cup thinly sliced cabbage
¼ cup red wine vinegar
1 tablespoon firmly packed brown sugar
½ teaspoon ground ginger
¼ teaspoon ground cloves
3 (14¼-ounce) cans no-salt-added beef broth
1 bay leaf
1 cup medium egg noodles, uncooked
¼ cup raisins
4 gingersnaps, crushed

Combine first 4 ingredients. Dredge meat in flour
mixture. Coat a Dutch oven with cooking spray. Place
over medium-high heat until hot; add meat, and cook
5 minutes or until browned, stirring often. Stir in
onion and next 7 ingredients. Bring to a boil; cover,
reduce heat, and simmer 30 minutes or until meat is
tender, stirring occasionally. Stir in noodles and
raisins. Cook 10 minutes or until noodles are tender;
remove and discard bay leaf. To serve, ladle soup into
individual bowls, and sprinkle with crushed cookies.
Yield: 4 (1½-cup) servings.

Per Serving: Calories 321 (18% calories from fat)
Fat 6.5g (Sat 2.0g Mono 2.4g Poly 0.6g) Chol 72mg
Protein 29.6g Carbohydrate 31.7g Sodium 379mg
Exchanges: 3 Lean Meat, 2 Starch, 1 Vegetable

Stroganoff Meatball Stew

1 pound ground round
½ cup soft breadcrumbs
2 tablespoons skim milk
1 tablespoon dried minced onion
1 teaspoon garlic powder
½ teaspoon salt, divided
　Vegetable cooking spray
¼ cup all-purpose flour
2 (14¼-ounce) cans no-salt-added beef broth
¼ teaspoon freshly ground pepper
2 cups cooked medium egg noodles (cooked
　　without salt or fat)
½ cup nonfat sour cream
1 (4-ounce) can sliced mushrooms, drained

Combine first 5 ingredients and ¼ teaspoon salt in a large bowl; stir well. Shape into 24 (1-inch) balls.

Coat a Dutch oven with cooking spray. Place over medium-high heat until hot. Add meatballs, and cook 8 minutes or until browned, turning often. Remove meatballs from Dutch oven; drain on paper towels. Wipe drippings from Dutch oven with a paper towel.

Add flour to Dutch oven; gradually add beef broth, pepper, and remaining ¼ teaspoon salt, stirring well with a wire whisk. Bring to a boil; reduce heat, and simmer, stirring constantly, 10 minutes or until mixture is thickened. Stir in noodles, sour cream, and mushrooms. Return meatballs to Dutch oven; cook until thoroughly heated. Yield: 4 (1½-cup) servings.

Per Serving: Calories 399 (20% calories from fat)
Fat 9.0g (Sat 2.9g Mono 3.5g Poly 0.9g) Chol 99mg
Protein 34.1g Carbohydrate 40.1g Sodium 459mg
Exchanges: 3 Lean Meat, 2 Starch, 2 Vegetable

Hearty Veal Stew

2 pounds lean boneless veal
1 teaspoon ground coriander
1 teaspoon ground cumin
1 teaspoon paprika
½ teaspoon salt
¼ teaspoon ground white pepper
　Vegetable cooking spray
1 tablespoon olive oil, divided
⅓ cup minced shallots
3 cloves garlic, minced
1 cup dry vermouth
2 (14¼-ounce) cans no-salt-added chicken broth
1 pound small round red potatoes
1 (16-ounce) package baby carrots
¼ cup chopped fresh flat-leaf parsley

Trim fat from meat; cut meat into bite-size pieces. Combine coriander and next 4 ingredients; dredge meat in coriander mixture.

Coat a Dutch oven with cooking spray; add 1 teaspoon oil. Place over medium-high heat until hot. Add half of meat; cook until browned on all sides, stirring often. Drain and pat dry with paper towels. Wipe drippings from Dutch oven with a paper towel. Coat Dutch oven with cooking spray; add 1 teaspoon oil, and repeat procedure with remaining meat.

Coat Dutch oven with cooking spray; add remaining 1 teaspoon oil. Place over medium-high heat until hot. Add shallots and garlic; sauté until tender. Add vermouth, broth, and meat; bring to a boil. Cover, reduce heat, and simmer 30 minutes. Add potatoes and carrots; cook, uncovered, 30 minutes or until meat and vegetables are tender. Stir in parsley. Yield: 5 (2-cup) servings.

Per Serving: Calories 456 (26% calories from fat)
Fat 13.0g (Sat 3.1g Mono 5.5g Poly 1.3g) Chol 169mg
Protein 49.5g Carbohydrate 31.3g Sodium 411mg
Exchanges: 5 Lean Meat, 2 Starch, 1 Vegetable

Lamb Ragoût

1½ pounds lean boneless lamb
1½ cups dry red wine
2 teaspoons cracked pepper
8 large round red potatoes, quartered
4 cups pearl onions
½ cup all-purpose flour
Vegetable cooking spray
1 teaspoon vegetable oil
4 cups chopped tomato
3 cups canned no-salt-added beef broth, undiluted
2 tablespoons brown sugar
½ teaspoon salt

Trim fat from meat. Cut meat into bite-size pieces; place in a shallow dish. Combine wine and pepper. Pour over meat, stirring to coat. Cover and marinate in refrigerator 2 hours.

Cook potato and onions in a Dutch oven in boiling water to cover 15 minutes. Drain and set aside.

Remove meat from marinade, reserving marinade. Place marinade in a small saucepan; bring to a boil, and set aside. Sprinkle flour over meat, stirring to coat. Coat Dutch oven with cooking spray; add oil. Place over medium-high heat until hot. Add meat, and cook 6 minutes or until browned; stirring often. Add reserved marinade, chopped tomato, and remaining 3 ingredients, stirring well. Bring to a boil; cover, reduce heat, and simmer 1 hour or until meat is tender. Add potato and onions; cook 10 minutes or until bubbly. Yield: 9 (1½-cup) servings.

Per Serving: Calories 239 (17% calories from fat) Fat 4.4g (Sat 1.4g Mono 1.6g Poly 0.7g) Chol 48mg Protein 19.4g Carbohydrate 30.4g Sodium 201mg
Exchanges: 2 Lean Meat, 2 Starch

ragoût (rah-GOO): a thick meat stew that usually, but not always, contains vegetables. It is often served with rice or bread.

Black-Eyed Pea
Gumbo

Black-Eyed Pea Gumbo

1 (¾-pound) pork tenderloin
  Vegetable cooking spray
2 (15-ounce) cans black-eyed peas, undrained
1 (14¼-ounce) can no-salt-added beef broth
1 (16-ounce) package frozen vegetable
  gumbo mix
1 tablespoon dried parsley flakes
2 teaspoons hot sauce
½ teaspoon dried thyme
½ teaspoon ground red pepper
2 cloves garlic, minced
2 bay leaves
2½ cups cooked long-grain rice (cooked without
  salt or fat)

Trim fat from pork; cut pork into bite-size pieces.
Coat a Dutch oven with cooking spray; place over
medium heat until hot. Add pork, and cook until
browned on all sides, stirring often.

Stir in peas and next 8 ingredients. Bring to a boil;
reduce heat, and simmer, uncovered, 20 minutes or
until vegetables are tender. Remove and discard bay
leaves.

To serve, place ½ cup rice into each of 5 bowls;
ladle 1½ cups gumbo over each serving. Yield:
5 servings.

Per Serving: Calories 424 (7% calories from fat)
Fat 3.3g (Sat 1.0g Mono 0.9g Poly 0.8g) Chol 44mg
Protein 31.6g Carbohydrate 65.8g Sodium 594mg
Exchanges: 3 Very Lean Meat, 4 Starch, 1 Vegetable

Barbecue Pork Stew

⅔ cup water
¼ cup firmly packed brown sugar
1 tablespoon paprika
3 tablespoons cider vinegar
3 tablespoons reduced-calorie ketchup
2 tablespoons low-sodium Worcestershire sauce
2 teaspoons garlic powder
2 teaspoons chili powder
1 teaspoon freshly ground pepper
½ teaspoon salt
1 (8-ounce) can no-salt-added tomato sauce
1½ pounds lean boneless pork loin
½ cup all-purpose flour
  Vegetable cooking spray
1 teaspoon vegetable oil
2½ cups chopped onion
2½ cups peeled, diced baking potato
1 (14½-ounce) can no-salt-added whole
  tomatoes, undrained and chopped
1 bay leaf
2 (15-ounce) cans no-salt-added kidney beans,
  undrained

Combine first 11 ingredients. Combine pork and flour
in a heavy-duty, zip-top plastic bag. Seal bag; shake
well to coat pork.

Coat a Dutch oven with cooking spray; add oil,
and place over medium heat until hot. Add pork and
onion; cook until onion is crisp-tender. Stir in tomato
sauce mixture, potato, tomato, and bay leaf. Bring to
a boil; cover, reduce heat, and simmer 1½ hours or
until pork is tender, stirring occasionally. Stir in
beans; cook until thoroughly heated. Remove and
discard bay leaf. Yield: 8 (1½-cup) servings.

Per Serving: Calories 418 (17% calories from fat)
Fat 8.0g (Sat 2.5g Mono 3.2g Poly 1.5g) Chol 51mg
Protein 30.2g Carbohydrate 57.3g Sodium 246mg
Exchanges: 2½ Lean Meat, 3 Starch, 2 Vegetable

Margarita Chicken Soup

Vegetable cooking spray
1 pound skinned, boned chicken breasts,
    cut into bite-size pieces
1 teaspoon ground coriander
½ teaspoon salt
¼ teaspoon pepper
2 cloves garlic, minced
1 small onion, sliced and cut in half
2 (14¼-ounce) cans no-salt-added chicken broth
2 cups cooked long-grain rice (cooked without
    salt or fat)
1 cup chopped fresh cilantro
2 tablespoons lime juice
1 tablespoon tequila
1 teaspoon sugar

Coat a large saucepan with cooking spray; place over
medium-high heat until hot. Add chicken and next 5
ingredients; sauté 15 minutes or until chicken is done
and onion is tender. Add broth. Bring to a boil; cover,
reduce heat, and simmer 15 minutes. Stir in rice and
remaining ingredients; cook 5 minutes or until thoroughly heated. Yield: 4 (1½-cup) servings.

Per Serving: Calories 275 (6% calories from fat)
Fat 1.7g (Sat 0.4g Mono 0.4g Poly 0.4g) Chol 66mg
Protein 29.5g Carbohydrate 31.1g Sodium 381mg
Exchanges: 3½ Very Lean Meat, 2 Starch

Chicken Chili Soup

Vegetable cooking spray
1 cup chopped onion
½ cup chopped green pepper
1 pound skinned, boned chicken breasts,
    cut into bite-size pieces
3 cups canned no-salt-added chicken broth,
    undiluted
1 tablespoon brown sugar
2 tablespoons red wine vinegar
2 tablespoons low-sodium Worcestershire sauce
1 teaspoon garlic powder
1 teaspoon chili powder
½ teaspoon salt
½ teaspoon ground cumin
½ teaspoon pepper
¼ teaspoon dry mustard
1 (15¼-ounce) can no-salt-added whole-kernel
    corn, drained
1 (15-ounce) can no-salt-added red kidney
    beans, drained
1 (14½-ounce) can no-salt-added whole
    tomatoes, undrained and chopped
1 (8-ounce) can no-salt-added tomato sauce

Coat a Dutch oven with cooking spray; place over
medium-high heat until hot. Add onion and green
pepper; sauté until tender. Add chicken and remaining ingredients, and stir. Bring to a boil; cover, reduce
heat, and simmer 20 minutes, stirring often. Yield:
6 (1¾-cup) servings.

Per Serving: Calories 229 (7% calories from fat)
Fat 1.8g (Sat 0.3g Mono 0.3g Poly 0.4g) Chol 44mg
Protein 23.6g Carbohydrate 28.2g Sodium 292mg
Exchanges: 2 Very Lean Meat, 1 Starch, 2 Vegetable

Chicken and Barley Soup

1 pound skinned, boned chicken breasts,
   cut into bite-size pieces
1 cup chopped onion
1 cup chopped celery
1 cup sliced carrot
1 cup chopped sweet red pepper
½ cup medium barley, uncooked
1 teaspoon dried crushed red pepper
½ teaspoon salt
½ teaspoon dried oregano
½ teaspoon dried thyme
¼ teaspoon pepper
¼ teaspoon turmeric
3 (14¼-ounce) cans no-salt-added
   chicken broth

Combine all ingredients in a large saucepan. Bring to a boil; cover, reduce heat, and simmer 15 minutes. Uncover and simmer 15 minutes or until barley is tender. Yield: 4 (2-cup) servings.

Per Serving: Calories 292 (6% calories from fat)
Fat 2.1g (Sat 0.5g Mono 0.4g Poly 0.7g) Chol 66mg
Protein 30.9g Carbohydrate 33.5g Sodium 420mg
Exchanges: 3 Very Lean Meat, 2 Starch, 1 Vegetable

Tortellini-Chicken Soup

Olive oil-flavored vegetable cooking spray
1 teaspoon olive oil
1¼ cups shredded carrot
1 cup chopped onion
1 cup sliced fresh mushrooms
½ teaspoon ground red pepper
¼ teaspoon salt
3 cloves garlic, minced
1 pound skinned, boned chicken breasts,
   cut into bite-size pieces
4 (10½-ounce) cans low-sodium chicken broth
1 bay leaf
¼ cup finely chopped fresh basil leaves
1 (9-ounce) package fresh cheese tortellini

Coat a Dutch oven with cooking spray; add oil. Place over medium-high heat until hot; add carrot and next 5 ingredients, and sauté until onion is tender. Add chicken, broth, and bay leaf. Bring to a boil; cover, reduce heat, and simmer 20 minutes or until chicken is done. Add basil and tortellini; cook 6 to 7 minutes or until pasta is tender. Remove and discard bay leaf. Yield: 6 (1½-cup) servings.

Per Serving: Calories 304 (19% calories from fat)
Fat 6.5g (Sat 1.4g Mono 1.5g Poly 0.7g) Chol 84mg
Protein 31.9g Carbohydrate 30.6g Sodium 343mg
Exchanges: 3 Lean Meat, 2 Starch, 1 Vegetable

Chicken
Divan
Soup

Chicken Divan Soup

Vegetable cooking spray
1¼ pounds skinned, boned chicken breasts,
    cut into bite-size pieces
¾ cup chopped onion
2 cloves garlic, minced
1 cup cooked long-grain rice (cooked without
    salt or fat)
½ teaspoon pepper
¼ teaspoon salt
2 (4-ounce) cans sliced mushrooms, drained
1 (16-ounce) package frozen chopped broccoli,
    thawed
1 (14¼-ounce) can no-salt-added chicken broth
1 (12-ounce) can evaporated skimmed milk
1 (10¾-ounce) can reduced-fat, reduced-sodium
    cream of chicken soup, undiluted

Coat a Dutch oven with cooking spray; place over medium-high heat until hot. Add chicken, onion, and garlic, and sauté until onion is tender. Add rice and remaining ingredients, stirring well. Bring to a boil; cover, reduce heat, and simmer 15 minutes. Yield: 6 (1½-cup) servings.

Per Serving: Calories 264 (10% calories from fat)
Fat 2.8g (Sat 0.8g Mono 0.5g Poly 0.7g) Chol 61mg
Protein 31.2g Carbohydrate 26.7g Sodium 591mg
Exchanges: 3 Very Lean Meat, 1½ Starch, 1 Vegetable

SOUP'S ON

Now you can buy canned cream soups that are made to fit your specific dietary needs. Use one of these varieties in recipes that call for regular canned cream soups. Look on the grocery shelves for—
•**low-sodium:** 25 milligrams of sodium and 7 grams of fat per ½-cup serving
•**reduced-fat, reduced-sodium:** 480 milligrams of sodium and 2 grams of fat per ½-cup serving
•**reduced-fat:** 940 milligrams of sodium and 3.5 grams of fat per ½-cup serving

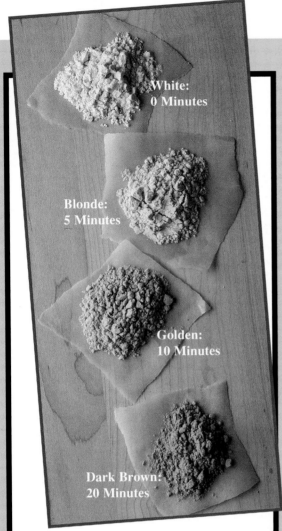

White:
0 Minutes

Blonde:
5 Minutes

Golden:
10 Minutes

Dark Brown:
20 Minutes

MAKE A LOW-FAT ROUX

Roux (roo), made from slowly cooked flour and fat, is the thickener of choice in many gumbo recipes. But you can brown flour in the oven without the fat. The longer it bakes, the darker and more flavorful it becomes.

As the flour bakes, its color changes from white to blonde to golden to dark brown in only 20 minutes in a 350° oven. This browned flour thickens the gumbo and adds a nutty, rich flavor.

Chicken Gumbo

Vegetable cooking spray
¾ pound smoked turkey sausage, sliced
1½ pounds skinned, boned chicken breasts
½ cup all-purpose flour
1 tablespoon vegetable oil
2½ cups chopped celery
2 cups chopped onion
2 cups chopped green pepper
½ cup chopped green onions
4 cloves garlic, minced
1 tablespoon Creole seasoning
1 tablespoon low-sodium Worcestershire sauce
2 teaspoons hot sauce
½ teaspoon pepper
3 bay leaves
3 (14¼-ounce) cans no-salt-added chicken broth
Gumbo filé (optional)
6 cups cooked long-grain rice (cooked without salt or fat)

Coat a large nonstick skillet with cooking spray. Add sausage, and cook 5 minutes or until browned on all sides. Remove sausage from skillet, and set aside. Add chicken to skillet, and cook 7 minutes on each side or until chicken is done. Remove chicken from skillet, and let cool slightly. Shred chicken; set aside.

Place flour on a baking sheet; bake at 350° for 20 minutes or until dark brown, stirring occasionally.

Coat a large Dutch oven with cooking spray; add oil. Place over medium-high heat until hot. Add celery and next 4 ingredients; sauté 8 minutes or until tender. Add browned flour, Creole seasoning, and next 4 ingredients, stirring well. Add broth and sausage. Bring to a boil; reduce heat, and simmer, uncovered, 1 hour. Add chicken, and simmer, uncovered, 30 minutes. Remove and discard bay leaves. Stir in filé, if desired. To serve, place ¾ cup rice in each of 8 bowls; ladle 1½ cups gumbo over each serving. Yield: 8 servings.

Per Serving: Calories 455 (24% calories from fat) Fat 12.2g (Sat 2.6g Mono 3.1g Poly 2.8g) Chol 78mg Protein 31.5g Carbohydrate 51.4g Sodium 587mg
Exchanges: 3 Lean Meat, 3 Starch, 1 Vegetable

Chicken
Gumbo

Curried Chicken Stew

Vegetable cooking spray
1⅔ cups chopped tomato
1 cup sliced onion
1 cup chopped sweet red pepper
1 cup frozen sliced okra
6 cloves garlic, minced
1¼ pounds skinned, boned chicken breasts,
    cut into bite-size pieces
4 cups canned no-salt-added chicken broth,
    undiluted
1 tablespoon curry powder
1 tablespoon finely chopped crystallized ginger
½ teaspoon salt
½ teaspoon ground red pepper
½ teaspoon black pepper
1 cup orzo (rice-shaped pasta), uncooked

Coat a Dutch oven with cooking spray. Add tomato and next 4 ingredients; sauté until tender. Stir in chicken and next 6 ingredients. Bring to a boil; cover, reduce heat, and simmer 20 minutes. Gradually stir in orzo, and cook 8 to 10 minutes or until orzo is tender. Yield: 6 (1½-cup) servings.

Per Serving: Calories 287 (8% calories from fat)
Fat 2.4g (Sat 0.5g Mono 0.5g Poly 0.7g) Chol 55mg
Protein 27.9g Carbohydrate 36.1g Sodium 271mg
Exchanges: 3 Very Lean Meat, 2 Starch, 1 Vegetable

Mexican Squash Stew

Vegetable cooking spray
4 (6-inch) corn tortillas, cut into ½-inch strips
1 pound skinned, boned chicken breasts, cut
    into 1-inch cubes
¼ cup all-purpose flour
4 cups canned no-salt-added chicken broth,
    undiluted
2 cups peeled, cubed acorn squash
1 cup sliced carrot
1 cup sliced onion
½ cup sliced celery
1½ teaspoons chili powder
1 teaspoon ground cumin
½ teaspoon salt
2 cloves garlic, minced
1 cup chopped fresh cilantro

Coat a baking sheet with cooking spray. Place tortilla strips on baking sheet; coat strips with cooking spray. Bake at 400° for 9 minutes or until crisp. Set aside.

Combine chicken and flour in a heavy-duty, zip-top plastic bag. Seal bag, and shake until chicken is well coated.

Coat a Dutch oven with cooking spray; place over medium-high heat until hot. Add chicken mixture; sauté 5 minutes or until chicken begins to brown. Remove chicken from Dutch oven; set aside.

Combine broth and next 8 ingredients in Dutch oven. Bring to a boil; cover, reduce heat, and simmer 10 minutes. Add chicken, and simmer 10 additional minutes or until vegetables are tender and chicken is done. Stir in cilantro, and top with tortilla strips just before serving. Yield: 4 (2-cup) servings.

Per Serving: Calories 303 (9% calories from fat)
Fat 2.9g (Sat 0.6g Mono 0.7g Poly 0.8g) Chol 66mg
Protein 31.1g Carbohydrate 36.1g Sodium 459mg
Exchanges: 3 Very Lean Meat, 2 Starch, 1 Vegetable

Ginger-Chicken Stew

Vegetable cooking spray
2 cups chopped tomato
1 cup sliced onion
1 cup sliced carrot
¼ cup chopped ripe olives
6 cloves garlic, minced
1½ pounds skinned, boned chicken breasts,
    cut into bite-size pieces
4 cups canned no-salt-added chicken broth,
    undiluted
1 tablespoon paprika
1 tablespoon finely chopped crystallized ginger
½ teaspoon salt
½ teaspoon ground red pepper
½ teaspoon black pepper
1 (7-ounce) jar roasted red peppers in water,
    drained and chopped
1 cup bulgur, uncooked
¼ cup plus 2 tablespoons plain nonfat yogurt

Coat a Dutch oven with cooking spray; place over medium-high heat until hot. Add tomato and next 4 ingredients; sauté 6 minutes or until onion is tender. Stir in chicken and next 7 ingredients. Bring to a boil; cover, reduce heat, and simmer 20 minutes. Stir in bulgur; cook 15 minutes or until bulgur is tender.

To serve, ladle soup into individual bowls, and top each serving with 1 tablespoon yogurt. Yield: 6 (2-cup) servings.

Per Serving: Calories 288 (9% calories from fat)
Fat 3.0g (Sat 0.6g Mono 0.9g Poly 0.8g) Chol 66mg
Protein 32.1g Carbohydrate 32.6g Sodium 375mg
Exchanges: 3 Very Lean Meat, 2 Starch, 1 Vegetable

Turkey-Zucchini Soup

1 teaspoon olive oil
¾ cup chopped onion
¾ cup chopped carrot
1 teaspoon dried oregano
½ teaspoon salt
½ teaspoon pepper
2 cups cubed cooked turkey breast
1 cup coarsely chopped zucchini
1 (14½-ounce) can no-salt-added whole
    tomatoes, undrained and chopped
1 (14¼-ounce) can no-salt-added chicken broth

Heat oil in a large saucepan over medium-high heat. Add onion and next 4 ingredients, and sauté until onion is tender. Add turkey and remaining ingredients. Bring to a boil; reduce heat, and simmer, uncovered, 15 minutes or until zucchini is tender. Yield: 4 (1¼-cup) servings.

Per Serving: Calories 195 (18% calories from fat)
Fat 4.0g (Sat 1.1g Mono 1.3g Poly 0.9g) Chol 59mg
Protein 27.2g Carbohydrate 10.7g Sodium 372mg
Exchanges: 3 Very Lean Meat, 2 Vegetable

Sausage Minestrone

Vegetable cooking spray
½ pound turkey kielbasa, cut in half lengthwise
    and sliced into thin pieces
1 cup chopped onion
2 cloves garlic, minced
1 cup chopped celery
1 cup chopped zucchini
1 cup shredded cabbage
1 teaspoon dried oregano
1 teaspoon dried basil
¼ teaspoon salt
2 (14¼-ounce) cans no-salt-added beef broth
1 (14½-ounce) can no-salt-added whole
    tomatoes, undrained and chopped
1 (8-ounce) can no-salt-added tomato sauce
2½ cups cooked elbow macaroni (cooked without
    salt or fat)
1 (15-ounce) can no-salt-added kidney beans,
    drained
3 tablespoons freshly grated Parmesan cheese

Coat a large Dutch oven with cooking spray; place over medium-high heat until hot. Add sausage, onion, and garlic; sauté until onion is tender.

Add celery and next 8 ingredients. Bring to a boil; cover, reduce heat, and simmer 35 minutes or until vegetables are tender, stirring occasionally. Stir in macaroni and beans; cook, uncovered, 5 minutes or until thoroughly heated. To serve, ladle soup into individual bowls, and sprinkle evenly with cheese. Yield: 7 (1½-cup) servings.

Per Serving: Calories 215 (9% calories from fat)
Fat 2.1g (Sat 0.7g Mono 0.2g Poly 0.3g) Chol 14mg
Protein 12.6g Carbohydrate 34.6g Sodium 494mg
Exchanges: 1 Lean Meat, 2 Starch, 1 Vegetable

BETTER-FOR-YOU BEANS

Beans are low in fat, high in fiber and protein, and packed with vitamins and minerals—all good reasons to include them in a heart-healthy diet. But if canned beans have been off-limits to you because of their sodium content, take heart...and take a few cans off the grocery shelf once again. Now convenient-to-use canned beans come in low-sodium versions.

Most low-sodium brands have about 10 to 15 milligrams of sodium in a ½-cup serving, as opposed to about 430 to 500 milligrams for the same amount of regular canned beans.

Sausage and Black Bean Stew

Vegetable cooking spray
½ pound turkey kielbasa, cut in half lengthwise
    and sliced into thin pieces
2 cups chopped tomato
1 cup chopped onion
1 teaspoon dried oregano
6 cloves garlic, minced
2 tablespoons all-purpose flour
2½ cups drained canned no-salt-added
    black beans
1 (14¼-ounce) can no-salt-added beef broth
¼ cup chopped green onions

Coat a Dutch oven with cooking spray; place over medium heat until hot. Add sausage, and cook until browned, stirring often. Drain and pat dry with paper towels. Set aside. Wipe drippings from Dutch oven with a paper towel.

Coat Dutch oven with cooking spray; place over medium-high heat until hot. Add tomato and next 3 ingredients; sauté until onion is tender. Add sausage and flour. Cook, stirring constantly, 1 minute. Add beans and broth; stir well. Bring to a boil; reduce heat, and simmer, uncovered, 10 minutes or until thickened, stirring often. To serve, ladle soup into individual bowls, and sprinkle each serving with 1 tablespoon chopped green onions. Yield: 4 (1½-cup) servings.

Per Serving: Calories 313 (18% calories from fat)
Fat 6.3g (Sat 2.7g Mono 0.1g Poly 0.5g) Chol 30mg
Protein 20.7g Carbohydrate 44.4g Sodium 616mg
Exchanges: 2 Lean Meat, 2 Starch, 2 Vegetable

Thai Hot-and-Sour Soup

1 pound unpeeled medium-size fresh shrimp
    Olive oil-flavored vegetable cooking spray
1 teaspoon olive oil
4 cloves garlic, minced
1 teaspoon dried crushed red pepper
1 cup chopped onion
1 cup sliced fresh mushrooms
1 cup peeled, seeded, and chopped
    tomato
½ cup drained canned bamboo shoots,
    cut into thin strips
1 teaspoon ground ginger
1 teaspoon hot sauce
¼ teaspoon dried lemon peel
4½ cups canned fat-free, no-salt-added chicken
    broth, undiluted
2 tablespoons low-sodium soy sauce
2 tablespoons lime juice

Peel and devein shrimp; set aside.

Coat a large saucepan with cooking spray; add oil. Place over medium-high heat until hot. Add garlic and red pepper; sauté 1 minute. Add onion and next 6 ingredients; sauté until onion is tender. Add chicken broth and soy sauce; bring to a boil. Cover, reduce heat, and simmer 25 minutes. Stir in shrimp and lime juice. Cook 3 minutes or until shrimp turn pink. Yield: 3 (2½-cup) servings.

Per Serving: Calories 221 (17% calories from fat)
Fat 4.2g (Sat 0.7g Mono 1.4g Poly 1.1g) Chol 172mg
Protein 26.1g Carbohydrate 14.8g Sodium 457mg
Exchanges: 3½ Very Lean Meat, 1 Starch

Cioppino

Cioppino

¾ pound unpeeled medium-size fresh shrimp
1 dozen littleneck clams
1 tablespoon cornmeal
   Olive oil-flavored vegetable cooking spray
2 teaspoons olive oil
1 cup chopped onion
1 cup chopped green pepper
½ teaspoon pepper
½ teaspoon dried oregano
½ teaspoon dried basil
¼ teaspoon salt
2 cloves garlic, minced
½ cup dry red wine
2 tablespoons dried parsley flakes
2 tablespoons low-sodium Worcestershire sauce
2 (14½-ounce) cans no-salt-added whole
   tomatoes, undrained and chopped
1 (8-ounce) can no-salt-added tomato sauce
½ pound fresh or frozen perch fillets, skinned
   and cut into 1-inch pieces

Peel and devein shrimp; set aside.

Scrub clams thoroughly, discarding any that are cracked or open. Place clams in a large bowl; cover with cold water, and sprinkle with cornmeal. Let stand 30 minutes. Drain and rinse clams; set aside. Discard cornmeal.

Coat a Dutch oven with cooking spray; add oil. Place over medium-high heat until hot; add onion and next 6 ingredients. Sauté 5 minutes or until onion is tender. Add wine and next 4 ingredients. Bring to a boil; cover, reduce heat, and simmer 10 minutes. Add fish; cook, covered, 5 minutes. Add shrimp and clams; cook, covered, 3 additional minutes or until shrimp turn pink. (Discard any clams that do not open.)
Yield: 8 (2-cup) servings.

Per Serving: Calories 266 (16% calories from fat)
Fat 4.6g (Sat 0.7g Mono 2.0g Poly 1.0g) Chol 161mg
Protein 32.6g Carbohydrate 23.9g Sodium 368mg
Exchanges: 4 Very Lean Meat, 1 Starch, 2 Vegetable

Shrimp and Crab Bouillabaisse

1 pound unpeeled medium-size fresh shrimp
6 cups water
   Olive oil-flavored vegetable cooking spray
1 teaspoon olive oil
2 cups chopped tomato
1 cup chopped onion
1 teaspoon ground coriander
1 teaspoon ground cumin
½ teaspoon pepper
3 cloves garlic, minced
3 cups canned no-salt-added chicken broth,
   undiluted
½ pound fresh lump crabmeat, drained
½ cup chopped fresh cilantro
¼ cup dry white wine
5 (1-ounce) slices French bread, toasted

Peel and devein shrimp. Bring water to a boil in a large saucepan; add shrimp, and cook 3 to 5 minutes or until shrimp turn pink. Drain well, and set aside.

Coat a Dutch oven with cooking spray; add oil. Place over medium-high heat until hot. Add tomato and next 5 ingredients; sauté 5 minutes or until onion is tender. Add broth; bring to a boil. Add shrimp, crabmeat, cilantro, and wine. Reduce heat, and simmer 2 minutes.

To serve, place 1 bread slice in each of 5 bowls; ladle 1½ cups soup over each serving. Yield: 5 servings.

Per Serving: Calories 229 (13% calories from fat)
Fat 3.3g (Sat 0.6g Mono 1.3g Poly 1.0g) Chol 135mg
Protein 22.9g Carbohydrate 24.0g Sodium 408mg
Exchanges: 2 Very Lean Meat, 1 Starch, 2 Vegetable

cioppino (chuh-PEE-no): a tomato sauce-based Italian fish stew; typically contains shrimp and clams, plus perch, flounder, sole, or snapper.

Vegetables

Tabbouleh
(page 221)

vegetables (VEJ-tah-buls): the good-for-you foods Mother always said you had to eat before you could have dessert. They often replace meat as the main ingredient in entrées.

Seasoned Vegetable Tacos (page 228)

Thai-Style Vegetables (page 233)

Fiesta Beans and Rice

2¼ cups water, divided
1½ cups long-grain brown rice, uncooked
1¼ cups canned vegetable broth, undiluted
1 cup sliced fresh mushrooms
1 cup finely chopped green pepper
1 teaspoon ground cumin
1 teaspoon dried oregano
1 teaspoon paprika
½ teaspoon salt
1 teaspoon olive oil
1 cup chopped onion
1 clove garlic, minced
¼ cup no-salt-added tomato paste
1 tablespoon chili powder
2 (8-ounce) cans no-salt-added tomato sauce
1 (15-ounce) can no-salt-added black beans, drained
¼ cup plus 2 tablespoons nonfat sour cream

Combine 1½ cups water, rice, and next 7 ingredients in a large saucepan. Bring to a boil; cover, reduce heat, and simmer 30 to 35 minutes or until rice is tender and liquid is absorbed.

Heat oil in a Dutch oven over medium-high heat. Add onion and garlic; sauté until tender. Add remaining ¾ cup water, tomato paste, and next 3 ingredients, stirring well. Bring to a boil; cover, reduce heat, and simmer 25 minutes, stirring occasionally.

Spoon rice mixture evenly into individual serving bowls, making a well in each serving with the back of a spoon. Spoon bean mixture evenly over rice, and top each serving with 1 tablespoon sour cream. Yield: 6 servings.

Per Serving: Calories 304 (9% calories from fat)
Fat 3.1g (Sat 0.5g Mono 1.2g Poly 0.9g) Chol 0mg
Protein 10.5g Carbohydrate 59.7g Sodium 200mg
Exchanges: 3 Starch, 2 Vegetable, ½ Fat

Three-Bean Barbecue Bake

2 teaspoons vegetable oil
1½ cups chopped onion
1 cup chopped green pepper
1 cup chopped sweet red pepper
2 cloves garlic, minced
¾ cup low-sodium ketchup
½ cup firmly packed brown sugar
¼ cup molasses
1 tablespoon cider vinegar
1 teaspoon dry mustard
1 (16-ounce) can Great Northern beans, drained
1 (16-ounce) can no-salt-added kidney beans, drained
1 (16-ounce) can lima beans, drained
Vegetable cooking spray

Heat oil in a large nonstick skillet over medium-high heat. Add onion, peppers, and garlic; sauté 5 minutes or until tender. Stir in ketchup and next 4 ingredients; bring to a boil. Stir in beans.

Pour mixture into an 11- x 7- x 1½-inch baking dish coated with cooking spray. Bake, uncovered, at 325° for 55 minutes or until bubbly. Yield: 4 servings.

Note: If you want a more traditional, yet low-fat baked bean dish, top the bean mixture with 5 slices turkey bacon before baking. Bake as directed above.

Per Serving: Calories 301 (7% calories from fat)
Fat 2.4g (Sat 0.4g Mono 0.5g Poly 1.1g) Chol 0mg
Protein 11.2g Carbohydrate 61.5g Sodium 316mg
Exchanges: 4 Starch, ½ Fat

White Bean Enchiladas

6 tomatillos, husked
13 (6-inch) corn tortillas, divided
1 cup water
½ cup plus 2 tablespoons canned vegetable broth, undiluted and divided
1 cup coarsely chopped green leaf lettuce
¼ cup chopped fresh cilantro
½ teaspoon cumin seeds
2 (4½-ounce) cans chopped green chiles
Vegetable cooking spray
1 teaspoon vegetable oil
1 cup chopped onion
3 cloves garlic, minced
1 (15-ounce) can cannellini beans, drained
2½ cups cooked brown rice (cooked without salt or fat)
1 cup (4 ounces) shredded part-skim mozzarella cheese
½ cup (2 ounces) shredded reduced-fat Monterey Jack cheese

Place tomatillos on a large baking sheet; bake at 500° for 7 minutes.

Place 1 tortilla on a baking sheet; bake at 300° for 3 to 4 minutes or until crisp. Break into pieces.

Place tomatillos, tortilla pieces, 1 cup water, ½ cup broth, and next 4 ingredients in container of an electric blender; cover and process until smooth, stopping once to scrape down sides. Transfer mixture to a saucepan; cook over low heat until thoroughly heated. Remove from heat; set aside, and keep warm.

Coat a large nonstick skillet with cooking spray; add oil. Place over medium-high heat until hot. Add onion and garlic; sauté until tender. Add remaining 2 tablespoons vegetable broth and beans; cook 3 to 4 minutes or until thoroughly heated. Remove from heat, and mash beans; stir in brown rice and cheeses.

Dip 1 tortilla in tomatillo mixture; spoon ⅓ cup rice mixture down center of tortilla, and roll up. Place, seam side down, in a 13- x 9- x 2-inch baking dish coated with cooking spray. Repeat procedure with remaining 11 tortillas, tomatillo mixture, and rice mixture. Spoon remaining tomatillo mixture over tortillas. Bake, uncovered, at 350° for 30 minutes. Yield: 4 servings.

Per Serving: Calories 378 (20% calories from fat) Fat 8.4g (Sat 3.5g Mono 1.7g Poly 1.5g) Chol 17mg Protein 17.0g Carbohydrate 60.0g Sodium 437mg
Exchanges: 3 Starch, 3 Vegetable, 1½ Fat

SUBTRACT MEAT AND ADD PROTEIN

It's easy to meet your protein needs without meat if you include a variety of high-protein foods like beans, grains, and low-fat dairy products. In fact, 1 cup of cooked kidney beans contains more protein than 2 ounces of lean ground beef.

Nutrition experts say that if you're a healthy woman age 25+, you need no more than 50 grams of protein each day. Men age 24+ need no more than 63 grams. (This recommendation is based on a diet of 2000 calories; you may not need as much as 50 or 63 grams of protein if you're on a lower calorie diet.) If you eat between 10 to 20 grams of protein at each meal, you're probably getting as much daily protein as you need.

Tabbouleh

Tabbouleh

½ cup dried lentils
2 cups water
1 cup bulgur, uncooked
2 cups boiling water
½ cup lemon juice
1 cup coarsely chopped fresh parsley
1 cup coarsely chopped fresh mint
1 cup cherry tomato halves
1 cup sliced canned artichoke hearts, drained
1 cup peeled, seeded, and diced cucumber
½ cup minced purple onion
½ teaspoon pepper
1½ tablespoons olive oil
2 cloves garlic, minced
   Fresh mint leaves (optional)
   Pita wedges (optional)

Combine lentils and 2 cups water in a medium saucepan. Bring to a boil; cover, reduce heat, and simmer 40 minutes or until lentils are tender. Drain, rinse under cold water, and drain again. Transfer to a large bowl.

Combine bulgur, boiling water, and lemon juice in a medium bowl; cover and let stand 30 minutes. Add bulgur mixture, parsley, and next 8 ingredients to lentils; toss well. Cover and chill at least 30 minutes. If desired, garnish with mint leaves, and serve with pita wedges. Yield: 4 (2-cup) servings.

Per Serving: Calories 274 (20% calories from fat) Fat 6.1g (Sat 0.9g Mono 3.9g Poly 0.8g) Chol 0mg Protein 10.4g Carbohydrate 50.3g Sodium 163mg
Exchanges: 3 Starch, 1 Vegetable, 1 Fat

Greek Vegetable Couscous

1½ cups water
½ cup canned vegetable broth, undiluted
2 cups couscous, uncooked
   Olive oil-flavored vegetable cooking spray
2 cloves garlic, minced
1½ cups chopped zucchini
1 cup peeled, seeded, and chopped tomato
1 cup chopped purple onion
1 (15-ounce) can garbanzo beans (chick-peas), drained
½ teaspoon ground cumin
½ teaspoon ground oregano
½ teaspoon dried crushed red pepper
¼ teaspoon black pepper
1½ cups crumbled basil- and tomato-flavored feta cheese
¼ cup sliced ripe olives
¼ cup chopped fresh parsley

Combine water and broth in a medium saucepan; bring to a boil. Remove from heat. Add couscous; cover and let stand 5 minutes or until couscous is tender and liquid is absorbed.

Coat a large nonstick skillet with cooking spray; place over medium-high heat until hot. Add garlic; sauté 1 minute. Add zucchini, tomato, and onion, and sauté 2 to 3 minutes or until onion is tender. Add garbanzo beans and next 4 ingredients; stir well. Add couscous; cook 3 minutes or until thoroughly heated. Top with cheese, olives, and parsley. Yield: 7 (1½-cup) servings.

Per Serving: Calories 330 (20% calories from fat) Fat 7.4g (Sat 3.9g Mono 1.7g Poly 0.8g) Chol 22mg Protein 14.4g Carbohydrate 53.3g Sodium 450mg
Exchanges: 3 Starch, 2 Vegetable, 1½ Fat

tabbouleh (tuh-BOO-luh): a traditional Greek grain salad made of bulgur and seasoned with tomatoes, parsley, and mint; often eaten scooped onto pita wedges.

Vegetable-Rice Medley

6 fresh asparagus spears
  Vegetable cooking spray
1 cup chopped onion
2 cloves garlic, minced
1 cup sliced fresh shiitake mushroom caps
1 cup long-grain brown rice, uncooked
1 cup canned vegetable broth, undiluted
½ cup water
½ cup dry white wine
1 teaspoon dried basil
1 teaspoon dried oregano
¼ teaspoon dried crushed red pepper
⅛ teaspoon salt
1 (10-ounce) package frozen black-eyed peas,
  thawed
1 cup sliced carrot
1 cup sliced zucchini
¼ cup chopped fresh parsley
⅔ cup grated Asiago cheese

Snap off tough ends of asparagus. Remove scales
from stalks with a knife or vegetable peeler, if
desired. Cut spears into 1-inch pieces; set aside.

Coat a large nonstick skillet with cooking spray.
Place over medium-high heat until hot. Add onion
and garlic; sauté until tender. Add mushrooms; sauté
2 minutes. Add rice and next 8 ingredients, stirring
well. Bring to a boil; cover, reduce heat, and simmer
35 minutes. Add asparagus, carrot, zucchini, and parsley. Bring to a boil. Cover, reduce heat, and simmer
15 minutes or until vegetables are crisp-tender.
Transfer vegetable mixture to a serving bowl; top
with cheese. Yield: 5 (1½-cup) servings.

Per Serving: Calories 321 (17% calories from fat)
Fat 5.9g (Sat 2.8g Mono 1.6g Poly 0.6g) Chol 10mg
Protein 15.8g Carbohydrate 53.0g Sodium 459mg
Exchanges: 1 Medium-Fat Meat, 3 Starch, 2 Vegetable

Artichoke-Tomato Pitas

4 (8-inch) pita bread rounds
1 (14-ounce) can artichoke hearts, drained and
  sliced
2 cups seeded, chopped plum tomato
½ cup sliced fresh basil
¼ cup fat-free Ranch-style dressing
1 cup (4 ounces) shredded part-skim mozzarella
  cheese

Place pita rounds on a large baking sheet. Place one-
fourth of artichoke, tomato, basil, and dressing down
center of each pita. Sprinkle each serving with ¼ cup
cheese. Broil 3 inches from heat (with electric oven
door partially opened) 2 to 3 minutes or until
cheese melts.

Remove from oven. Roll up each pita; wrap bottom
of each pita roll in wax paper or decorative tissue
paper, and serve immediately. Yield: 4 servings.

Per Serving: Calories 477 (14% calories from fat)
Fat 7.5g (Sat 3.2g Mono 1.5g Poly 1.2g) Chol 16mg
Protein 16.8g Carbohydrate 80.6g Sodium 713mg
Exchanges: 5 Starch, 1 Vegetable, 1½ Fat

Broccoli Phyllo Pie

2 teaspoons vegetable oil
2 cups chopped fresh mushrooms
1 cup minced onion
2 cloves garlic, minced
3 tablespoons all-purpose flour
1⅓ cups 1% low-fat milk
2 (10-ounce) packages frozen chopped
    broccoli, thawed and drained
½ teaspoon salt
¼ teaspoon ground pepper
2 egg yolks, lightly beaten
¼ cup plus 2 tablespoons freshly grated
    Parmesan cheese
4 egg whites
¼ teaspoon cream of tartar
    Vegetable cooking spray
13 sheets frozen phyllo pastry, thawed

Heat oil in a nonstick skillet over medium heat. Add mushrooms, onion, and garlic; sauté 7 minutes. Sprinkle flour over vegetable mixture; stir well. Stir in milk; cook over medium heat, stirring constantly, until thickened and bubbly. Stir in broccoli, salt, and pepper. Let cool. Stir in egg yolks and cheese.

Beat egg whites and cream of tartar at high speed of an electric mixer until stiff peaks form. Fold beaten egg white mixture into broccoli mixture.

Coat a 10-inch springform pan with cooking spray; place 1 sheet of phyllo in pan (keep remaining phyllo covered). Coat phyllo with cooking spray. Layer 9 more sheets on top of first sheet, coating each with cooking spray and fanning each slightly to the right. (The over-hanging sheets will form a circle around the pan.) Gently press phyllo into pan, forming a shell; fill with broccoli mixture. Top with remaining 3 sheets, coating each with cooking spray and fanning each to the right. Fold edges over top to enclose filling. Coat top of phyllo with cooking spray.

Bake, uncovered, at 400° for 25 minutes. Cover and bake 35 minutes; let stand 10 minutes. Serve warm. Yield: 8 servings.

Per Serving: Calories 209 (28% calories from fat) Fat 6.5g (Sat 2.0g Mono 1.8g Poly 1.9g) Chol 60mg Protein 11.1g Carbohydrate 27.3g Sodium 444mg
Exchanges: 1 Medium-Fat Meat, 1 Starch, 2 Vegetable

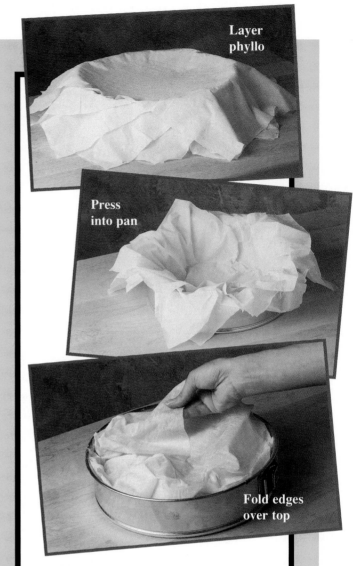

Layer phyllo

Press into pan

Fold edges over top

MAKING A PHYLLO PIE

Follow these easy steps for preparing a golden, flaky phyllo pastry shell. First, place one sheet of phyllo in the pan, and coat it with cooking spray.
•**Layer** more sheets of phyllo on top of the first, fanning each sheet to the right so that the overhanging phyllo makes a circle around the pan.
•**Press** the phyllo into the pan to make a shell, and pour in the filling. Top with more phyllo.
•**Fold** the phyllo edges over the top, and bake.

Onion Gratin in Bread Bowls

6 (1½-ounce) kaiser rolls
2 tablespoons reduced-calorie margarine,
    divided
1 tablespoon sugar
3 medium onions, peeled and cut in half
    crosswise
¼ teaspoon coarsely ground pepper
1 cup dry Marsala, divided
¼ cup all-purpose flour
2 cups 1% low-fat milk
1 teaspoon chopped fresh thyme
¾ cup (3 ounces) shredded reduced-fat
    Swiss cheese
    Paprika (optional)

Cut a ¼-inch slice from the top of each roll. Hollow out centers of rolls, leaving ½-inch-thick shells; reserve tops and inside of rolls for another use. Bake bread shells at 350° for 7 to 9 minutes or until golden. Set shells aside.

Melt 1 tablespoon margarine in a large ovenproof nonstick skillet over low heat; sprinkle sugar over melted margarine. Arrange onion halves, cut sides down, over sugar mixture. Sprinkle onions with pepper, and drizzle with ½ cup wine. Cover and cook over medium-high heat 10 minutes, shaking skillet occasionally to keep onions from sticking. Add remaining ½ cup wine. Reduce heat to medium; uncover and cook 8 additional minutes. Place skillet in oven, and bake, uncovered, at 350° for 12 to 15 minutes or until onion is tender. Remove onion from skillet, and set aside.

Melt remaining 1 tablespoon margarine in skillet over low heat. Add flour, stirring well with a wire whisk. Gradually add milk, stirring well; add thyme. Cook over medium heat, stirring constantly, until thickened.

Spoon 2 tablespoons sauce into each toasted bread shell; reserve remaining sauce. Place 1 onion half, cut side up, in each bread shell. Sprinkle cheese evenly over onion halves. Broil 5½ inches from heat (with electric oven door partially opened) 5 to 7 minutes or until cheese melts. Sprinkle with paprika, if desired. To serve, spoon remaining sauce evenly over bread shells. Yield: 6 servings.

Per Serving: Calories 320 (24% calories from fat)
Fat 8.6g (Sat 2.7g Mono 1.7g Poly 1.7g) Chol 12mg
Protein 14.1g Carbohydrate 47.4g Sodium 387mg
Exchanges: 1 High-Fat Meat, 3 Starch

SPREAD THE NEWS

To reduce your risk of heart disease, you need to eat less fat—especially saturated fat.

The American Heart Association recommends that you use margarine products that contain no more than 2 grams of saturated fat per tablespoon. Soft margarines (tub or liquid) are better for your heart than stick margarines because they contain less saturated fat.

Potatoes Latino

18 thin fresh asparagus spears
6 large round red potatoes (about 2½ pounds),
    cut into ¼-inch-thick slices
    Vegetable cooking spray
1 cup chopped purple onion
2 cloves garlic, minced
1 whole fresh Anaheim chile, seeded and minced
½ teaspoon ground cumin
½ teaspoon dried oregano
2 cups chopped fresh tomato
¼ cup canned no-salt-added chicken broth,
    undiluted
3 tablespoons cider vinegar
1 cup (4 ounces) shredded reduced-fat Monterey
    Jack cheese
2 tablespoons chopped fresh cilantro

Snap off tough ends of asparagus. Remove scales
from stalks with a knife or vegetable peeler, if
desired. Cut spears into 1-inch pieces. Set aside.

Cook potato in a Dutch oven in boiling water to
cover 10 minutes. Add asparagus; cook 5 minutes or
until potato is tender and asparagus is crisp-tender.
Drain and set aside.

Coat Dutch oven with cooking spray; place over
medium-high heat until hot. Add onion, garlic, and
chile; sauté until crisp-tender. Add cumin and
oregano; sauté 1 minute. Stir in tomato, broth, and
vinegar. Bring to a boil; reduce heat, and simmer,
uncovered, 5 minutes. Add potato mixture; toss
lightly to coat. Sprinkle with cheese and cilantro.
Serve warm. Yield: 6 servings.

Per Serving: Calories 261 (15% calories from fat)
Fat 4.4g (Sat 2.2g Mono 0.1g Poly 0.4g) Chol 12mg
Protein 11.3g Carbohydrate 46.9g Sodium 145mg
Exchanges: 3 Starch, 1 Vegetable, 1 Fat

Greek Spinach Pie

1 (10-ounce) package frozen chopped spinach,
    thawed and drained
1 cup 1% low-fat cottage cheese
⅔ cup nonfat buttermilk
½ cup frozen egg substitute, thawed
½ cup crumbled basil- and tomato-flavored
    feta cheese
¼ teaspoon pepper
1 egg white
½ cup chopped onion
1 tablespoon chopped fresh oregano
1 teaspoon salt-free lemon-pepper seasoning
1 large clove garlic, minced
    Olive oil-flavored vegetable cooking spray
6 sheets frozen phyllo pastry, thawed
2 tablespoons plus 1 teaspoon fine, dry
    breadcrumbs, divided
3 plum tomatoes, cut lengthwise into wedges

Press spinach between paper towels to remove excess
moisture; set spinach aside.

Position knife blade in food processor bowl. Add
cottage cheese and next 5 ingredients; process until
smooth. Add spinach, onion, and next 3 ingredients;
process 45 seconds.

Coat an 11- x 7- x 1½-inch baking dish with cooking spray. Cut phyllo sheets in half crosswise. Place 1
half-sheet of phyllo in bottom of dish (keep remaining
phyllo covered). Lightly coat phyllo with cooking
spray, and sprinkle with 1 teaspoon breadcrumbs.
Repeat layers six times, coating each with cooking
spray and sprinkling with 1 teaspoon breadcrumbs.
Top with 1 half-sheet of phyllo; lightly coat with cooking spray. Spread spinach mixture over phyllo in pan.
Top spinach mixture with remaining 4 phyllo half-
sheets, coating each with cooking spray. Bake at 350°
for 40 minutes or until golden. Serve with tomato
wedges. Yield: 4 servings.

Per Serving: Calories 252 (22% calories from fat)
Fat 6.2g (Sat 3.0g Mono 1.3g Poly 1.3g) Chol 16mg
Protein 19.7g Carbohydrate 30.5g Sodium 725mg
Exchanges: 2 Lean Meat, 1 Starch, 3 Vegetable

Squash Parmesan

6 medium-size yellow squash
4 medium zucchini
2 eggs
¼ cup water
⅔ cup fine, dry breadcrumbs
½ cup grated Parmesan cheese
¼ cup minced fresh basil
2 tablespoons minced fresh parsley
¼ teaspoon dried crushed red pepper
3 cloves garlic, minced
2 teaspoons olive oil
  Vegetable cooking spray
2 (15-ounce) cans no-salt-added crushed
  tomatoes
¼ cup freshly grated Romano cheese

Cut each squash and zucchini lengthwise into 4 slices; set aside.

Combine eggs and water, stirring well. Combine breadcrumbs and next 5 ingredients; stir well. Brush squash and zucchini slices with egg mixture. Dredge in breadcrumb mixture, covering vegetables completely; reserve remaining breadcrumb mixture.

Heat oil in a large nonstick skillet over medium-high heat. Add squash and zucchini to skillet; cook 2 to 3 minutes on each side or until lightly browned. Alternately layer squash and zucchini in a 13- x 9- x 2-inch baking dish coated with cooking spray.

Pour tomato over squash and zucchini. Top with remaining breadcrumb mixture. Cover and bake at 350° for 35 minutes. Uncover and sprinkle with Romano cheese. Bake 25 minutes. Let stand 10 minutes before serving. Yield: 6 servings.

Per Serving: Calories 233 (29% calories from fat)
Fat 8.5g (Sat 3.6g Mono 3.3g Poly 0.8g) Chol 86mg
Protein 13.6g Carbohydrate 28.1g Sodium 389mg
Exchanges: 1 High-Fat Meat, 1 Starch, 2 Vegetable

Artichoke-Stuffed Tomatoes

4 large tomatoes
¾ cup diced yellow squash
⅓ cup (1.3 ounces) shredded part-skim
  mozzarella cheese
¼ cup chopped fresh parsley
¼ cup fine, dry breadcrumbs
¼ cup grated Parmesan cheese
1 tablespoon sliced green onions
1 teaspoon dried basil
1 teaspoon olive oil
¼ teaspoon dried Italian seasoning
1 (14-ounce) can artichoke hearts, drained
  and sliced

Cut a ¼-inch slice from stem end of each tomato; discard stem ends. Scoop out pulp, leaving shells intact. Discard pulp and seeds. Invert tomato shells on paper towels to drain.

Combine squash and remaining 9 ingredients; stir well, and spoon evenly into tomato shells. Place shells in a 9-inch square pan. Bake, uncovered, at 350° degrees for 45 minutes or until tomatoes and stuffing are thoroughly heated. Yield: 2 servings.

Per Serving: Calories 313 (30% calories from fat)
Fat 10.4g (Sat 4.5g Mono 3.9g Poly 1.2g) Chol 19mg
Protein 18.3g Carbohydrate 43.3g Sodium 831mg
Exchanges: 1 High-Fat Meat, 2 Starch, 2 Vegetable

Vegetable Lasagna with Mushroom Sauce

2 medium-size sweet red peppers
12 cloves garlic, unpeeled (about 1 head)
4 large baking potatoes, sliced lengthwise into
    ¼-inch-thick slices
    Vegetable cooking spray
1 teaspoon olive oil
1 cup chopped onion
1 (8-ounce) package presliced fresh mushrooms
½ cup dry white wine
½ cup water
1 cup skim milk
¼ cup all-purpose flour
2 tablespoons chopped fresh parsley
1 (10-ounce) package frozen chopped spinach,
    thawed and drained
1 (15-ounce) carton nonfat ricotta cheese
1 cup 1% low-fat cottage cheese
½ cup freshly grated Parmesan cheese
½ teaspoon salt
¼ teaspoon pepper
1 cup sliced yellow squash (about 1 medium)
1 cup chopped fresh broccoli
1 cup (4 ounces) shredded part-skim mozzarella
    cheese

Cut peppers in half lengthwise; remove and discard seeds and membranes. Place peppers, skin sides up, on a baking sheet, and flatten with palm of hand. Broil 5½ inches from heat (with electric oven door partially opened) 15 to 20 minutes or until charred. Place in ice water until cool; peel and discard skins. Slice peppers into thin strips.

Arrange garlic cloves and potato in a single layer on a large baking sheet; bake at 400° for 30 minutes or until potato is tender. Remove from oven; let cool. Peel garlic cloves.

Coat a large nonstick skillet with cooking spray; add oil. Place over medium-high heat until hot. Add onion, and sauté 5 minutes or until tender. Add mushrooms and garlic; sauté 2 minutes. Add wine and water.

Combine milk and flour; stir well with a wire whisk. Add flour mixture to mushroom mixture in skillet; bring to a boil, and cook 5 minutes or until thickened and bubbly. Stir in parsley, and set aside.

Press spinach between paper towels to remove excess moisture. Combine spinach, ricotta cheese, cottage cheese, Parmesan cheese, salt, and pepper in a medium bowl; stir well, and set aside. Combine roasted pepper strips, squash, and broccoli; stir well, and set aside.

Coat a 13- x 9- x 2-inch baking dish with vegetable cooking spray. Spread ¼ cup mushroom sauce in baking dish. Arrange half of potato slices over mushroom sauce. Spread half of cheese mixture over potato. Arrange half of broccoli mixture over cheese mixture, and top with half of remaining mushroom sauce. Repeat layers with remaining potato slices, cheese mixture, broccoli mixture, and mushroom sauce. Top with mozzarella cheese. Cover and bake at 350° for 30 minutes. Uncover and bake 15 additional minutes. Let stand 10 minutes before serving. Yield: 8 servings.

Per Serving: Calories 338 (16% calories from fat) Fat 5.9g (Sat 3.2g Mono 1.8g Poly 0.4g) Chol 21mg Protein 24.5g Carbohydrate 50.3g Sodium 547mg
Exchanges: 2 Lean Meat, 3 Starch, 1 Vegetable

Fold foil in half

TACO SHELL TRICK

Crispy corn taco shells are full of flavor and full of fat because they're usually fried. But you don't have to sacrifice that rich corn taste. Just use our secret for making low-fat, full-flavor shells.

• **Fold** a 12- x 10-inch piece of aluminum foil in half lengthwise. Then open it slightly, and twist the foil at each end to form a boat shape.

• **Make** a boat for every taco shell that you need.

Make a boat

Place in boat

• **Place** a 6-inch corn tortilla in each boat, and press it gently to mold into the shape of the foil.

Put a small piece of crushed foil inside each tortilla boat so the boat will hold its shape while baking.

Seasoned Vegetable Tacos

    8 (6-inch) corn tortillas
1½ cups frozen whole-kernel corn, thawed
    1 cup diced zucchini
    1 cup shredded carrot
    2 teaspoons chili powder
    ½ teaspoon garlic powder
    ½ teaspoon onion powder
    ¼ teaspoon salt
    ¼ teaspoon ground oregano
    ¼ teaspoon sugar
    ½ cup water
    1 (15-ounce) can no-salt-added kidney beans
    4 cups shredded iceberg lettuce
    1 cup chopped tomato
    1 cup (4 ounces) shredded reduced-fat Cheddar
      cheese
    ½ cup nonfat sour cream
    ½ cup no-salt-added salsa

Cut 8 (12- x 10-inch) pieces of aluminum foil; fold each piece in half lengthwise. Open foil slightly, and twist ends to form boats. Place foil boats on a large baking sheet, flattening bottoms. Place corn tortillas inside boats, pressing gently to form shells. Bake at 350° for 15 to 20 minutes or until crisp. Set aside.

Combine corn and next 10 ingredients in a large nonstick skillet; bring to a boil. Cook, uncovered, 5 minutes or until vegetables are tender.

Place ½ cup lettuce in each taco shell. Spoon ½ cup corn mixture into each. Top each with 2 tablespoons tomato, 2 tablespoons cheese, 1 tablespoon sour cream, and 1 tablespoon salsa. Yield: 4 servings (serving size: 2 tacos).

Note: We thought it was great fun to make our own low-fat taco shells, but you can always serve the hearty bean mixture with fat-free tortilla chips instead.

Per Serving: Calories 446 (16% calories from fat) Fat 7.9g (Sat 3.5g Mono 0.5g Poly 1.3g) Chol 18mg Protein 26.6g Carbohydrate 71.8g Sodium 726mg **Exchanges:** 2 Lean Meat, 4 Starch, 2 Vegetable

Seasoned
Vegetable
Tacos

Veggie Egg Rolls

1 teaspoon dark sesame oil
½ cup shredded carrot
½ cup diced water chestnuts
½ cup diced zucchini
½ cup chopped bean sprouts
¼ cup sliced green onions
1¾ cups cooked long-grain rice (cooked
    without salt or fat)
¼ cup frozen egg substitute, thawed
2 tablespoons low-sodium soy sauce
1 teaspoon ground turmeric
12 egg roll wrappers
    Vegetable cooking spray
    Low-sodium soy sauce (optional)
    Hot mustard (optional)

Heat oil in a large nonstick skillet over medium-high heat. Add carrot and next 4 ingredients; sauté until crisp-tender. Remove from heat. Add rice and next 3 ingredients; stir well.

Mound ¼ cup rice mixture in center of each egg roll wrapper. Fold one corner of wrapper over filling, then fold left and right corners over filling. Push filling toward center of wrapper. Lightly brush exposed corner of wrapper with water. Tightly roll filled end of wrapper toward exposed corner; gently press corner to seal securely.

Place egg rolls on a large baking sheet coated with cooking spray. Coat tops of egg rolls with cooking spray. Bake at 350° for 20 minutes or until lightly browned. Serve warm. If desired, serve with low-sodium soy sauce or hot mustard. Yield: 4 servings.

Note: If you want to add a powerful flavor punch to the egg rolls, serve about 2 teaspoons of spicy hot mustard with each one. Just remember that each teaspoon of mustard has 51 milligrams of sodium.

Per Serving: Calories 470 (7% calories from fat)
Fat 3.8g (Sat 0.5g Mono 0.7g Poly 1.2g) Chol 10mg
Protein 14.9g Carbohydrate 91.2g Sodium 836mg
Exchanges: 5 Starch, 2 Vegetable, 1 Fat

Vegetable Garden Sandwiches

1 cup shredded zucchini
1¼ cups soft sourdough breadcrumbs
1 cup grated carrot
½ cup cooked long-grain brown rice (cooked
    without salt or fat), chilled
¼ cup plus 2 tablespoons (1½ ounces) shredded
    reduced-fat Swiss cheese
¼ cup finely chopped purple onion
2 tablespoons chopped fresh parsley
1 tablespoon finely chopped fresh mint
⅛ teaspoon pepper
1 egg
1 egg white
    Vegetable cooking spray
2 tablespoons Dijon mustard
2 tablespoons reduced-fat mayonnaise
8 (1-ounce) slices sourdough bread, toasted
4 green leaf lettuce leaves
8 tomato slices

Press zucchini between paper towels to remove excess moisture. Combine zucchini, breadcrumbs, and next 9 ingredients in a large bowl, mixing well.

Shape mixture into 8 (3-inch) patties. Coat a nonstick skillet with cooking spray; place over medium-high heat until hot. Cook patties 3 minutes on each side or until browned.

Combine mustard and mayonnaise; spread evenly on one side of 4 bread slices. Place 1 lettuce leaf and 2 tomato slices on coated side of each bread slice. Top each with 2 vegetable patties and a remaining bread slice. Serve immediately. Yield: 4 servings.

Per Serving: Calories 334 (21% calories from fat)
Fat 7.9g (Sat 1.9g Mono 0.6g Poly 0.5g) Chol 64mg
Protein 15.1g Carbohydrate 51.8g Sodium 734mg
Exchanges: 1 High-Fat Meat, 3 Starch, 1 Vegetable

Sun-Dried Tomato Pesto Quesadillas

12 sun-dried tomato halves (packed without oil)
¾ cup boiling water
¼ cup chopped green onions
¼ cup chopped fresh parsley
¼ cup chopped fresh basil
¼ cup grated Parmesan cheese
1 tablespoon slivered almonds, toasted
½ teaspoon olive oil
4 cloves garlic, chopped
1 cup nonfat ricotta cheese
¼ cup crumbled goat cheese
3 (10-inch) flour tortillas
Vegetable cooking spray
½ cup (2 ounces) shredded part-skim mozzarella cheese

Combine tomato halves and boiling water in a small bowl; let stand 10 minutes. Drain.

Position knife blade in food processor bowl; add tomato, green onions, and next 6 ingredients. Process until mixture is minced. Set aside.

Combine ricotta cheese and goat cheese; stir until smooth. Place 2 tortillas on a baking sheet coated with cooking spray. Spread cheese mixture evenly over 2 tortillas. Spoon tomato mixture evenly over cheese mixture. Place 1 tortilla, tomato side up, on top of the other tomato-topped tortilla. Top with remaining tortilla; sprinkle with mozzarella cheese. Bake at 425° for 8 to 10 minutes or until cheeses melt and tortillas are golden. Slice into wedges, and serve immediately. Yield: 4 servings.

Per Serving: Calories 305 (32% calories from fat) Fat 10.7g (Sat 4.5g Mono 3.7g Poly 1.6g) Chol 24mg Protein 20.6g Carbohydrate 34.6g Sodium 583mg
Exchanges: 2 Medium-Fat Meat, 2 Starch, 1 Vegetable

TOMATO TIDBITS

Dried tomatoes, commonly called "sun-dried tomatoes," add a zesty flavor to recipes. Although they are not always dried in the sun, they are usually dried without the use of salt, fat, or seasonings. You'll find them in bits, strips, or halves. You may also see marinated dried tomatoes, but these are not the best choice for low-fat cooking because they contain vegetable or olive oil.

Thai-Style
Vegetables

Thai-Style Vegetables

6 ounces rice vermicelli, uncooked
12 cups warm water
   Vegetable cooking spray
2 teaspoons vegetable oil, divided
½ cup sliced green onions
1 teaspoon peeled, minced gingerroot
2 cloves garlic, minced
2 cups julienne-sliced sweet red pepper
1 Anaheim chile, seeded and chopped
1 (10-ounce) package frozen English peas,
   thawed
½ cup water
2 teaspoons curry powder
1 teaspoon ground cumin
1 cup shredded Chinese cabbage
1 cup diced extra-firm tofu
3 tablespoons low-sodium soy sauce
1 (8-ounce) can sliced water chestnuts, drained

Place vermicelli in a large bowl; cover with 12 cups water. Let stand 10 minutes or until vermicelli is soft. Drain and cut vermicelli into pieces. Set aside.

Coat a wok or large nonstick skillet with cooking spray; drizzle 1 teaspoon oil around top of wok, coating sides. Heat at medium-high (375°) until hot. Add green onions, gingerroot, and garlic; stir-fry 2 minutes. Add pepper and chile; stir-fry 2 minutes. Add peas and ½ cup water; stir-fry 4 minutes or until peas are tender and liquid is evaporated. Remove mixture from wok.

Drizzle remaining 1 teaspoon oil around top of wok. Add curry powder and cumin; stir-fry 1 minute. Add vermicelli, cabbage, and remaining 3 ingredients; stir-fry 2 minutes. Add pepper mixture; stir-fry 1 minute or until thoroughly heated. Yield: 4 servings.

Note: Rice vermicelli, a kind of noodle made from rice flour, is also called long rice, Chinese vermicelli, or rice sticks.

Per Serving: Calories 334 (14% calories from fat) Fat 5.2g (Sat 0.8g Mono 1.3g Poly 2.5g) Chol 0mg Protein 12.1g Carbohydrate 61.1g Sodium 422mg
Exchanges: 3 Starch, 3 Vegetable, 1 Fat

TOFU—WHAT'S IN IT FOR YOU?

Tofu, a soybean curd made from soy milk, is packed with protein and B vitamins, is low in sodium and saturated fat, and is cholesterol free. Recent research suggests that tofu may even have cholesterol-lowering power.

Look for one or all three types of tofu in the produce section of your grocery store.

• **Soft** tofu's texture makes it just right as a substitute for creamy ingredients in dips, puddings, soups, and salad dressings.

• **Firm or Extra-Firm** tofu works well cut into cubes, sliced, or crumbled, and used in salads, stir-fries, and pasta.

Recipe Index

S: **S**UPER•**Q**UICK

M: **M**AKE•**A**HEAD

S: **S**UPER•**Q**UICK

M: **M**AKE•**A**HEAD

Subject Index

Acknowledgments & Credits

Oxmoor House wishes to thank the following merchants and individuals:

Antiques & Gardens, Birmingham, AL
Barbara Eigen Arts, Jersey City, NJ
Biot, New York, NY
Bridges Antiques, Birmingham, AL
Bromberg's, Birmingham, AL
Carolyn Rice Art Pottery, Marietta, GA
Cassis & Co., New York, NY
Christine's, Birmingham, AL
Cyclamen Studio, Berkeley, CA
Goldsmith/Corot, Inc., New York, NY
Lamb's Ears Ltd., Birmingham, AL
Le Creuset of America, Inc., Yemassee, SC
The Loom Company, Aletha Soulé, New York, NY
M's Fabric Gallery, Birmingham, AL
Savoir Vivre International, San Francisco, CA

Additional photography:
Brit Huckaby: pages 27, 42, 62, 63, 184, 206, 209, 214

Additional photo styling:
Iris Crawley O'Brien: page 214

Additional copy editing:
Keri Bradford Anderson

Source of Nutrient Analysis Data:
Computrition, Inc., Chatsworth, California.
Primarily comprised of *Composition of Foods:
Raw, Processed, Prepared*. Agriculture Handbook
No. 8 Series. United States Department of Agriculture,
Human Nutrition Information Service, 1976–1993.